Form and Feeling in Japanese Literati Culture

Matthew Mewhinney

Form and Feeling in Japanese Literati Culture

palgrave
macmillan

Matthew Mewhinney
Florida State University
Tallahassee, FL, USA

ISBN 978-3-031-11921-7   ISBN 978-3-031-11922-4   (eBook)
https://doi.org/10.1007/978-3-031-11922-4

Cover Image: James David Lee, *As stars descend to the ocean floor – you can watch it from the
window*, Ink, pigment, and rainwater on paper; 41 x 30.5 cm

This Palgrave Macmillan imprint is published by the registered company Springer Nature
Switzerland AG.
The registered company address is: Gewerbestrasse 11, 6330 Cham, Switzerland

In memory of Robert L. Backus (1928–2014),
mentor and friend

PREFACE

This study grew out of my curiosity about Japanese novelist Natsume Sōseki (1867–1916), the writer treated in Chap. 5 and the coda of this book. I wanted to know what had informed his literary creativity, his imagination, and the poetic nature of his prose. Over the course of my research, I discovered that much of his inspiration derived from his longing for the aesthetic attitude and sensibility of poet-painters in Japanese literati (*bunjin*) culture from the Late Edo period (1750s–1867). By his lifetime in the Meiji period (1867–1912), literati culture had declined and survived primarily as an antiquarian avocation.

Sōseki has been called a *bunjin* because he practiced aesthetic forms from the literati repertoire, including Chinese calligraphy, poetry, and painting. While these were not his main contribution to modern Japanese literature, they did inform it. In public, he was first and foremost a novelist; he was also a scholar of English literature, a literary theorist, and a philosopher. During a single decade, he produced thirteen major works of fiction, each distinct in theme and style. In private, he produced works of calligraphy, Chinese-style paintings, and impressionist watercolor paintings, exchanging them with the members of his coterie.

These public and private streams merged in Sōseki's production of poetry. Over his lifetime he composed more than 2000 poems across multiple genres. His practice in haiku and especially *kanshi* (Chinese poems, or Sinitic verse) allowed him to participate in—and to memorialize—the moribund literati tradition. He integrated these poetic genres to write several long works of prose, two of which I treat in Chap. 5 as modern prose poems.

In summer of 2011 the Kanagawa Museum of Modern Literature (Kanazawa Kindai Bungakukan) put on an exhibit entitled "Calligraphy and Painting of Sōseki and other *Bunjin*." At the exhibit, I had the opportunity to view Sōseki's works of calligraphy and Chinese-style paintings, alongside those by other modern writers who participated in literati culture. Among all this company, Sōseki is the most highly regarded by literary history—a reputation based upon the fact that he was one of the last modern writers to compose *kanshi*. His poems earned the praise of Yoshikawa Kōjirō (1904–1980), a renowned scholar of Chinese poetry, who in a 1974 interview thus compared Sōseki's *kanshi* to those composed by other poets in the Japanese tradition: "Though *kanshi* to Sōseki was likely an avocation, his poems are truly outstanding."[1]

I sought to discover for myself what was so "outstanding" about Sōseki's *kanshi* and why this genre of poetry attracted Japanese readers when the literati tradition had disappeared. I read his poems in the original and then translated them into English, an experience that taught me about the affordances of *kanshi* as a poetic form in modern Japanese literature.

When I use the word "form" in this book, I mean two things. The first is the term's most common use in Japanese literary studies, which refers to the arrangement of words on the page that identifies a literary work in the context of its tradition: the seventeen-syllable (5-7-5) poetic form is known as haiku; the Chinese poetic form in Japan is known as *kanshi*. In this sense, form is used almost interchangeably with the word genre, which refers to a normative category determined by expectations of what a literary work should do. Haiku and *kanshi* are genres of both traditional Japanese poetry and Japanese literati culture.

The second way I use the term "form" refers to something more abstract—that is, "how a poem works as a poem." Scholar Helen Vendler writes that "form is content as deployed," which I understand as the process of bringing words into action.[2] US poet laureate Robert Hass has put this idea more poetically, as "the way the poem embodies the energy of the gesture of its making."[3] More recently, poet and scholar Lucy Alford has described form as an event that invites the reader's attention: "What is formed *by* and *in* poetic language is an event of attention generated in the acts of both reading and writing."[4] These definitions inform my own, namely form as that which mediates the aesthetic experience of a poem and that which enlists the reader to participate in that experience. In other words, form is not just the words on the page; it is what those words "do" in the process of reading.

When reading Sōseki's *kanshi*, I find most compelling their irony, an experience that comes into being only by reading their form. His *kanshi* are simultaneously ancient and modern: their external shape—the way they look on the page—is identical to how Chinese poems look in the old literati tradition; at the same time, how they work as poems—what they "do" in the process of reading—distinguishes them from that tradition, making them new.

The poem below is a pentasyllabic ancient-style verse (*gogon koshi*) that Sōseki composed in 1899 before embarking on a long voyage from Tokyo to England, where he would study for two miserable years before returning to Japan:

> Ever since my eyes have known the letters of East and West,
> My heart has borne the anxiety of both past and present.
> A shameful twenty years of darkness and confusion;
> At thirty I know where I stand, enough to look back.
5 > As I sit and meditate upon weal and woe,
> The open mind weighs the interplay of the pliant and rigid.
> Birds fly into the clouds without a trace,
> Fish swim, streams flow as they please.
> In a world that began without human affairs,
> White clouds take their time indifferently.

me ni tōzai no ji o shiri	眼識東西字
kokoro ni kokon no urei o idaku	心抱古今憂
nijūnen kondaku o haji	廿年愧昏濁
jiryū wazuka ni kōbe o megurasu	而立纔回頭
seiza shite fukuhaku o mi	靜坐觀復剝
kyokai gōjū o ekisu	虛懷役剛柔
tori irite kumo ato naku	鳥入雲無迹
uo yukite mizu onozukara nagaru	魚行水自流
jinkan motoyori buji	人間固無事
hakuun onozukara yūyū	白雲自悠悠 5

The poem exemplifies how Sōseki's *kanshi* represent modern thoughts and feelings in ancient poetic form. In the opening couplet, the speaker describes language as a site of tension between past and present. This dissonance between Chinese characters and the Western alphabet (*tōzai no ji*) is a self-referential comment on the anachronism of *kanshi* in modern literary expression that opens a rift between sign and signified. As the speaker holds on to an ancient poetic form, the metaphorical ground on which it stands simultaneously crumbles, leaving the speaker and the poetic meaning of the poem in a liminal state of suspension.

The rest of the poem represents the speaker's modern sensibility as he perceives the world through metaphors of loss. He looks back on his life, contemplating the space between "weal and woe" and "the pliant and rigid," binaries that represent internal feelings and perceptions of the external world. With an "open mind," the speaker paints an elegiac landscape, representing a natural world no longer in reach. The speaker's longing to return to a time when "Birds fly into the clouds without a trace, / Fish swim, streams flow as they please" resonates with nineteenth-century Romantic poetry, which Sōseki had read as a scholar of English literature. His lyricism is informed as much by Anglo-European Romanticism as by the Chinese and Japanese literary traditions.

The speaker realizes that it is no longer possible to return to the way the natural world used to be and ends the poem with "white clouds," an image of formlessness. He suggests that the world moved more slowly in earlier times, before humans made their mark, evoking the feelings of William Wordsworth's "The World is Too Much with Us."

In the literati tradition, the image of white clouds would have afforded the speaker hope of Daoist or Buddhist transcendence, transporting him to the immortal realm or the Pure Land, but here he realizes that this traditional ideal is no longer a possibility in the modern world, where humanity has become alienated from nature. This loss is implied by the sound of the onomatopoeic phrase that ends the poem, *yūyū* (translated as "indifferently"), which also means "longing across a vast distance." In the present, white clouds are signs not of transcendental time and place but rather of inexpressible feelings of loss and metaphors for longing.

Sōseki's *kanshi* says much more than it at first seems to be saying: it is a modern poem in ancient form. Although this book is not about Sōseki's *kanshi* per se, it is about how *kanshi* and other aspects of literati culture informed his poetic sensibility and that of three other Japanese writers: Yosa Buson, Ema Saikō, and Masaoka Shiki. Like Sōseki, these writers worked in, or drew from, the *kanshi* form, making a claim to the literati tradition in order to become the poets they wanted to be. This volume demonstrates how they made these claims through close examinations of their poetic forms.

Tallahassee, FL, USA   Matthew Mewhinney

NOTES

1. Yoshikawa, *Yoshikawa Kōjirō zenshū*, 23: 567.
2. Vendler, *The Ocean, the Bird, and the Scholar*, 13.
3. Hass, *A Little Book on Form*, 3.
4. Alford, *Forms of Poetic Attention*, 3.
5. Natsume Sōseki, *Sōseki zenshū*, 18: 211–212. Translation mine.

REFERENCES

Alford, Lucy. *Forms of Poetic Attention.* New York: Columbia University Press, 2020.

Hass, Robert. *A Little Book on Form: An Exploration into the Formal Imagination of Poetry.* New York: Ecco, 2017.

Natsume Sōseki. *Soseki zenshū.* 29 vols. Tokyo: Iwanami Shoten, 2003.

Yoshikawa Kōjirō. *Yoshikawa Kōjirō zenshū.* 27 vols. Tokyo: Chikuma Shobō, 1976.

Vendler, Helen. *The Ocean, the Bird, and the Scholar: Essays on Poets and Poetry.* Cambridge, MA: Harvard University Press, 2015.

Notes on Style

The revised Hepburn system is used for transliterating Japanese terms and pinyin is used for transliterating Chinese terms; when otherwise unclear from context, the respective language for those terms is indicated by the abbreviations J. and Ch. Names of Japanese and Chinese persons are given in the traditional order, surname first and given name (or penname) second. When using one-name references to Japanese and Chinese authors in the text I follow customary usage: Buson for Yosa Buson, Wang for Wang Wei.

All Japanese poems under examination appear with an English transliteration, followed by the original Japanese (or Chinese) text. All *kanshi* (Chinese poems, or Sinitic verse) composed by a Japanese poet appear with an English transliteration of the *kundoku*—the "Japanese reading gloss" that approximates how the poem might have been read aloud in Japanese. In all cases, the *kundoku* derives from the editor(s) of the source collection, not the *kanshi* poet. Modifications to the *kundoku* made by the author of the present volume are noted.

ACKNOWLEDGMENTS

Many people have helped nurture this project from its fledgling form as a dissertation to its final form as a book. I am grateful to Alan Tansman for his close attention to my work, overseeing the project from start to finish, reading draft after draft, and offering valuable feedback every time. His curiosity and criticisms have invigorated the writing and revision process. I warmly thank Paula Varsano, H. Mack Horton, Dan O'Neill, Anne-Lise François, Kevis Goodman, and Jonathan Zwicker for their questions, guidance, and inspiration at various stages of the project. I extend thanks to the anonymous reviewer and editors at Palgrave Macmillan and Amyrose McCue Gill at TextFormations for their crucial work on the manuscript in the final stages before publication.

My passion for writing this book grew in the company of scholars who believe in the value of literature. I was honored when Keith Vincent and Wiebke Denecke hired me in 2018–2019 to teach their courses in the Department of World Languages and Literatures at Boston University. There I was able to explore new ideas with the intellectual support of my wonderful colleagues: Sarah Frederick, Sunil Sharma, Will Waters, Yuri Corrigan, Yoon Sun Yang, Peter Schwartz, Roberta Micallef, Anna Zielinska-Elliott, Margaret Litvin, Sassan Tabatabai, Abigail Gillman, Ines Garcia de la Puente, Noga Ganany, Petrus Liu, and Catherine Yeh.

I have benefited from many conversations with scholars of the four Japanese writers under examination here. Nakajima Kunihiko, Ikezawa Ichirō, Kōzen Hiroshi, Daniel Poch, and Sonja Arntzen generously shared their expertise with me, especially on Sōseki. I thank Matthew Fraleigh and Rob Tuck—fellow enthusiasts of modern *kanshi* and literati culture—for reading an early draft of the manuscript, finding errors, and offering helpful suggestions. Nick Albertson, Scott Mehl, Marianne Tarcov, and Andrew Campana have stirred new excitement for modern Japanese poetry—I would hope that my chapters on Shiki and Sōseki can join the conversation.

Since my arrival at Florida State University in 2019, research for this study has been funded by the Council on Research & Creativity, the Winthrop-King Institute, and my home department of Modern Languages & Linguistics. I thank my senior colleagues Rob Romanchuk, Reinier Leushuis, Andrew Epstein, Laura Lee, Lisa Wakamiya, and Annika Culver for their mentorship and feedback on the book. I also thank Sarah Stanley and Jonathan DaSo at Strozier library for assistance with the Sōseki Poetry Project and for expanding the Japanese collection.

Portions of this manuscript have appeared in print elsewhere. A part of Chap. 2 was published in "The Pheasant's Call and the Sound of Sympathy," *Japanese Language and Literature* 56, no.1 (Spring 2022): 1–41. A part of Chap. 5 was published in "Evincing Experience: Lyric in Natsume Sōseki's *Recollecting and Such*," *Proceedings of the Association for Japanese Literary Studies* 20 (2019): 157–167.

Completing the manuscript during a global pandemic was challenging, but the encouragement of friends from Berkeley made it possible in the end: Kerry Shannon, Brian Hurley, Shelby Oxenford, Nick Constantino, Margi Burge, Pedro Bassoe, Matt Wild, Jon Pitt, Daryl Maude, Brendan Morley, Bonnie McClure, and Sebastian Peel, all reminded me that the work is worthwhile.

John Nathan opened the door to Japanese literature for me as an undergraduate at UC Santa Barbara; his voice continues to inspire me to approach translation as an art. Robert Backus was a mentor and friend for many years until his passing in 2014; I miss our long chats about haiku, *kanshi*, and translation—I dedicate this book to him.

Lastly, I thank my parents Michael and Linda Mewhinney and my brother Ryan in San Francisco for their love and support and for being patient with me and my studies. The monthly care-packages of cookies and coffee were nourishment for both body and mind. Emma has been my lovely companion here in Tallahassee—thinking about poetry has made more sense after long walks with her.

CONTENTS

LIST OF FIGURES

CHAPTER 1

Introduction

This book is about what poetry can do. The aim is to show how, at a specific series of moments in Japanese literary history, poetry gave form to feeling while making a claim to an earlier literary tradition. Each chapter focuses on a single writer, examining how he or she expressed his or her lyricism through a poetic persona representing an idiosyncratic and lyric self by means of the poetic artifice afforded by the Japanese literati (*bunjin*) tradition.

Yosa Buson (1716–1783) and Ema Saikō (1787–1861) participated in a *bunjin* renaissance during the late eighteenth and early nineteenth centuries, or the Late Edo period (1750s–1867). Masaoka Shiki (1867–1902) and Natsume Sōseki (1867–1916) carried forth this legacy, practicing literati forms during the late nineteenth and early twentieth centuries, or the Meiji period (1867–1912). At this time, many Japanese writers were abandoning traditional forms for modern vernacular prose, precipitating the decline and eventual disappearance of the literati tradition.

All four of these figures have been called *bunjin*, a term that literary historians have used to characterize artists in the Japanese tradition who shared a set of practices and sensibilities that included composition in a variety of genres of poetry and painting drawn from both Japanese and Chinese traditions. Participation in *bunjin* culture involved cultivating an aesthetic attitude of "eccentricity" (*ki*), which artists displayed by experimenting with—and stretching the boundaries of—*bunjin* forms in the

M. Mewhinney, *Form and Feeling in Japanese Literati Culture*, https://doi.org/10.1007/978-3-031-11922-4_1

process of seeking an idiosyncratic language with which to represent sense, feeling, and emotion.

Form and Feeling in Japanese Literati Culture argues that these experiments with *bunjin* forms, performed in the name of eccentricity, required an ironic mode. Each writer created poetic forms using tropes drawn from the literati repertoire, an approach that constituted all four as *bunjin* subjects and endowed them with a sense of belonging to that tradition. At the same time, their chosen poetic forms reveal the personal qualities of each author's irony—namely, how each poet embraced the literati tradition by distancing him or herself from it in a unique way. The present volume contends that these writers' chosen poetic forms and their poetics of irony transformed the lineaments of lyric expression in *bunjin* culture and advanced the emergence of modern prose poetry in Japanese literature.

The four chapters of this book demonstrate that the lyricism of these writers relies on both clear and occluded kinds of poetic oppositions—including juxtaposition, contradiction, interruption, and incongruity—to represent feelings of anxiety, longing, and grief that reveal each poet's aesthetic and ironic distance from the literati tradition. D.C. Muecke defined the "art of irony" as "the art of saying something without really saying it. It is an art that gets its effects from below the surface, and this gives it a quality that resembles the depth and resonance of great art triumphantly saying much more than it seems to be saying."[1] Muecke has shown how irony in the Anglo-European tradition takes many forms and has many functions, comparing its elusiveness to that of vapor: "Getting to grips with irony seems to have something in common with gathering the mist; there is plenty to take hold of if only one could."[2] That very openness—the protean nature of irony—is what creates an indeterminacy of meaning and compels the reader to return to the page again and again. Irony, I argue, also afforded these four writers in the Japanese tradition a means of representing a lyric self that was open to multiple interpretations.

The notion of irony as central to the artifice of a great work of art allows us to think about its role in our performance as human beings. US philosopher Jonathan Lear has argued that irony is fundamental to the human condition, occurring when we "pretend," or make claims about who we are and the shape of our lives.[3] Lear defines "to pretend" as "to put oneself forward" or "to make a claim," adding that "pretense goes to the heart of human agency."[4] The idea is that putting oneself forward as a certain kind of person sets one up for a fall, occasioning irony when "pretense simultaneously expresses and falls short of its own aspiration."[5] I suggest that the idiosyncratic poetic forms created by the four Japanese writers under consideration here reveal a similar kind of irony, but that these authors' pretense as *bunjin* simultaneously expresses and *exceeds* its own aspiration. In other words, in trying to meet the expectations of the literati tradition, these poets' aesthetic attitudes took them beyond it, as is revealed by their experimentations with literary forms. Producing this kind of irony, I propose, was the only way that these four writers could represent an eccentric and lyric self and become the poets they wanted to be.

Form and Feeling opens new spaces for thinking about *bunjin* lyricism and the relationships among poetic form, irony, and the representation of self, sense, and feeling. Highlighting a critical moment in Japanese literary history—the transition from early modern (1603–1867) to modern (1867–present)—this book poses a larger question for literary studies by exploring how loss occasions poetry: Why did these four writers feel the need to forge new poetic forms in order to become the poets they wanted to be? One answer might be to say that this is what all great artists do: they make use of all available resources to say something new in a new way. I propose that another answer might be found by considering the decline of the literati tradition during the late nineteenth century, which Buson and Saikō might have foreseen and Shiki and Sōseki witnessed firsthand. By the early twentieth century, the literati tradition had disappeared; Sōseki lamented its loss in his final poem from 1916, the subject of the coda to this book.

LATE EDO LITERATI CULTURE

What has come to be regarded today as Japanese literati (*bunjin*) culture emerged in the early eighteenth century, but the term *bunjin* was used to refer to historical figures long before the Edo period (1603–1867), also known as early modern Japan. *Bunjin* is the Japanese transliteration of the Chinese term *wenren*, which has come to refer to "scholar-officials" from as early as the Song dynasty (960–1279). *Wenren* were elite polymaths who served as government officials and excelled in literature, philosophy, and politics.[6]

In the twentieth century the term *bunjin* gained cultural currency among literary historians, who used it to characterize various writers and thinkers who displayed mastery of multiple aesthetic forms and an aesthetic attitude that aspired toward the ideals of Late Edo literati culture.

Cheryl Crowley has remarked that this flexible application of the term makes its meaning opaque, but she has nonetheless found it compelling because it puts writers in conversation with the literary and visual culture of the Edo period.[7] I use the term to refer specifically to the performances of Buson, Saikō, Shiki, and Sōseki as *bunjin*: it was an ideal that each writer sought to achieve personally and to demonstrate poetically via experiments with form.

Edo *bunjin* modeled themselves on amateur fourteenth-century Chinese scholar-artists who disengaged from politics to concentrate on self-cultivation in the arts, literature, and philosophy. By the early eighteenth century these *bunjin* had formed an artisan culture devoted to creative pursuits in multiple genres across poetry, painting, and calligraphy. This culture blossomed in the early nineteenth century in the works of Kameda Bōsai (1752–1826), Tanomura Chikuden (1777–1835), Nishina Hakukoku (1791–1845), Kamei Nanmei (1743–1814), and Ōta Nanpo (1749–1823), all of whom have been studied as *bunjin* representative of the Edo period.[8]

Bunjin showcased their creativity through their reverence for ancient and classical traditions. As Leon Zolbrod has put it, "by moving forward, they took a step backward."[9] This reverence for the past was informed by the rise of classicism in two intellectual spheres over the course of the long eighteenth century. In the sphere of Chinese learning (*kangaku*), Confucian scholar Ogyū Sorai (1666–1728) criticized the heterodox schools of Neo-Confucian thought and called for a return to antiquity and to the Chinese classics in a doctrine that came to be known as the School of Ancient Language learning (*kobunjigaku*), or simply Ancient learning (*kogaku*).[10] Sorai and his followers were inspired by the Ancient Phraseology (Ch. *guwenci*; J. *kobunji*) movement of the Ming dynasty (1368–1644); they praised the poetry of the High Tang (eighth century) and promoted the imitation of classical models.[11]

Debates over this approach in Confucian circles paralleled a rising movement of nativism known as National learning (*kokugaku*). Kamo no Mabuchi (1697–1769) and Motoori Norinaga (1730–1801), National learning philologists and scholars, looked toward ancient and classical Japanese texts in an attempt to establish a native Japanese tradition.[12] The aim of their project was to distinguish Japanese literature and thought from the long-revered Chinese tradition.

Although the aesthetic ideals of *bunjin* culture derived primarily from the Chinese tradition, being *bunjin* meant having an open mind. *Bunjin* attended cultural salons that brought together scholars of Confucian thought and National learning, along with intellectuals from other fields of knowledge, including medicine.[13] This openness to distinct spheres of learning enriched creativity. While it was common for Confucian scholars also to be *bunjin*—such as Saikō's mentor Rai San'yō (1780–1832)—the ideal of free expression in *bunjin* culture prevented its participants from subscribing rigidly to a single doctrine or ideology.

This freedom of thought expanded with the wider availability of different kinds of books from abroad. In the early eighteenth century the Kyōhō Reforms loosened restrictions on the importation of books from China and Europe, including texts on *materia medica* and illustrated manuals for painting. Books from China introduced Japanese artists to the rich literary and visual culture of the Ming dynasty, which profoundly informed the development of *bunjin* aesthetics throughout the eighteenth century.

Participants in this artisan culture reproduced Ming aesthetics in their poetry and painting. Poetry in literati culture by and large referred to traditional Chinese poetry, or *shi*. This term was used to distinguish the genre from *uta*, or "song," another name for *waka*, or Japanese court poetry. When British and European poetry were imported in the nineteenth and twentieth centuries, *shi* came to refer to all poetry. In order to distinguish Chinese poetry from other genres, the term *kanshi*, or "Chinese poetry," was coined in the Meiji period.[14] Edo literature scholar Ikezawa Ichirō considers composition in *kanshi* to be a defining characteristic of a *bunjin*.[15]

Kanshi was the genre of poetry that *bunjin* conventionally combined with visual representation, as in the Chinese tradition. *Bunjin* learned how to paint from illustrated manuals; they emulated genres of traditional Chinese painting that included calligraphic inscriptions of *kanshi* lines either composed by the post-artist himself or quoted from another. Today these works have come to be called *bunjinga*, or literati painting. The genre includes mountain-stream landscapes (*sansuiga*) as well as ink-wash paintings (*suibokuga*) of natural objects ranging from rocks to blossoms to bamboo. Landscape paintings are also referred to as *nanga*, short for "Southern School of painting" (*nanshūga*), which blossomed in the Song dynasty.[16]

Mastering multiple forms was at the heart of being a *bunjin*, and by the late Edo period, literati culture had reached new heights of diversity. The literati repertoire originally comprised only Chinese aesthetic forms; by the Edo period it had also come to include Japanese genres of poetry, prose, and painting. By Japanese poetry I mean *haikai* (unorthodox verse), which is an umbrella term for all genres that derive from *haikai-no-renga*, or unorthodox linked verse. The opening verse of a linked-verse sequence is called a *hokku* and came to be called haiku in the Meiji period. When poets combined *hokku* with classical Japanese prose, they were writing in a prose poem genre called *haibun*. By Japanese painting I mean *haiga* (*haikai* painting), which comprised simple, cartoon-like images alongside *haikai* inscriptions. Zolbrod has observed that Buson used the simple representational mode of *haiga* to express more complex emotions than did other artists.[17]

LATE EDO LYRICISM

As Earl Miner remarked: "In the end what happens in a language and a literature is more important than the labels, although we find it difficult to say what happens without using our customary tokens."[18] Buson's and Saikō's compositions in the aforementioned forms and genres exemplify what I call the "lyricism" of Late Edo literati culture. Art historian James Cahill once described Chinese and Japanese literati painting, including works by Buson, as a "lyric journey."[19] In his 1990 study of comparative poetics, Miner used the term "lyric" to describe the foundations of East Asian literature. Since the 1980s, most scholars of traditional Japanese poetry have focused on the social, biographical, material, or political circumstances of poetic production, rather than on its affective or expressive dimension.[20] This may suggest that there is some ambivalence about applying the terms "lyricism" or "lyric" to traditional Japanese poetry—including that of literati culture—which some scholars would describe as a performance of tropes in the poetic tradition, rather than an expression of personal thoughts and feelings. However, I contend that Late Edo poets like Buson and Saikō drew from earlier kinds of lyricism in the tradition, composing poems that represent a self through the artifice of subjective and personal expression, or what is indeed commonly known as "lyric," that is, poetry that displays "heightened emotion and authentic sentiment" and "expresses a state of mind or a process of perception, thought, and feeling."[21]

Buson expressed his lyricism primarily in genres of *haikai*; Saikō in genres of *kanshi*. Their poetry absorbed the aesthetics of traditional Chinese painting as well as the poetics of late imperial Chinese poetry. In the *hokku* below, Buson deployed modes of lyricism from both the Chinese and Japanese poetic traditions, creating a poetic form that also represents an anxious state of mind:

The sea in spring
All the day long swells
Long swells.

haru no umi / hinemosu notari / notari kana
春の海終日のたりのたりかな [22]

Buson composed this poem around 1762, at the height of his career, and returned to it at different moments in his life: it appeared in his personal letters, in many anthologies of his poetry, and as an ekphrastic inscription on several paintings.

It was common for *bunjin* to combine words with painting, text with image. In one of his *haiga* (Fig. 1.1), Buson inscribed the *hokku* within the blank space depicting the sea.[23] Like the sea in all its vastness, the blankness promises openness and possibility. Buson rendered the poem in fluid brush strokes, representing an imaginary sea swell—the smooth long waves after a storm.

The poem's form—what makes the poem work as a poem—figures the blank space on the canvas as a space of calm and concern. The onomatopoeia *notari notari* (swells/Long swells) represents the slow heaving motion of the ocean. The eighth-century word *hinemosu* (all the day long) describes this rhythm as ancient, sending ripples of the present into the past, and back again. The poetic exclamation *kana* caps and contains this timeless rhythm, allowing it to reverberate, to swell ceaselessly. Spring is the season of hope and longing, which can be heard in the homophone *umi*, meaning both "sea" and "weariness"—the latter evoking the springtime languor, expectancy, and melancholy of an abandoned woman in Chinese poetry.[24] In tune with poetic convention, the sound of the sea heaving eternally is as much a soothing hymn as it is a plangent song.[25]

Through its form, the poem becomes an allegory for the anxiety of living up to *bunjin* ideals during the late eighteenth century. Buson spent his career living in the shadow of Matsuo Bashō (1644–1694), the great *haikai* poet of the seventeenth century. Crowley has shown that Buson was writing during a time of anxiousness over the loss of Bashō, when the *haikai* tradition was in desperate need of revival.[26] In Buson's poem, the calm rhythm of the sea swell is simultaneously the wavering of an anxious mind and the beating of a longing heart. Echoing the endless undulation of waves in its content, the poem rises and falls in its form, suggesting that these feelings of anxiety and longing will rise and fall forever.

Fig. 1.1 Yosa Buson. *Sea in Spring*, hanging scroll; ink and light color on paper; Image: 27.31 × 23.5 cm.; Minneapolis Institute of Art. Mary Griggs Burke Collection, Gift of the Mary and Jackson Burke Foundation. Public Domain

By creating a poetic form of ceaseless rising and falling waves, Buson makes a claim to the literati tradition while moving beyond it. The way the poem was received by his contemporaries highlights the aesthetic distance and irony of its form. Late Edo literatus Miyake Shōzan (1718–1801) included the poem in *Ancient Anthology of Haikai* (1763; Haikai kosen), recognizing it as an exemplary *hokku*. In *bunjin* style, Shōzan wrote a commentary in classical Chinese prose (*kanbun*), praising the poem for its representation of a traditional Chinese landscape and for its lyricism, revealing how Buson had with it transformed the *haikai* genre:

Bland and bold.
平淡而逸 [27]

By characterizing Buson's poem as "bland" (*heitan*), Shōzan suggests that it is both a representation of a traditional Chinese landscape painting and a moral expression of an inner self. *Heitan* refers to the ideal of "blandness" (Ch. *pingdan*) that Chinese literati painters have represented in landscape painting since the Song dynasty. John M. Rosenfield has described the representation of blandness as akin to the expression of sincerity: "Decorative opulence and displays of virtuoso technique were signs of vulgarity, because silk and colors could be bought and technique could be acquired through practice. Superficial visual appeal distracted both artist and viewer from penetrating into the moral and metaphysical heart of a subject."[28]

Shōzan's commentary shows how Buson's poem stands in for a Chinese painting, as much as it stands out as a poem from the heart, qualities that characterize the lyricism of his poetry. The word "bold" (*itsu*) stresses how Buson aspired toward the *heitan* ideal; the other meanings of *itsu* throw this aspiration into relief. In literati culture *itsu* was metonymic for the ideals of *ikkaku*, or "untrammeled personality," and *in'itsu*, or "eremitic." Another meaning is "transcendent," echoing Buson's ideal of "transcending the vulgar" (*rizoku*) in *haikai* poetry, which he aspired toward by evoking Chinese tradition in his *haikai*.

The word "bold" also suggests that the poem's voice is distinct. In this way, Buson's lyricism speaks to the heightened awareness of self in Late Edo *bunjin* culture that several scholars have described using different idioms. Ibi Takashi has discussed how *bunjin* concentrated on the workings of "the self's inner psychological life" (*jiko no naimenteki na seishin seikatsu*).[29] Lawrence Marceau has argued that *bunjin* could display a "bohemian" attitude working as independent artists practicing multiple forms; he describes Takebe Ayatari (1719–1774) as one such *bunjin* who practiced prose fiction, Chinese and Japanese poetry, and painting.[30] W. Puck Brecher has examined how a focus on the self gave rise to idiosyncratic artists who embraced aesthetic attitudes of strangeness in performances of "eccentricity" (*ki*) and "madness" (*kyō*).[31] These aspects of *bunjin* culture are reflected in the way Buson crafted a *hokku* that gives voice to an idiosyncratic and lyric self.

The increasing focus on the self that characterizes Late Edo lyricism can be seen on the material level of *haikai* production, in the evolution of *hokku* as an independent genre. The *haikai* genre was distinct from its poetic progenitors *waka* and *renga* because it allowed poets the freedom to talk about a wide range of topics, from the sonorous splash of a frog leaping into an ancient pond, to the aesthetic clash of plum blossom petals falling on piles of horse dung. During the Edo period *haikai* surged in popularity and precipitated the decline of poetry as a necessarily collective and social practice.[32] This can be seen in how *haikai* poets, including Buson, were already composing *hokku* individually, with the latent possibility of linking them to a fourteen-syllable verse at a future linked-verse session.[33] *Haikai* poets compiled collections (*kushū*) of their *hokku*, showing that the form could stand alone, like Buson's poem on the spring sea.

The increasing emphasis on writing about matters of the self in the Edo period encouraged experimentation with new theories of lyric expression. In particular, two currents in late imperial Chinese lyricism informed Late Edo *bunjin* culture: the poetics of "natural sensibility" (Ch. *xingling*; J. *seirei*)—that is, the expression of personality by writing from personal experience of everyday life—and the poetics of "blending of feeling and scene" (Ch. *qing jing jiao rong*)—that is, combining representations of the natural world with those of personal states of mind.

Seirei poetics called for spontaneous poetic expression—drawing inspiration from one's inner nature to communicate heart, mind, and soul. Nakamura Shin'ichirō has observed that these poetics fundamentally transformed the philosophy of Late Edo *kanshi*, arguing that *kanshi* from the late eighteenth century onward diversified in topic and embraced "individuated expression" (*koseiteki hyōgen*) and "modern consciousness" (*kindai ishiki*), a poetics that he likened to Romanticism.[34] Ibi Takashi has traced *seirei* poetics to the writings of late Ming dynasty poet Yuan Hongdao (1568–1610; penname Zhonglang):

> Whatever the heart-mind wants to express, the wrist can convey it.... If you apprehend a place with the heart-mind, and convey the heart-mind with the wrists, then there is nothing that natural sensibility cannot totally transmit. This is what is called 'true poetry.'[35]

In the Qing dynasty (1644–1912), Yuan Hongdao's ideas were expounded upon by another poet of the same surname, Yuan Mei (1716–1797),[36] who declared: "Poetry is what expresses one's nature and emotion. It is enough to look no further than one's self [for the material of poetry]. If its words move the heart, its colors catch the eye, its taste pleases the mouth, and its sound delights the ear, then it is good poetry."[37] Late Edo literati culture absorbed these ideas, giving rise to poetry that mediated subjective representations of the world.

In the late eighteenth century, Buson displayed his "natural sensibility" by representing feelings in a *hokku* on the spring sea. As Saikō's works show, decades later, *seirei* poetics also called for representations of the everyday, allowing poets to use poetry as autobiography. In a separate collection, Buson's poem appeared with the headnote "At Suma Bay," suggesting that he had composed the poem on a journey to Suma.

Buson's headnote inspired later readers to interpret his poem as a record of his personal observations. In the late nineteenth century, Masaoka Shiki celebrated Buson for his "objective beauty" (*kyakkanteki bi*), or representation of things as they are. Shiki and his colleagues Takahama Kyoshi (1874–1959) and Kawahigashi Hekigotō (1873–1937) agreed that the poem was an empirical record of Buson observing (as opposed to imagining) the spring sea, but they disagreed about the exact object of representation: Shiki saw light waves lapping on the shore, Kyoshi saw a heaving swell far off in the bay, and Hekigotō saw a sweeping view of the entire sea.[38] In 1950 R. H. Blyth joined the conversation and praised the poem for "expressing our feelings by the spring sea and the nature of the spring sea without leaning either to the subjective, or to the objective."[39]

My reading of Buson's poem as ekphrasis allows for the sea to be imaginary, a representation infused with personal feeling from the heart, wherein the painting of the spring sea merges with an anxious mind. This is a lyricism informed by the Chinese poetics of "blending feeling and scene," which can be traced to Qing dynasty poet Wang Fuzhi (1619–1692):

> In spite of the fact that 'feeling' is in the mind and 'scene' is with things, 'scene' engenders 'feeling' and so does 'feeling' engender scene. Whether the 'feeling' evoked is sorrow or joy, whether the 'scene' encountered is one that thrives or withers, they reside and hide in each other's dwelling.[40]

Wang's idea emerged in the late seventeenth century, but he applied to all Chinese poetry his theory that "feeling" (*qing*) and "scene" (*jing*) are inseparable.[41] As Cecile Sun describes in her reading of Wang, the poem enacts "the mutually affective dynamism between man and nature to generate a flow of meaning between 'feeling' and 'scene' that never stagnates"[42]—Buson's endless undulation of waves.

These currents in late imperial Chinese lyricism also informed the works of Saikō, who composed *kanshi* and painted in various genres of traditional Chinese painting; she is most known for her ink-brush paintings of bamboo. In the early nineteenth century, Saikō incorporated the poetics of "natural sensibility" in poems where she constructed an "authentic voice" insofar as it met the conventions of women's poetry and the expectation that her self-representation was truthful, as Mari Nagase has argued.[43] Nagase has shown how this at times gave rise to contradictions between Saikō's authentic self as a woman and the feminine persona she constructed. I read these contradictions as the cornerstone of Saikō's irony.

Saikō's poetry also shows how Late Edo lyricism was enhanced by the rise of scientific empiricism in natural history and *materia medica*, which influenced Japanese poetry and painting throughout the nineteenth century.[44] As the daughter of a scholar of Dutch learning (*rangaku*) and a physician, Saikō was conversant with early nineteenth-century science and medicine. The fruits of such knowledge can be found in her poems where the lyric subject intensely scrutinizes a living form and communicates that experience through the senses. By the late eighteenth century, these methods of empirical observation had dovetailed with the pictorial realism of Dutch-style painting (*ranga*). By the early nineteenth century, these trends inspired *bunjin* painters to represent a "true view" (*shinkei*)—an authentic representation that was true to the heart and mind of a literati painter, or in other words, his or her subjective experience.[45]

MEIJI LYRICISM

From the early nineteenth century, *bunjin* culture was absorbing intellectual and poetic currents beyond the borders of the Chinese and Japanese traditions. By Meiji in the late nineteenth century, *bunjin* forms had incorporated new images from the British and European Romantic traditions in particular.[46] The empirical and realist modes of representation that had emerged in the Late Edo period were brought to further fruition by a new literary language of realism that "unified speech and writing" (*genbun'itchi*).

Shiki and Sōseki began writing at this time, when *bunjin* culture had become an antiquarian practice: *kanshi*, in all its forms, had come to be regarded as outmoded; meanwhile, *haikai* had become modernized as haiku and had come to be recognized as its own modern lyric genre. Komuro Yoshihiro has shown how the legacy of *hokku* that represented a poet's idiosyncratic style can be seen in the genre of "*bunjin* haiku" in the modern period.[47] Even though haiku and *kanshi* had been transformed by the lyricism of Buson and Saikō, they still belonged to the category of traditional poetic convention. As modern *bunjin*, Shiki and Sōseki transformed this tradition by combining these poetic genres and conventions with literary realism.

Shiki and Sōseki modernized *haibun* by bringing haiku and *kanshi* together with a new vernacular language of modern prose infused with the imported lyricism of British and German Romanticism as well as the realism of the nineteenth-century Anglo-European novel. This lyricism emphasized the individual and his or her subjective experience, and was informed by ideas such as the "Romantic artist," whose poetry was devoted to the "spheres of natural beauty and personal feeling,"[48] as well as by the notion of the poetic imagination as a "blending, fusing power."[49] Romanticism also brought ideas from eighteenth-century natural history and biology, including that of "organic form," a morphological metaphor for a poetic form that, in the words of Samuel Taylor Coleridge (1772–1834), "shapes as it develops from within,"[50] and that thereby seemed to represent the poet's inner world "naturally."

Shiki and Sōseki absorbed these Romantic ideas and created modern *bunjin* forms—"organic forms" that unfolded according to the poet's senses and feelings rather than to a predetermined poetic form. Shiki wrote lyrical essays about his inner life in modern vernacular prose saturated by poetic genres drawn from the literati repertoire. Sōseki wrote a lyrical novel about a Romantic artist who composes haiku and *kanshi* in his quest to find natural beauty in addition to a memoir that, through the composition of haiku and *kanshi*, attempts to recollect senses and feelings. I treat these works by Shiki and Sōseki as experimental prose poems that mediate sense and feeling organically through a contrapuntal narrative motion between poetic moments marked by haiku and *kanshi*, and narrative progress made through modern vernacular prose. These prose poems display the sensory dimensions and lyric affordances of modern literary form, which could represent the diverse range of senses and personal feelings of a living organism.

Becoming the Poets They Wanted to Be

As Kenneth Burke wrote: "We cannot use language maturely until we are spontaneously at home in irony."[51] The four writers treated in this book displayed mastery of *bunjin* forms and represented a longing to feel at home in *bunjin* culture, which they did ironically. Each of them stood on the periphery of literati culture—a liminal position that these poets performed in a lyric voice that was anxious about living up to its ideals. And still their poetic forms exceeded the expectations of the literati tradition by transforming it through irony.

For most of Japanese literary history, being a *bunjin* was a possibility exclusive to the elite class, which in the Edo period was the warrior class (*bushi*). After the Kyōhō reforms of the early eighteenth century, the privilege was extended to members of the lower social classes. Not much is known about Buson's background, but biographers claim that he came from a farming village at Kema, near Osaka. Committing to *bunjin* ideals was a special aspiration, and his endeavors as a *haikai* teacher and poet likely added to his anxiety about attaining it. Buson's poetry thus represents an anxious longing to belong to literati culture by trying to bridge the *haikai* and *kanshi* genres.

Saikō was, in contrast, a member of the warrior class. She was the eldest daughter of Ema Ransai (1747–1838), an accomplished physician in the Ōgaki domain in Mino (present-day Gifu), a region rich in samurai culture and known for its many scholars, writers, and artisans. Until Late Edo, literati culture had been exclusive to men. Saikō's father was a savant of both Confucian and Dutch learning, and he raised his daughter like a son, encouraging her to learn the ways of *bunjin*. She produced her first painting, of bamboo, at age five and spent her early years studying painting with Kyoto masters. At age twenty-seven she learned how to compose *kanshi* under the tutelage of Rai San'yō, who served as her mentor until his death. As scholars Atsuko Sakaki and Mari Nagase have shown, in choosing to compose *kanshi* Saikō deviated from traditional gender norms and diverged from the expectations of women poets who wrote in this genre.[52] Saikō was not the only woman in the period to participate in literati culture, but her poetry reveals the loneliness of a woman writing in a genre whose expectations had been set by men, and represents the anxiety of a woman *bunjin*.

Compared to Buson, Shiki, and Sōseki, Saikō stands out for several reasons: she is a woman, she did not compose *haikai*, and she is not as well known in literary history. Ironically, though, it is Saikō who was the most connected to literati culture in the traditional sense, as she only practiced traditional Chinese forms. Through San'yō, she gained recognition among Late Edo's most esteemed *bunjin*, all of whom praised her talents as a *keishū*, or "talented woman of the inner chamber," the feminine poetic persona Saikō performed in her poetry. She also lived during the relatively cosmopolitan early nineteenth century, when literati culture had come to include aesthetic thought beyond the Chinese and Japanese traditions, leading painters to experiment with new realist modes of representation in the European style. By limiting herself to the *kanshi* form and its poetic conventions, Saikō could express her brand of irony by concealing it in the very artifice that made irony so difficult to convey.

Buson's influence on Shiki and Sōseki has been noted by several scholars, including Mark Morris and Morimoto Tetsurō.[53] I propose that Saikō's irony, read together with that of Buson, can shed new light on how Shiki and Sōseki experimented with the literati tradition in the modern period, when its tropes had become calcified relics of the past, yet the meaning of its tropes could still take figurative turns through irony.[54]

Shiki and Sōseki were both born in 1867, the last year of the Edo period and the first year of Meiji. They were modern writers who aspired toward *bunjin* ideals in an age when traditional culture had entered a state of collapse. Although the Edo class system had become defunct with modernization, coming from a warrior-class family still had its benefits. Shiki was the eldest son of a samurai of the Matsuyama domain (present-day Ehime); his maternal grandfather was a Confucian scholar. This pedigree gave Shiki the opportunity to acquire profound knowledge of the Chinese classics, which he exhibited in nearly 2000 compositions of *kanshi*. In literary history Shiki is remembered as a poet and reformer of *haikai* and *waka*. The fact that his prolific production in *kanshi* is rarely mentioned highlights the gulf between literati culture and the framing of modern Japanese literature.[55]

Shiki and Sōseki became close friends at Tokyo Imperial University. They shared their appreciation for Late Edo literati culture by composing and exchanging *kanshi* and haiku. Sōseki came from a merchant-class family, making him a member of the bourgeoisie. He learned the Chinese classics as a part of his primary education and eventually shifted his studies to English letters. He became a scholar and critic of English literature and spent two years abroad in London as an ambassador for the Japanese Ministry of Education. After returning from England in the years following Shiki's death in 1902, Sōseki began his career as a novelist. In his spare time, he composed 208 *kanshi* and more than 2000 haiku, and produced works of calligraphy as well as paintings in the literati style. Today he is known only for his novels, leading his most recent biographer in English to regard him as "modern Japan's greatest novelist."[56]

Shiki's participation in *bunjin* culture revealed a deep sense of irony, and Sōseki's a much darker one. Both men made their claim to the literati tradition when it entered a ghostlike existence after many writers had abandoned traditional forms for modern vernacular prose with the rise of the novel. In the late nineteenth century, Shiki and Sōseki thus confronted a paradoxical question: "Among the *bunjin*, is there a *bunjin*?" The first part of the question acknowledges *bunjin* as a possibility; the second casts doubt on that very possibility. For Shiki, and especially for Sōseki as a novelist, participating in *bunjin* culture required the forging of new forms. Both writers kept the literati tradition alive by attempting to create modern prose poems, organic forms that represented anxiety, longing, and grief in a self-referential way and that heralded the mournful end of literati culture.

THE STRUCTURE OF THE PRESENT BOOK

Form and Feeling begins in the Late Edo period, when literati culture reached its height in Japan. Chapter 2 shows how Yosa Buson participated in this artistic renaissance, transforming the poetics of juxtaposition in *haikai*. I show how Buson combined diction, images, and genres from *bunjin* painting, creating *haikai* forms that merged an anxious state of mind with representations of the natural world in literati painting—as we have already seen in the poem discussed above. I argue that these experimental syntheses made Buson's *haikai* ekphrastic and that he used ekphrasis to long for *bunjin* culture and to bring new visual dimensions to *haikai* poetry.

Chapter 3 remains in Late Edo but shifts focus to Ema Saikō and how her poetics of contradiction ironized the *kanshi* genre, expressing a sensuality beyond the reach of poetic convention or topos. As a woman she was required to adhere to the conventions of women's poetry, but she did not limit herself to them. Saikō created poems that represented her existential self by asserting her sense and sensibility as a literata writing through the very literary artifice that entrapped the representation of self in poetic convention. This chapter shows how Saikō refigured the tropes of sensual experience in the inner chamber as a lyricism that revealed the irony of being a woman *bunjin*.

The book then moves to the Meiji period to examine how modern writers used literary form as allegory for cultural collapse by creating new kinds of opposition, including interruption and incongruity. Chapter 4 shows how Masaoka Shiki represented his own ill body as a metaphor for the dissolution of literati culture. Shiki created organic forms that combined the poetic artifices of the literati tradition with the realism of modern vernacular prose. I argue that these literary forms simulate a living and dying organism through a discursive style of narrative prose interrupted by poetic references, quotations, and other tropes from Romanticism and the *bunjin* tradition. I contend that the contrapuntal narrative motion of his prose poems creates an organic rhythm through which Shiki both mediated his senses and feelings and represented the decline of literati culture.

Chapter 5 examines the farthest reaches of *bunjin* culture's modern, Meiji-era transformation in the works of Natsume Sōseki. I show how Sōseki worked the language of literati culture into the weave of prose in both seamless and interruptive ways, creating poetic narratives of harmonious dissonance. Sōseki represented grief through a lyricism that combined haiku and *kanshi* with modern vernacular prose, which I examine in his novel *Pillow of Grass* (1906; Kusamakura) and in his memoir *Recollecting and Such* (1910; Omoidasu koto nado). The oscillation between prose and poetry in both narratives creates an organic rhythm between stasis and movement that evokes the alternation of loss and restoration in the grieving process, and that simulates the beating pulse of a living organism. This chapter shows how *Pillow of Grass* and *Recollecting and Such* are works of irony because they end without the artificiality of literary closure, suggesting that the grieving process can only be represented through the organic open-endedness afforded by the prose poem.

Form and Feeling concludes with a coda that examines Sōseki's final *kanshi*, the single lyric form from literati culture that he shared with Buson, Saikō, and Shiki. I read the poem as an allegory for—and enactment of—the future of form and feeling in literati culture in the absence of *kanshi*. The poem concludes with the poet singing a song to white clouds, an ironic and paradoxical ending that intimates the possibility that literati culture might survive only as a disembodied echo in the ether of Japanese cultural memory.

NOTES

1. Muecke, *The Compass of Irony*, 5.
2. Ibid., 3.
3. Lear, *A Case for Irony.*
4. Ibid., 10.
5. Ibid., 13.
6. In Japan, Sugawara no Michizane (845–903 CE) is one example of a *bunjin* who was a scholar, poet, and politician. See Borgen, *Sugawara no Michizane.*
7. Crowley, "Knowing Elegance," 239–250.
8. See Tokuda, *Bunjin*; Ikezawa, *Edo bunjinron.*
9. Zolbrod, *Reluctant Genius*, "Eighth Installment," 61.
10. Backus, "The Kansei Prohibition." On the rise of orthodoxy in Edo Confucianism, see Backus, "The Motivation."
11. For more on Sorai and eighteenth-century Confucianism, see Flueckiger, *Imagining Harmony*, 61–115.
12. For more on Mabuchi and Norinaga, see Flueckiger, *Imagining Harmony*, 145–209.
13. For a social history of Edo salon culture, see Nosco, *Individuality in Early Modern Japan*, 81–96.
14. For more on nineteenth-century *kanshi*, see Gōyama, *Bakumatsu-Meijiki*. For an overview of Sinitic prose and poetry in Japanese literary history, see Takigawa, *Bunka sōchi.*
15. Ikezawa Ichirō, "Nihon ni okeru 'bunjin' to wa," 167.
16. Literati painting in the Edo period is generally referred to as *nanga* (lit. southern painting) or *bunjinga* (lit. literati painting). Both terms denote the same style of painting practiced by eighteenth-century *bunjin*, including Buson, Sakaki Hyakusen (1697–1753), Ike no Taiga (1723–1776), and Maruyama Ōkyo (1733–1795). *Nanga* is a mixture of styles developed by two schools of painting in the Song dynasty: the Northern school and the Southern school. The Northern school comprised professional artists who painted with technical precision. The Southern school comprised amateurs, or scholar-gentlemen, who valued subjective expression. They painted from the heart and inscribed poems on their paintings. Painting styles from both schools mixed during the Yuan (1279–1368), Ming (1368–1644), and Qing (1644–1912) dynasties. It was during this period when *nanga* and other Chinese paintings were first imported to Japan. These paintings served as the bedrocks of *bunjin* aesthetics throughout and beyond the Edo period.
17. Zolbrod, *Reluctant Genius*, "Sixteenth Installment," 52–53.
18. Miner, *Comparative Poetics*, 92.
19. Cahill, *The Lyric Journey.*

20. One exception is Levy, *Hitomaro*. Levy's argument for lyricism was challenged in Ebersole, *Ritual Poetry*.
21. Brewster, *Lyric*, 2–3; Abrams, *A Glossary of Literary Terms*, 108–9. The entry for "lyric" from the *Oxford English Dictionary*: "Adj. 1. Of or pertaining to the lyre; adapted to the lyre, meant to be sung; pertaining to or characteristic of song. Now used as the name for short poems (whether or not intended to be sung), usually divided into stanzas or strophes, and directly expressing the poet's own thoughts and sentiments. Hence, applied to the poet who composes such poems." The adjective "lyrical" is an older synonym of "lyric."
22. Yosa Buson, *Buson zenshū*, 4: 25. From here on *BZ*.
23. For more Buson *haiga* featuring the same poem, see *BZ*, 6: 408, 448.
24. This *umi* 倦み appears in Li Qingzhao's (1084–1155) "To the Tune 'Spring in Wuling': "When the winds stop, the ground is fragrant, the flowers all are down, / as the day wears on I'm too lazy [*juan* 倦] to comb my hair. / The objects are right, the people wrong, everything is over now! / About to speak, tears first flow." Egan and Shields, *The Works of Li Qingzhao*, 162.
25. Buson scholars Muramatsu Tomotsugu and Yamamoto Kenkichi have remarked on the feelings of "melancholy" (*mono-uge*) and "longing" (*akogare-gokoro*) in the poem. Yosa Buson, *Buson shū*, 102; Yamamoto, *Yosa Buson*, 69.
26. Crowley, *Haikai Poet Yosa Buson*.
27. *BZ*, 8: 115.
28. Rosenfield, *Mynah Birds*, 26.
29. Ibi, *Edo no bunjin saron*, 4.
30. Marceau, *Takebe Ayatari*.
31. Brecher, *The Aesthetics of Strangeness*.
32. Robert Tuck has examined the relationship between *kanshi* and haiku and late nineteenth-century media, evincing that poetry as social practice continued and crossed national boundaries in the nineteenth and twentieth centuries. See Tuck, *Idly Scribbling Rhymers*.
33. *Renga* (linked verse) was a collaborative poetic form that reached its zenith in the medieval period. In *renga*, two or more poets gathered to compose sequences of alternating long (5-7-5) and short (7-7) stanzas, which they repeated to a decided limit. The standard form of *renga* was 100 verses (*hyakuin*). In exceptional cases, poets also practiced "solo composition" (*dokugin*)—for an example see Carter, *The Road to Komatsubara*.
34. Nakamura, *Edo kanshi*, 67–271.
35. The quote comes from the preface to a collection of Yuan's poems by Jiang Yingke (1553–1605; penname Jinzhi). Ibi, *Edo Shiikaron*, 68.

36. For a recent discussion of Yuan Mei's poetic theories, see Schmidt, *Harmony Garden*, 227–236.
37. Liu, *The Art of Chinese Poetry*, 73. The kernel of Yuan Mei's statement resonates with the oldest theory of lyric expression in Chinese found in the preface to *Classic of Poetry* (Shijing): "poetry expresses the heart's intent" (*shi yan zhi*); but here he adds a new concern for sensuous embodiment. In other writings, Yuan Mei extends this concern for the sensual to the depiction of romance between men and women, which resonates with themes of vernacular fiction of the late imperial period. Ibi notes that this is the main difference between Yuan Hongdao's *xingling* and Yuan Mei's *xingling*: the latter's emphasis on emotion evoked by the love between men and women.
38. Masaoka Shiki, *Shiki zenshū*, 17: 258–259. I thank Keith Vincent for bringing this to my attention.
39. Blyth, *Haiku*, 2: 135.
40. Sun, *The Poetics of Repetition*, 190.
41. This blending and mutual dependency between feeling and scene is also found in the ideas of late Qing intellectual and poet Wang Guowei (1877–1927). Wang Guowei embraced Wang Fuzhi's idea of blending lyricism and visuality, and he connected it with the aesthetic philosophies of Immanuel Kant (1724–1804) and Arthur Schopenhauer (1788–1860) in the Western tradition. Wang, *The Lyrical in Epic Time*, xv, 303.
42. Sun, 190.
43. Nagase, "Truly, they are a lady's words," 279–305.
44. By empiricism, I am referring to the new concentration on a single object and setting it apart from its environment in eighteenth-century literati painting. Federico Marcon has examined the epistemology of nature in early modern Japan and argues that between the early seventeenth and the mid-nineteenth centuries, the discipline of natural history became more secular and objective, separating itself from spiritual and philosophical understandings of the natural world. He notes that this method of cataloguing natural objects resembled and rivaled contemporaneous developments in European science. In his discussion on scholars of *materia medica*, or *honzōgaku* (the study of medicinal herbs), Marcon argues that by the eighteenth century, naturalists began to depart from lexicographical work, and instead ventured into the wild to catalogue objects in nature: "To these scholars, nature was no longer conceivable as an organic, meaningful, and homopoietic space of supernatural and mystifying relations but as a multitude of objects—myriads of things (*banbutsu*)." Marcon, *The Knowledge of Nature*, 10.
45. This also gave rise to a poetics of the quotidian, the influences of which can be seen in the diversity of objects that appear in Edo poetry and in the expression of feelings and scenes of everyday life. As Suzuki Ken'ichi has

shown, the *kanshi, haikai,* and *waka* genres expanded their vocabulary to include images and soundscapes outside of the poetic tradition. Suzuki, *Edo shiika no kūkan*; Suzuki, *Edo shiikashi no kōsō.*

46. After the importation of British and European Romanticism in the nineteenth century, *kanshi* incorporated aesthetics and images from the English, French, and German poetic traditions. For more on how the range of content in classical Chinese text expanded to translate European texts by the nineteenth century, see Fraleigh, "Rearranging the figures on the tapestry."

47. Komuro, *Bunjin haiku no sekai*, 5–11.

48. Williams, *Culture & Society*, 30.

49. This is Romantic poet Samuel Taylor Coleridge's (1772–1834) theorization of the poetic imagination as a "synthetic, a "permeative," and a "blending, fusing power." Abrams, *The Mirror and the Lamp*, 169.

50. Ibid., 213.

51. Burke, *Language as Symbolic Action*, 12.

52. Sakaki, "Women in the Heterosocial Literary Field of Early Modern Japan"; Nagase, "Women Writers of Chinese Poetry in Late-Edo Period Japan."

53. Morris, "Buson and Shiki: Part One," "Buson and Shiki: Part Two." Morimoto, *Tsuki wa higashi ni.*

54. Shiki's and Sōseki's modern prose experiments likely were also informed by the ironic narratives of seventeenth-century *haikai* poet and fiction writer Ihara Saikaku (1642–1693). For a study of Saikaku's irony, see Gundry, *Parody.* Saikaku's legacy during Meiji, however, was more visible in popular fiction and melodrama—for example, the works of Ozaki Kōyō (1869–1903), Izumi Kyōka (1873–1939), and other writers of the literary coterie Kenyūsha, or "Friends of the Inkstone."

55. The recent work on nineteenth-century *kanshi* by Matthew Fraleigh and Robert Tuck has attempted to close this gap. See Fraleigh, *Plucking Chrysanthemums*, and Tuck, *Idly Scribbling Rhymers.*

56. Nathan, *Sōseki.*

References

Abrams, M.H. *The Mirror and the Lamp: Romantic Theory and the Critical Tradition* (Oxford: Oxford University Press, 1971.
———. *A Glossary of Literary Terms.* Fort Worth, TX: Harcourt Brace, 1993.
Backus, Robert L. "The Kansei Prohibition of Heterodoxy and Its Effects on Education." In *Harvard Journal of Asiatic Studies* 39, no. 1 (Jun., 1979a): 55–106.
———. "The Motivation of Confucian Orthodoxy in Tokugawa Japan." In *Harvard Journal of Asiatic Studies* 39, no. 2 (Dec., 1979b): 275–338.

Blyth, R.H. *Haiku*. 4 vols. Tokyo: Hokuseido Press, 1950.

Brecher, W. Puck. *The Aesthetics of Strangeness: Eccentricity and Madness in Early Modern Japan*. Honolulu: University of Hawaii Press, 2013.

Brewster, Scott. *Lyric*. New York: Routledge, 2009.

Borgen, Robert. *Sugawara no Michizane and the Early Heian Court*. Cambridge, MA: Harvard University Press, 1986.

Burke, Kenneth. *Language as Symbolic Action: Essays on Life, Literature, and Method*. Berkeley, CA: University of California Press, 1966.

Cahill, James A. *The Lyric Journey: Poetic Painting in China and Japan*. Cambridge, MA: Harvard University Press, 1996.

Carter, Steven D. *The Road to Komatsubara: A Classical Reading of the Renga Hyakuin*. Cambridge, MA: Harvard University Asia Center, 1987.

Crowley, Cheryl. *Haikai Poet Yosa Buson and the Bashō Revival*. Boston: Brill, 2007.

———. "Knowing Elegance: The Ideals of the *Bunjin* (Literatus) in Early Modern Haikai." In *New Essays in Japanese Aesthetics*, edited by A. Minh Ngyuyen, 239–250. New York: Lexington Books, 2017.

Ebersole, Gary. *Ritual Poetry and The Politics of Death in Early Japan*. Princeton, NJ: Princeton University Press, 1989.

Egan, Ronald and Anna Shields, eds. *The Works of Li Qingzhao*. Boston: De Gruyter Mouton, 2019.

Fraleigh, Matthew. *Plucking Chrysanthemums: Narushima Ryūhoku and Sinitic Literary Traditions in Modern Japan*. Cambridge, MA: Harvard University Asia Center, 2016.

———. "Rearranging the figures on the tapestry: what Japanese direct translation of European texts can tell us about *kanbun kundoku*." *Japan Forum* 31, no. 1 (2019): 4–32.

Flueckiger, Peter. *Imagining Harmony: Poetry, Empathy, and Community in Mid-Tokugawa Confucianism and Nativism*. Stanford, CA: Stanford University Press, 2011.

Gōyama Rintarō. *Bakumatsu-Meijiki ni okeru Nihon kanshibun no kenkyū*. Tokyo: Izumi Shoin, 2014.

Gundry, David. *Parody, Irony, and Ideology in the Fiction of Ihara Saikaku*. Boston: Brill, 2017.

Ibi Takashi. *Edo Shiikaron*. Tokyo: Kyūko Shoin, 1998.

———. *Edo no bunjin saron: chishikijin to geijutsuka tachi*. Tokyo: Yoshikawa Kōbunkan, 2009.

Ikezawa Ichirō. *Edo bunjinron: Ōta Nanpo o chūshin ni*. Tokyo: Kyūko shoin, 2000.

———. "Nihon ni okeru 'bunjin' to wa." In *Koten bungaku no jōshiki o utagau*, edited by Matsuda Hiroshi, et al., 164–167. Tokyo: Bensei Shuppan, 2017.

Komuro Yoshihiro. *Bunjin haiku no sekai*. Tokyo: Hon'ami Shoten, 1997.

Lear, Jonathan. *A Case for Irony*. Cambridge, MA: Harvard University Press, 2011.

Levy, Ian Hideo. *Hitomaro and the Birth of Japanese Lyricism*. Princeton, NJ: Princeton University Press, 1984.

Liu, James J.Y. *The Art of Chinese Poetry*. Chicago: The University of Chicago Press, 1962.

Nagase, Mari. "Women Writers of Chinese Poetry in Late-Edo Period Japan." PhD diss., University of British Columbia, 2007.

———. "'Truly, they are a lady's words': Ema Saikō and the Construction of an Authentic Voice in Late Edo Period Kanshi." *Japanese Language and Literature* 48, No. 2 (October 2014): 279–305.

Nakamura Shin'ichirō. *Edo kanshi*. Tokyo: Iwanami Shoten, 1998.

Nathan, John. *Sōseki: Modern Japan's Greatest Novelist*. New York: Columbia University Press, 2018.

Nosco, Peter. *Individuality in Early Modern Japan: Thinking for Oneself*. New York: Routledge, 2018.

Marceau, Laurence E. *Takebe Ayatari: A Bunjin Bohemian in Early Modern Japan*. Ann Arbor: Center for Japanese Studies, University of Michigan, 2004.

Marcon, Federico. *The Knowledge of Nature and the Nature of Knowledge in Early Modern Japan*. Chicago: The University of Chicago Press, 2015.

Masaoka Shiki. *Shiki zenshū*. 25 vols. Tokyo: Kōdansha, 1976.

Miner, Earl. *Comparative Poetics: An Intercultural Essay on Theories of Literature*. Princeton, NJ: Princeton University Press, 1990.

Morimoto Tetsurō. *Tsuki wa higashi ni: Buson no yume, Sōseki no maboroshi*. Tokyo: Shinchōsha, 1992.

Morris, Mark. "Buson and Shiki: Part One." *Harvard Journal of Asiatic Studies* 44, no. 2 (December 1984): 381–425.

———. "Buson and Shiki: Part Two." *Harvard Journal of Asiatic Studies* 45, no. 1 (June 1985): 255–321.

Muecke, D.C. *The Compass of Irony*. London: Metheun & Co., Ltd., 1969.

Rosenfield, John M. *Mynah Birds and Flying Rocks: Word and Image in the Art of Yosa Buson*. Lawrence, KS: Spencer Museum of Art, The University of Kansas, 2003.

Sakaki, Atsuko. "Women in the Heterosocial Literary Field of Early Modern Japan." *U.S.-Japan Women's Journal English Supplement* 17 (1999): 3–38.

Schmidt, J.D. *Harmony Garden: The Life, Literary Criticism, and Poetry of Yuan Mei (1716–1798)*. New York: Routledge, 2016.

Sun, Cecile Chu-chin. *The Poetics of Repetition in English and Chinese Lyric Poetry*. Chicago: The University of Chicago Press, 2011.

Suzuki Ken'ichi. *Edo shiika no kūkan*. Tokyo: Shinwasha, 1998.

———. *Edo shiikashi no kōsō*. Tokyo: Iwanami Shoten, 2004.

Takigawa Kōji, Nakamoto Dai, Fukushima Riko, and Gōyama Rintarō, eds. *Bunka sōchi toshite no Nihon kanbungaku*. Tokyo: Bensei Shuppan, 2019.

Tokuda Takeshi, ed. *Bunjin: Kameda Bōsai, Tanomura Chikuden, Nishina Hakukoku, and Kamei Nanmei.* Vol. 1, *Edo Kanshisen.* 5 vols. Tokyo: Iwanami Shoten, 1997.

Tuck, Robert. *Idly Scribbling Rhymers: Poetry, Print, and Community in Nineteenth-Century Japan.* New York: Columbia University Press, 2018.

Wang, David. *The Lyrical in Epic Time: Modern Chinese Intellectuals and Artists Through the 1949 Crisis.* New York: Columbia University Press, 2015.

Williams, Raymond. *Culture & Society: 1780–1950.* New York: Columbia University Press, 1983.

Yamamoto Kenkichi. *Yosa Buson.* Tokyo: Kōdansha, 1987.

Yosa Buson. *Buson shū.* Edited by Muramatsu Tomotsugu. Vol. 17, *Kanshō Nihon no koten.* 18 vols. Tokyo: Shōgaku tosho, 1981.

———. *Buson zenshū.* Edited by Ogata Tsutomu, et al. 9 vols. Tokyo: Kōdansha, 1992.

Zolbrod, Leon M. *Reluctant Genius: The Life and Work of Buson, A Japanese Master of Haiku and Painting,* "Eighth Installment." In *Modern Haiku* 26, no. 1 (Winter-Spring, 1995): 60–65.

———. *Reluctant Genius: The Life and Work of Buson, A Japanese Master of Haiku and Painting,* "Sixteenth Installment." In *Modern Haiku* 29, no. 1 (Winter-Spring 1998): 48–54.

CHAPTER 2

Yosa Buson and the Colors of a *Bunjin* Mind

In poetry there is painting, in painting there is poetry.
—Su Shi (1037–1101)

Haikai *is a living being.*
—*Yosa Buson, "Preface to Correct Use of Haikai Topics"* (1782)

It's as if every part were aware of all the others.
—Rainer Maria Rilke, *Letters on Cézanne* (1907)

This chapter examines how Yosa Buson (1716–1783) embraced literati (*bunjin*) culture in the late eighteenth century by experimenting in genres of *haikai*—an umbrella term for all genres that derive from *haikai-no-renga* (unorthodox linked verse), including *hokku*, the "opening verse" to a linked-verse sequence. I argue that Buson mediated perception and feeling through the representational world of *bunjin* painting, creating ekphrastic poetic forms that expressed an anxious longing to belong to the literati tradition. These experiments opened new visual dimensions of *haikai* lyricism.

Buson was a professional painter of Chinese-style landscapes (*bunjinga*); he acquired *haikai* under the tutelage of many masters. In literary history, he is known for inheriting the legacy of Matsuo Bashō (1644–1694), the great *haikai* poet of the seventeenth century, and reviving his poetry in the eighteenth century.[1] What is less known is how Buson distinguished himself in the *haikai* tradition as a *bunjin* by composing sensuous, colorful, and multigenred poems that drew inspiration from Chinese poetry and painting.[2] In Japan during the eighteenth century, art and culture from the Chinese Ming dynasty (1368–1644) was very much in vogue. Buson's own practice in the Chinese arts exposed him to late imperial Chinese theories of lyricism, including the "blending of feeling and scene" (Ch. *qing jing jiao rong*) that describes the merging of a poet's personal state of mind with scenes he beholds in the natural world.

The introduction to this book includes an example of this Chinese lyricism at work in a *hokku* that blends the feeling of longing with the long swells of the spring sea. This poem offers one example of how Buson transformed the *haikai* genre. The playful conventions of *haikai* allowed poets to substitute images from the tradition of Japanese court poetry (*waka*) for those drawn from personal observations of nature and everyday life. Buson both followed and transformed these conventions by taking natural images and poetic genres (specifically *kanshi*) drawn from *bunjinga* and combining them with genres of *haikai*, including *hokku*, *haiga* (*haikai* painting), and *haishi* (hybrid or composite forms comprising *haikai* and *kanshi*). For example, the onomatopoeia *notari notari* (swells/Long swells) in the earlier *hokku* represents ordinary speech that falls outside the conventional stock vocabulary of *waka* and *renga*. And as Miyake Shōzan (1718–1801) observed in his *kanbun* commentary, the "blandness" of that *hokku* evokes the representational world of Chinese landscape painting. This chapter explores how Buson's experimental combinations made *haikai* ekphrastic by examining the ways his *hokku*, *haiga*, and *haishi* evoked formal and aesthetic features of *bunjinga*, including representations of color, poetic topoi, and tropes from the poetic genre of *kanshi*.

SEEING AND IMAGINING COLOR

The vogue of late imperial Chinese art and culture included texts on Chinese herbal medicine. This gave rise to *honzōgaku*, or *materia medica*—the study of the medicinal properties of the natural world—which inspired intellectuals and poets alike to catalogue nature in a scientific and desacralized way.[3] Buson absorbed this empirical science and composed *hokku* that examined the colors of natural objects, exploring the possibilities of visual perception through the modes of painting. The *hokku* genre, by convention, examines the contiguity of images through poetic juxtaposition. Buson followed this convention by juxtaposing natural objects from the representational world of *bunjin* painting, creating a new poetics of suggestion that required the reader to imagine colors and colorful landscapes. These *hokku* transformed *haikai* conventions by affording their author a means of representing empirical investigations of color and anxieties about seeing through the eyes of a literati painter.

In the two *hokku* below the speaker examines the colors of tea flowers (*cha no hana*) and plum blossoms (*ume*):

Tea flowers—
Yellow or white,
Hard to tell.

cha no hana ya / ki ni mo shiro ni mo / obotsukana
茶の花や黄にも白にもおぼつかな [4]

Wild plum blossoms:
Not white,
Not red.

noji no ume / shiroku mo akaku mo / aranu kana
野路の梅白くも赤くもあらぬ哉 [5]

Both poems make color the object of uncertainty, questioning both the clarity of the speaker's perception and the necessity to make definitive claims about colors perceived. Adopting the stance of an empirical scientist, the speaker seeks to specify the colors of natural objects, making the perception of color itself the crux of the poem. The *hokku* above seek to name a color, but do not succeed in doing so, thereby encouraging the reader to imagine what the tea flowers and plum blossoms might look like.

The first *hokku* opens with an image of tea flowers (*cha no hana*)—a *kigo*, or "seasonal referent," for winter. The poem's second measure labels the colors yellow and white (in a variant the color order is switched), which the speaker describes as *obotsukana* in the third measure: the stem of the adjective *obotsukanashi*, meaning "indistinct." The speaker beholds a patch of green tea flowers but cannot tell whether they are yellow or white. He may be too far away to see them, or they have yet to bloom and he is gazing at their buds. When in bloom, tea flowers display white petals and yellow pistils, but here the speaker questions the certainty of his perception, ending the poem with a visual image that is vague and indistinct, encouraging the reader to imagine that the buds may be both yellow and white, or neither.

The second *hokku* opens with an image of plum blossoms (*ume*), a *kigo* for early spring. Here again, the speaker beholds a natural object and questions its color. The speaker in this poem may not be certain about the color he sees, but he is certain about the colors he does not see: red and white. In his many poems on plum blossoms, Buson usually specifies whether they are red or white. Scholars Ogata Tsutomu and Morita Ran claim that the speaker sees a color in between red and white, perhaps pink,[6] but there is also a possibility that the *ume* have yet to bloom. Taken literally, the poem states that the blossoms are neither red nor white.

The indecision or lack of perceptual clarity about color evokes the humor of the *haikai* genre, the wit of *haikai-no-renga* (unorthodox linked verse), which Robert Backus has described as the "fun" that evolved as a way to lighten the aristocratic weight of orthodox *renga* before the Edo period. In orthodox *renga*, attitudes and feelings toward any object worth discussing were made normative by convention:

> This sense of a proper response to a sanctified category of objects considered to be beautiful, which generations of aristocratic poets had imparted to the Japanese mind, created a situation made to order for humor. Sanctity affronted shocks the believer and gives the recreant a laugh.[7]

The sanctified category of objects to which Backus refers is the finite number of things that appear in *waka* and *renga*, including tea flowers and plum blossoms. Ironizing the conventions of their evocation is what makes the poet and reader laugh.

Until the Edo period, traditional poetry conditioned the way poets thought about natural objects. But with the rise of empirical observation and the emergence of *haikai* as an autonomous genre of poetry, Buson was able to blend traditional imagery and their figurative associations with a new way of seeing: taking an object and scrutinizing its individual form such that he could represent thought and feeling, often in an ironic and humorous way. Thus *haikai* furnished a space for playful critique, imbuing poetry with wit, irony, and sarcasm. This playfulness can also be found in Buson's attitude toward *haikai* rules: he once wrote that when the rules do not work, the rule is to break the rules.[8]

In the second *hokku*, the speaker presents himself as a *bunjin* who does not take himself too seriously. Although a joke is no longer funny after someone tells you the punch line, an explanation of what plums mean in the literati tradition will elucidate how the *hokku* pokes fun. Buson composed countless poems on plum blossoms, including one where red petals blaze on piles of horse dung.[9] As one of the "Four Gentlemen" (*shikun-shi*)—orchids (*ran*), bamboo (*take* or *chiku*), chrysanthemums (*kiku*), and plums (*ume* or *bai*)—plum blossoms are cherished objects in the *bunjin* tradition and are associated with Confucian virtues. In *haikai*, however, even the sanctity of *ume* can become the butt of a joke.

In making a claim about what color the plum is not, the *hokku* alludes to a line in an earlier Chinese poem whose political meaning contradicts the interpretive openness that the *hokku* suggests. Northern Song literatus Tang Geng (1070–1120) wrote, in another poem on plum blossoms: "Their white is not yet white; their red is not yet red." Ogata and Morita write that here the white refers to plums and the red refers to peaches; they interpret the claim that neither has ripened to their full color as a metaphor that tinges the line with political satire. In Tang Geng's cultural context as a scholar-official in the Song dynasty (960–1279), this interpretation is plausible. But Buson was no scholar-official—he was an artist, like other *bunjin* in the eighteenth century. Moreover, he composed a *hokku* in which the plum blossoms are modified by "wild" (*noji*; lit. "a track on a moor"). In the context of Buson's poem, the plums have the potential to symbolize the virtues of a Confucian literatus, but because they are wild and uncultivated, and do not display the colors conventionally associated with their blossoms, the speaker is suggesting that they offer something else, which the reader is left to imagine. The speaker merely exclaims (with the emphatic *kana*) that the wild plum blossoms are neither red nor white. And this is when the reader chuckles.

The *hokku* above show how color serves as an object of empirical inquiry in Buson's *haikai*, and how the poetic juxtaposition of colors of natural objects from literati painting explores the possibility of perception. Buson also composed *hokku* in which such poetic juxtaposition could create confounding, sensual perceptions of landscape in the poetic imagination. For example, the *hokku* below suggests a conflict resolution between the colors black and white by hinting at their blending into gray in the final measure:

White plum blossoms—
Black ink fragrant
At Goose Cormorant Inn.

hakubai ya / sumi kanbashiki / kōrokan
白梅や墨芳しき鴻臚館 [10]

Scholars Morita and Ogata read the poem as a recollection or representation of the time when Japanese literati from distant provinces gathered together to compose poetry at Kōrokan, a hotel patronized by foreign officials (Japanese, Tang, and Silla) during the Heian period. With this historical setting in mind, the poem could be describing a scene where white plum blossoms are in full bloom around the hotel, the scent of black ink fills the air, and poets hailing from near and far sit together to compose verses.

By placing objects in an oppositional relationship with each other, the *hokku* gives form to the act of painting and to the experience of viewing it. A reader may imagine a painter just finished rendering the plum, its white blossoms and its dark branches still wet with the ink whose strong scent permeates the studio, the name of which aurally registers as "Kōrokan," a word in Chinese that translates to "Goose Cormorant Inn." The speaker may be thinking of the Heian hotel called Kōrokan, which literally translates to "Goose Belly Inn," but the author chooses to use a homonym for the middle graph *ro* that refers to a waterfowl in the cormorant family.

Anthologies feature the original *ro* 鸕 (cormorant), but annotators claim that it is an error, and that Buson really meant *ro* 臚 (belly). Since the *haikai* poet has the freedom to pun, the image of a cormorant gives the poem another visual layer, bringing resolution to the colors in opposition. Geese and cormorants are birds that both have black, white, and shades of gray in their plumage. By moving from the white of the plum blossom, to the black of the ink, and then to a mixture of the two colors in a static image of two birds, the poem represents the process of ink-wash painting, the act of blending colors, and the act of bringing two opposites into resolution.

Buson's resolution of black and white in the poem's third measure reveals how form and color balance each other in traditional Chinese painting. Early theorist of Chinese painting Zong Bing (375–444 CE) declared: "Write form from form, paint color from color."[11] In a discussion of the role of color in traditional Chinese vis-à-vis classic and modern Western painting, François Jullien observes that early Chinese texts thought of painting in terms of "an alliance between form and color," a dynamic relationship of complementarity and opposition. Early treatises list six "colors" that form three oppositional pairs: black and white, dry and wet, thick and thin. In ink-wash paintings, the literatus dilutes black ink to produce variations of lightness, density, clarity, and opacity. Buson represents this process in his *hokku* when black and white reappear in variegated but unified form in the plumage of two birds. In this way, Buson's use of black and white resonates with the idea in traditional Chinese painting that the painter must balance the tension between oppositional colors.[12]

The *hokku* below offers an example of how Buson uses complementary colors to explore the possibilities of perception and abstraction, in this instance to create an optical illusion:

> Red plum blossoms—
> The lowering sun strikes through
> The pines and the oaks.
>
> *kōbai ya / irihi no osou / matsu kashiwa*
> 紅梅や入日の襲ふ松かしは [13]

This *hokku* opens with the same *kigo*, making it a poem of early spring, and specifies the color of the plum blossoms as red. The poem's first measure ends with *ya*, the *kireji*, or "cutting word," which sets up the image of red plum blossoms as a visual riddle for the eye. The first measure presents an immediate image of red, and the third measure a mediated image of green, but by the end of the poem, the oppositional relationship between these complementary colors is neutralized by a visual distortion, creating an optical illusion. As the rays from the setting sun (*irihi*) penetrate the forest of the green pines and oaks, they refigure, temporally and spatially, the image of red plum blossoms.

The second measure ends with the verb *osou*, which means "to assail," "to invade," or "to strike." An older meaning of the verb means "to layer" and was used to describe the act of putting on layers of kimono. This meaning refigures the sunset as a slow scene of overlapping tapestries; the speed with which fabric falls upon and hugs another layer of fabric on the body is echoed by the speed of light gradually falling upon the tree branches. The end of the poem suggests that the red plum blossoms may in fact not be there at all: the sunset may be either a figure for the red glow of the plum blossoms, or the plum blossoms may be merely figures for the sunset. Here again Buson displays his ability to use the *hokku* form to explore the limits of perception through the abstractions afforded by the poetic juxtaposition of colors.

The *hokku* below offers a final example of how Buson uses the poetic juxtaposition of color, this time to evoke a polychromatic panoramic landscape:

> Fresh leaves greening,
> A stream shimmering white, barley
> Tinged with yellow.
>
> *wakaba shite / mizu shiroku mugi / kibamitari*
> 若葉して水白く麦黄ミたり[14]

The poem directs the eye to a dynamic landscape in green, white, and yellow, opening with an image of young leaves or fresh verdure (*wakaba*), a *kigo* for early summer. The word *wakaba* is a metonym for *shinryoku* (lit. the new green), suggesting that the color of the first measure is green. Unlike the previous two poems, where the first measure ended with a *kireiji*, the first measure in this *hokku* ends with *shite*, a verb that marks the state of action (the leaves "being green" or "greening") and serves as a linking conjunction between images in a poem, connecting the image of the green leaves to the following measures.

As the leaves green before the eye, a stream shimmers with the color white. Here, white is also used to describe bright light: white (*shiroku*) describes the summer sunlight coruscating from the stream, which the reader might imagine flowing by the green leaves. The second measure is enjambed, ending with the barley (*mugi*) that becomes the subject of the third measure, where the speaker describes stalks of barley as tinged with yellow (*kibamitari*). The absence of a *kireji* allows the poem to move without pause in one direction from image to image, culminating in a consummate scene of early summer: a bright shimmering stream flanked by trees with green leaves and a field of yellow barley.

As Makoto Ueda and other Buson scholars have noted, the poem paints a picture more akin to a modern oil painting than to a traditional literati landscape.[15] On the one hand, this view seemingly places the *hokku* at odds with the landscape paintings produced by Buson, whose style draws from the principles outlined in late imperial Chinese painting manuals and treatises. In her discussion of the "true view paintings" (*shinkeizu*) of eighteenth-century literatus Ike no Taiga (1723–1776), Melinda Takeuchi observes that eighteenth-century painters synthesized three principles of composition: "*shai* (painting the idea), *shasei* (painting life) and *ikkaku* (the artist's untrammeled personality)."[16] To paint the "idea" of an object means to communicate its essence by blending convention with the artist's feelings. To paint the "life" of an object means to "apprehend the spirit-resonance of nature's forms in order to probe the essential truth of nature." "Spirit-resonance" (J. *kiin*; Ch. *qi yun*) is the first of the "Six Laws" (*Liu fa*) of Chinese painting, outlined by painter and critic Xie He in the late fifth century. By the Edo period, the meaning of "spirit-resonance" varied depending on the artist, but in general it referred to a spiritual communion between artist, object, and painting.[17] These principles of representation in painting blend with the empiricism of Buson's *hokku*, in which the speaker subjectively engages with a panoramic scene by examining the colors that make it move, the colors that constitute a living form in the poetic imagination.

The five *hokku* in this section each focus on color perception and how the absence and presence of color stimulates the imagination. In the initial two poems on tea flowers and plum blossoms, the poet questioned the colors that constitute these traditional poetic objects. Such poems comically ironized the certainty of empirical perception by requiring the reader to visualize what the speaker might or might not be seeing. The last three *hokku* examined in this section showcase what visual acrobatics are possible when the poet plays with a wider palette of colors: balancing opposition and complementarity, visualizing the concrete and the abstract, and imagining a panoramic view that transcends the *haikai* genre.

WHITE, DEATH, AND LYRIC TIME

Among the colors in Buson's *hokku*, white is the most prominent. Indeed, Yamashita Kazumi has called Buson "The Poet of White" (*shiro no shijin*), an appellation that became the title of Yamashita's 2009 monograph on Buson's poetry.[18]

At the end of his life Buson left three *hokku* that suggest white to differing degrees of perceptual clarity. The third poem ends with suspension—waiting for white to appear. Although white is not the primary focus of any of these poems, the color is visible in the poems that suggest it, but not in the poem that names it. This curious relationship with white may be the result of sensory loss or be symptomatic of a lyric mind meditating on mortality through contradiction. Although biography does not necessarily weight the meaning of a poem, a set of poems that mark the end of a poet's life may encourage the reader to consider the effect of impending death on aesthetic choices.[19]

Wallace Stevens once remarked that, "to a large extent, the problems of poets are the problems of painters, and poets must often turn to the literature of painting for a discussion of their own problems."[20] Buson came to terms with his imminent demise by figuring the color white in three verses that draw on Chinese and Japanese poetry as well as on the tradition of literati painting. I propose that the three *hokku* be read as one poem or as a pseudo *renku*, or linked-verse sequence, since Buson on his deathbed uttered them one after another to his pupil Matsumura Goshun (1752–1811; also Gekkei):

> The winter warbler
> Long ago on Wang Wei's   *fuyu uguisu / mukashi ōi ga / kakine kana*
> Hedge fence.   冬鶯むかし王維が垣根哉
>
> Warbler—
> Why do you rustle   *uguisu ya / nani gosotsukasu / yabu no shimo*
> Frost on the bush?   うぐいすや何ごそつかす藪の霜
>
> The night to dawn
> White on the plum   *shira ume ni / akuru yo bakari to / narinikeri*
> Is all I have left.   しら梅に明る夜ばかりとなりにけり [21]

These poems date to the hour before dawn on December 25, 1783. Buson selected the third *hokku* to be his "death poem" (*jisei no ku*), but the figurative resonances among all three invite the reader to consider their relationship to one another, how they cohere as a single work—and yet how they also diverge into three distinct comments on the color white—and how they figure white in terms of painting. At the critical moment before his death, Buson represented a lyric mind thinking in verses not as individual poems but as a set or a sequence. Conventionally, *renku* (also known as *haikai-no-renga*) was communal like orthodox *renga* and it did not solely comprise *hokku*: two or more poets sat down together to compose sequences of alternating long (5-7-5) and short (7-7) stanzas, which they repeated to a decided limit.[22] Buson, alone, uttered just three *hokku*, representing a mind struggling between different beginnings, or a mind finding a form, forming a single amorphous poem from three strands of thought.

The first *hokku* stands in for a Chinese painting, and the color white is suggested in its representational landscape—the retrospective image of the winter warbler perched on Wang Wei's hedge fence. By invoking Tang poet Wang Wei (ca. 699–761 CE), the speaker calls to mind Su Shi's pronouncement about the chiastic relationship between poetry and painting: "In poetry there is painting, in painting there is poetry."[23] In the *hokku*, the speaker represents this relationship vis-à-vis two images: the winter warbler and Wang Wei's hedge fence, both of which are figured as things from long ago (*mukashi*).[24] The image of the winter warbler is a *kigo* for winter; the reader may imagine the bird perched on a snowy hedge branch. The snow and other images associated with winter are suggested by the allusions to the hedge fence.

The figure of the winter warbler disrupts the lyric subject's situatedness in the present by transporting him, the poem, and the reader through the history of representations (both in poetry and painting) of Wangchuan Villa by extracting elements from a source painting, likely a late imperial Chinese imitation, and stands in as its own representation. In this way, "Wang Wei's / Hedge fence" (*ōi ga / kakine*) functions like an *utamakura*—a device in *waka* that refers to poetic topoi.

After being transported through these earlier representations, the lyric subject is theoretically able to experience time as an object in a painting. Imagining himself as the winter warbler, the speaker merges with the landscape of Wangchuan Villa. In his discussion of Song dynasty painting, Edward Casey observes that the painter transmits himself, or his spirit, into his painting in order to give it its so-called verisimilitude: "The transmission of spirit sought by the painter is *the transmission of the spirit that inheres in a place* with which one is fully resonant—hence that is continually in motion, given that resonance and motion are inseparably allied."[25] In his formulation, Casey draws from the rhetoric in medieval Chinese painting manuals stating that the painter is one with the landscape because they share the same spirit.

As a reader of medieval Chinese manuals on painting—the ideas that were reproduced in Ming dynasty Chinese treatises that circulated among Late Edo *bunjin*—Buson was informed by the same spiritual and aesthetic beliefs. But writing in an age when the subject's relationship to nature had grown increasingly secular, the speaker realizes that his self-identification with Wangchuan Villa is mediated by time and representation. As he imagines a painting through the figure of the winter warbler, he becomes aware of the gulf between his present moment and the distant past (*mukashi*).

While the first *hokku* stands in for a painting of Wang's villa, as a *hokku* it also comments on how representation in poetry performs what representation in painting cannot: sound. And yet, the first *hokku* is curiously silent, especially given that most of Buson's poems that feature the warbler directly reference birdsong.[26] This silence, however, is soon disquieted by the noise the warbler makes in the second *hokku*, in which the white image of frost functions as an amplifier of sound. In this *hokku*, the speaker does not specify a season and begins with just *uguisu* (warbler). In some anthologies, this makes the poem a spring poem,[27] with the repetition of the same bird suggesting that the warbler in the second *hokku* is the warbler from the first *hokku*, but in the future, at a later time in early spring.

Unlike the first poem, which does not feature a *kireji* and which moves from image to image without pause, the second poem starts with the warbler and inserts a *ya*—a pause for exclamatory emotion. In his study of eighteenth-century *haikai* poetics, Herbert Jonsson has argued that while *kireji* (namely, *ya*, *kana*, and *keri*) are emotive, whether they "cut" or break the continuity of a poem depends on the poem.[28] Buson's own writing on the subject reveals his liberal attitude toward *kireji*: that in some poems they "cut," and in others they do not.[29] In this *hokku* the *ya* functions as a pause to facilitate the transition to a lyric address in the form of a question: "Why do you rustle?" I return to the complexities of lyric address in Buson's poetry in greater detail at the end of the chapter, but in this *hokku* the speaker is addressing the warbler that he recalls as the winter warbler in representations of the villa and that he now imagines in an early spring scene.[30]

The meaning of the poetic address depends on how the reader interprets the question that forms it. In the *bunjin* tradition, birds have allegorical and symbolic value. Literati painted and composed poems about birds because writers self-identified with them; being one with the bird meant being one with nature. Warblers are one of the metonyms for early spring, the most important of which are plum blossoms, the favorite flower of the literatus.[31] In historical terms, the immediate audience of the drama between the speaker and the warbler is Goshun, to whom Buson uttered the verse. But the reader reciting at home is now the audience that overhears the speaker asking the warbler: "Why do you rustle?" Most interpretations of the poem read the interrogative particle *nani* as "what,"[32] but in medieval *waka* and poems from the Chinese tradition, *nani* can also mean "why." The poem also provides an object for the verb, which makes the entire verse read like a straightforward question. But the syntax of 5-7-5 allows room for pauses in thought, one of those unmarked pauses Buson's suggests in his discussion of *kireji*. Indeed, the pause between the second and third measures amplifies the interrogative tone of the question.

The question momentarily suspends the poem before delivering an answer that blends sound and color. After the pause the reader discovers the object of the warbler's rustling: "Frost on the bush" (*yabu no shimo*). Buson employed the verb *gosotsukasu*, the causative form of *gosotsuku*, which translates to the intransitive verbs in English "to rustle" or "to whisper." The silence in the first verse is slightly disturbed by the faint rustling, but that sound ultimately leads to an image of frost, of white. The speaker's question highlights frost as the object mediating and amplifying the rustling sound. The reader could dismiss the question as banal—imagining that the speaker is just asking the warbler why it does what it naturally does—but Buson made an aesthetic choice to end with frost, which concludes the *hokku* with the jarring sound of white, white noise.

The suspension produced by the question is echoed by the answer, rendering the *hokku* in a state of temporal and semantic limbo that mirrors its formal position between two *hokku*. The suspension can be read as an ironic self-critique of poetic practice: the question to the warbler also asks what noise the warbler is *not* making, self-reflexively turning the question onto the poem's speaker. A survey of Buson's *hokku* on warblers rapidly reveals that a warbler makes a specific sound: a cry, a chirp, a warble. Because this warbler does not warble, the tone of the question harbors an unarticulated complaint: the bird is not singing its usual spring song. By asking the warbler why he is making faint and bothersome noises, disturbing the frost, the speaker poses a similar question about his own activity, revealing a feeling of failure on his part as a *bunjin* who is not singing, only muttering meaningless whispers.

Following this temporal suspension that forbodes feelings of doubt and disappointment, the third and final *hokku* absents the warbler entirely and makes present the speaker singing in its place. The speaker sings his heart out and figures himself as a landscape, entering the representation of an early spring scene at a moment of suspension: waiting for night to dawn white on the plum blossoms. The color white appears in name, but ironically as an object of longing because the temporal contingency of the predawn prevents the speaker from seeing white come to light.[33]

The third poem diverges from the resonance between the earlier *hokku*, and yet harmonizes the dissonances between them, also standing out as its own lyric poem. Right on the heels of the image of frost (*shimo*) that caps the second *hokku*, an image of white plum blossoms (*shiraume*) opens the third. The assonance between *shimo* and *shira* is deliberate: Buson rendered "plum blossoms" as *shiraume* and not their Chinese name *hakubai*, which appeared in the *hokku* with the fragrant black ink. Although the white is clear in the image of the plum blossoms, the verb *akuru* makes them the indirect object of dawning, a verbal pun of sorts that makes the visibility of the color white contingent upon the morning light. Buson performed the same relationship between light and white with the figure of the shimmering stream in the *hokku* about fresh green leaves and yellow barley. Unlike the scene in that *hokku*, though, the time here is not day, with the sun shining bright over the landscape, but the in-between hours of night and dawn, a time and space set in partial darkness. Time mediates the tension between the blackness of night and the white of the plum blossoms that is contingent upon the sunrise.

Unlike the first and second *hokku* in the sequence there is no warbler here, and the *kigo* that categorizes the poem as spring is waiting to be seen. In Buson's painting and poetry, dark is invariably placed in tension with light. Other poems by Buson use darkness as a space of wonder, of contemplation, a place where things happen and play on the senses.[34] In this *hokku* the darkness of night occludes the white of the plum—a tension shared by other poems—but the plaintive cry of the speaker mediated by the emphatic *keri* that caps the verse desires this darkness to end. Indeed, the verb *akuru* offers assurance that night will dawn.

Here, the color white straddles the boundary of new and old by evoking ineffability, possibility, and the unknown. The purpose of using cliché images in premodern Japanese poetry is to ensure that one poem be communicable with the collective, that the feelings expressed by one writer would be known and shared by all. In Edo period *haikai*, the warbler is within and without this tradition; here Buson defamiliarizes the bird by not letting it sing. The song would only confirm what an eighteenth-century reader already knows about the warbler: its beautiful song. The sound *shira* (white) in *shira-ume* (white plum) evokes the verb *shira-zu*, the negated form of the verb "to know" or "to be aware." It is misleading to say that white plum blossoms (*shiraume*) always suggest the unknown, but in the context of this poem—how the word rhymes in assonance with the curious rustle of frost (*shimo*) in the previous verse, and how it is paired with the darkness of night, waiting to be visible—white is the object of knowing.

Associations with white in the *hokku* carry meanings from the past—from *waka* and the Chinese tradition—including blandness, absence, and plenitude. In his discussion of colors in traditional Chinese painting, François Jullien writes that white is sometimes considered a "negative" color,[35] referring to the negative space in a painting, the "white" space (barely or left entirely untouched by the brush) that furnishes room for thought. As an aesthetic category, the negative is also associated with the ideal known as *pingdan* (J. *heitan*), meaning "plainness; blandness."[36] Song dynasty literatus Mei Yaochen (1002–1060) commented on the difficulty of representing *pingdan* in poetry:

In composing a poem, in the present as in the past,	作詩無古今
Only the creation of the plain and bland is hard.	唯造平澹難 [37]

Pingdan is "hard," indeed. Jullien writes that blandness "is the phase when different flavors no longer stand in opposition to each other but, rather, *abide within* plenitude."[38] The plenitude that the flavor of blandness provides is redolent of the ideas of absence or emptiness: the Chinese aesthetic category of *xu* (J. *kyo*) that is often used to describe literary works about ghosts, the supernatural, immortals, clouds, and other celestial bodies. These works often allude to Buddhist iconography, where white is symbolic of death. With such meanings in mind, white, emptiness, and blandness in this context evokes experiences beyond the limits of mortal perception, times and places where distinctions do not exist and everything melts into harmonious plenitude. By composing a *hokku* in which the object of longing is that the night dawn white on the plum, Buson sets up all the elements of a landscape—one of blandness and plenitude, just waiting to unfold at the will of time.[39]

Time is the larger dynamic force subtended by these three *hokku* in one form. At the end of his life, Buson composed a poem that begins as a representation of a painting where painter and landscape are fused, and then uses lyric address to question what was, what is, and what will be. The speaker speaks in the lyric present and apprehends time in three ways. The first *hokku* is retrospective, a representation of representations standing in for Wang's painting of Wangchuan Villa. The second *hokku* moves forward in time, out of winter and into early spring, when a warbler rustles frost on the bush, which disturbs the speaker and provokes the question "why." The third *hokku* is, on the one hand, a reply to the unspoken question, about why the warblers are not singing; on the other, it is a plangent cry uttered with the speaker's final breath: "It is now become the moment when I realize that all I have left before I die is for the night to dawn white on the plum." While the three *hokku* each treat time in distinct ways, as a single poem, a coherence formed by the figurative resonances between each line, the verses speak in the eternal lyric present, wherein all time—past, present, and future—happens at once.

EKPHRASIS UPON EKPHRASIS

Beginning with this section, my examination turns to Buson's lyricism in poetic forms that combine *haikai* with other genres from the literati repertoire. Buson created lyric forms that play with the intertextuality between the *haikai* and *kanshi* genres as well as with the ekphrastic relationship between poetic inscription and painted image. Late in his career, he created a *haiga*, or *haikai* painting (see Fig. 2.1), that pairs a painted image of rocks with a *haibun* (*haikai* prose) inscription in order to represent a multimedia and sensual experience of poetic topoi in the Japanese and Chinese traditions. John M. Rosenfield has described such versatility with both traditions as Buson's "*haikai* imagination."[40] I argue that the *haibun* inscription works as an ekphrastic description of the painted rocks, and that the *haiga* as a whole constitutes an ekphrastic form that comments on the history of representation of poetic topoi in the literati tradition.

> Each and every word in the Earlier and Later Rhapsodies on Red Cliff is sublime. The line 'The mountains tall, the moon small; the water level fallen, rocks protruding' is especially wondrous, like a lone crane flashing forth from a flock of fowl.
> Long ago when I journeyed to Michinoku, I was wandering under the willows and suddenly recalled the following poem:
>
> > Willow leaves scatter,
> > A clear stream sere, rocks

Strewn here and there.
yanagi chiri / shimizu kare ishi / tokoro-dokoro

赤壁前後の賦字々みな絶妙あるか中に山高月小水落石出といふものこ
とにめてたく孤霍の群鶏を出るかことし
むかしみちのくに行脚せしに遊行柳のもとに忽右の句をもおもひ出て
柳ちり清水かれ石ところどころ [41]

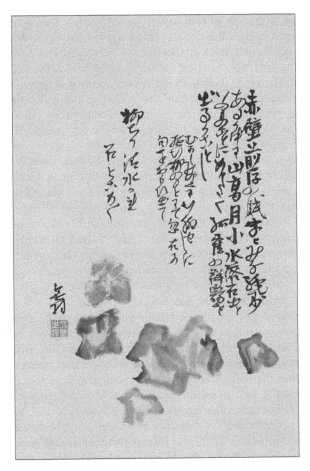

Fig. 2.1 Yosa Buson. *Willow Leaves Scatter* (Yanagi chiri); hanging scroll; ink and
light color on paper; 58.6 × 36.7 cm.; Itsuō Art Museum, Ikeda

In the *bunjin* tradition, *haiga* conventionally pairs a simple image with an inscription in prose or poetry. The simple image here is of rocks, which are featured prominently in *nanga* landscapes and object studies in late imperial Chinese painting manuals. Buson in fact did produce object studies of rocks, and in some ways this *haiga* represents a rock study.[42] By making rocks the sole image of the piece, Buson evoked the eighteenth-century idea that single objects are autonomous and totalizing landscapes, giving the rocks their own autonomy as living objects not as part of a larger landscape, but as a landscape of their own.[43]

The image comprises five (or six) rocks strewn across the bottom of the page. In rough brush strokes the painter rendered the rocks in chiaroscuro, giving form to them by blending light and dark, bold and faint shades of ink. The large rock(s) in the center confound(s) perception: One rock or two? Seamlessly fused, but also standing as overlapping, autonomous forms, the two rocks offer a visual metaphor for Buson's *bunjin* style: elements blended into a composite whole that transcends the containment of a particular genre.

The autonomy of the rocks as a landscape of their own is checked by the *haibun* inscription, which mediates a communion with other genres, transporting the rocks through the Chinese and the Japanese poetic traditions.[44] The inscription has three parts: a comment on "Rhapsody on Red Cliff" (Chibi fu) and "Later Rhapsody on Red Cliff" (Hou Chibi fu) composed by Song dynasty literatus Su Shi (1037–1101); allusions to the travelogue *The Narrow Road to the Deep North* (1689; Oku no hosomichi) by Matsuo Bashō (1644–1694) and a *waka* by early medieval poet Saigyō (1118–1190); and a quotation of a *hokku* that Buson composed in 1743, a few decades before he made this *haiga*.

Su Shi's rhapsodies are about travel, history, and the poetic imagination.[45] "Rhapsody on Red Cliff" opens with a tranquil scene in autumn of 1082: Su Shi and his guests are boating beneath Red Cliff, drinking wine, reciting poetry, and savoring the landscape. Then they enter a conversation that evokes the idea of impermanence, but also bespeaks the idea that there is continuity in human existence. Ronald Egan has suggested that this continuity is made possible by visiting a historical site, which places the subject in communion with a greater human consciousness and continuity.[46] By visiting Red Cliff, the literatus enters an affective space and forms a connection with the people who once inhabited it centuries ago.

"Later Rhapsody on Red Cliff" opens with a dreary scene of delayed celebration in winter of 1082: Su Shi and two guests wander across a desolate landscape, frost falls and dew forms on bare tree limbs; the moon glows bright in the dark sky. The companions lament not having any food or wine with which to enjoy the evening, but soon enough they find some, and go boating again beneath Red Cliff. This time, however, they encounter a changed landscape:

> Thereupon we took the wine and fish and wandered again below Red Cliff. The river flows, water rushing; sheer cliffs rise a thousand feet. The mountains tall, the moon small; the water level fallen, rocks protruding. How long has it been since our last visit? The landscape seemed completely unfamiliar.
> 於是攜酒與魚, 復遊於赤壁之下. 江流有聲, 斷岸千尺. 山高月小, 水落石出.
> 曾日月之幾何, 而江山不可復識矣. [47]

Buson's inscription quotes one of the four-character couplets from the passage above: "The mountains tall, the moon small; the water level fallen, rocks protruding." Although the speaker in the Su Shi passage had traveled to Red Cliff just months before, the landscape has changed from autumn to winter, a seasonal change that has rendered the scene "unfamiliar." The sublimity of the moment, in part, is engendered by how this seasonal change has imbued the landscape with a feeling of awesome boundlessness.

Their depictions of the experience of visiting Red Cliff place the two rhapsodies in tension with each other: the former offers a clear message of transience, whereas the latter is open ended and enigmatic.[48] Buson echoes the enigmatic feeling of the later rhapsody with a metaphor describing the sublimity of Su Shi's poetry: "Like a lone crane flashing forth from a flock of fowl."[49] This line alludes to the conclusion of the later rhapsody, where a lone crane appears in the east, swoops down toward the boatmen, soars across the river, and emits a loud cry before disappearing into the west. Although the color of the bird is not specified in Buson's inscription, the crane in the rhapsody is described as wearing a "black skirt" and "white robe." The rhapsody ends with the poet dreaming of a Daoist, whose feathery wardrobe reminds the poet of the crane. When the poet asks the Daoist whether he disguised himself as the crane, the Daoist just smiles. Su

Shi's ending has left traditional commentators befuddled: Ming dynasty poet Yuan Hongdao (1568–1610) claimed that the meaning of "Later Rhapsody on Red Cliff" was opaque even to the author himself.[50] With the desolate winter landscape and the Daoist transformation in mind, one can imagine what Buson found sublime about the two rhapsodies.

In addition to transporting the speaker to the rhapsodies on Red Cliff, Buson's inscription uses the lone crane to index the representation of birds in literati painting. The crane is considered auspicious and beautiful; it has been a subject of painting since at least the Tang dynasty.[51] In the Song dynasty, the crane was often associated with Confucian sagacity because of its dignified poses; soon after, with the development of Daoism in literary expression, the crane came to represent all the ideals associated with the immortals: purity, loftiness, longevity, and auspiciousness. By the Ming dynasty it had also become associated with the virtues of a scholar-official, a literatus, and thus in the eighteenth century, the crane carried all these meanings. By comparing the sublimity of Su Shi's rhapsodies to the sublimity of a crane, Buson's inscription extolls the rhapsody's evocation of the ineffable, overlaid with symbolic self-representation in literati painting.

Evoking the space of literati painting, the image of the flying crane shifts the scene from Red Cliff to representations of Ashino in the Japanese tradition and begins another chain of allusions across genres and forms. Buson alludes to a journey he made in 1743, retracing Bashō's travelogue *The Narrow Road to the Deep North*. The inscription features the phrase "wandering under the willows" (*yugyō yanagi*), an *utamakura* for Ashino, a poetic toponym known for its willows.[52] In his travelogue, Bashō recorded his experience in Ashino by composing a *hokku*:

> The whole paddy
> Sown with seeds, I part
> From the willow.

> *ta ichimai / uete tachisaru / yanagi kana*
> 田一枚植て立去る柳かな [53]

The *hokku* represents a moment of lingering under the shade of a willow and then parting from it. The *utamakura* for Ashino ties Bashō's poem to a Noh play of the same title, in which an itinerant priest retraces the steps of medieval poet Saigyō, encountering his spirit in the form of a willow. The association between Saigyō and willows comes from his *waka*:

Along the path
A clear stream flows
In the shade of a willow;
Stop for a moment, I thought,
Then ended up lingering.

michi no be ni / shimizu nagaruru / yanagi kage / shibashi tote koso / tachidomaritsure
道のべに清水ながるる柳かげしばしとてこそ立ちとまりつれ [54]

Saigyō's poem represents a summer scene where the speaker finds shade under a willow tree. By the end of the poem, what was intended to be a brief respite from the heat becomes a much longer stay. Like the itinerant priest in the Noh play, Bashō traces Saigyō's journey to Ashino. Saigyō's *waka*, the Noh play, and Bashō's *hokku* all depict willows as a space through which a traveler comes and goes. These works also echo Su Shi's rhapsodies in how their speakers tarry in a space of cultural significance—a space that stirs the poetic imagination.

The poem that concludes Buson's inscription thereby blends the autumn and winter scenes in Su Shi's rhapsodies, while also alluding to the summer willows in Bashō, the Noh play, and Saigyō, all in the space of seventeen syllables. The *hokku* exemplifies the power of allusion to transport the poet through and across the Chinese and Japanese literary traditions, blurring distinctions among time, space, genre, form, and medium.

The poem's form represents a cold and desolate landscape in a sequence of images: scattered leaves, a sere stream, and rocks. What makes a *hokku* a *hokku* is its *kigo*, or seasonal referent. Like *waka*, *hokku* are organized in anthologies (*kushū*) by the season. In the case of this poem, however, this method of categorization would clarify the seasonal ambiguity: the image of willow leaves scattering (*yanagi chiri*) is a *kigo* for autumn, while the image of the sere stream (*shimizu kare*) is a *kigo* for winter.[55] This seasonal ambiguity allows the poem to be both, neither, or in between autumn and winter.

This suspension of seasons mirrors the *hokku*'s dynamic relationship with other poems. Buson's poem relates to Saigyō's *waka* through opposition and contrast: the willows in Saigyō's poem have leaves, which provide shade over a clear, full-flowing stream; the willows in Buson's poem have scattered their leaves on a dried up stream. Where Saigyō evokes fullness, heat, and light, Buson evokes emptiness, cold, and darkness. By placing the *hokku* in an inscription that references Su Shi's rhapsodies, the *hokku* stands in for both rhapsodies. Although willows do not appear in either of Su Shi's pieces, one can picture willows in the autumn scene of the first rhapsody and see them shed their leaves like the trees in the second. The river is full in the first rhapsody, and empty in the second, like in Buson's verse. The *hokku* echoes the unfamiliar landscape in the later rhapsody by representing the seasonal change from autumn to winter in a single poem.[56]

Buson's *hokku* references poems in both the Japanese and Chinese traditions.[57] Su Shi's rhapsodies show how a traveler can join a larger human continuity by connecting to the affective space of a historical site; Bashō and Saigyō's poems use the *utamakura* for Ashino as a portal to collective experience. Edward Kamens has argued that the *utamakura* in one poem evokes a specific place, as well as the collective of poems that share that place, linking the single poem to the entire continuum of Japanese poetry.[58] In the same way that the site of Red Cliff mediated a connection with Cao Cao's fallen soldiers and the later representations of Red Cliff in Chinese poetry and painting, as an *utamakura* "Red Cliff" connects Buson's *hokku* to other poems about Red Cliff in the Japanese and Chinese traditions.

In 1680, Bashō composed a *hokku* that alludes to the same line from Su Shi's later rhapsody:

Rocks sere,
River dry—
Winter is missing.

ishi karete / mizu shibomeru ya / fuyu mo nashi
石枯れて水しぼめるや冬もなし[59]

Bashō's *hokku* represents a scene so dry, cold, and dreary that there is no space for "winter." The *hokku* is categorized as a winter poem, but the speaker doubts the winteriness of sere rocks and a dry river. Scholars Ōtani

Tokuzō and Nakamura Shunjō have argued that the poem comments on a misplaced metaphor: that the verbs *karete* (to be sere) and *shibomeru* (to dry up) are used to describe trees and vegetation during winter, but not rocks or rivers. Buson's *hokku*, however, is not making a claim about either autumn or winter; rather, it roams across multiple times and places.

Buson's inscription also challenges the boundaries of allusive variation by transporting the *hokku* to other poetic genres and their representations. As Kamens has observed, even when a Japanese poem does not feature an explicit allusion, it can "replicate" the familiar structure or "enact" the familiar attitude of another poem in the tradition.[60] As a representation of Red Cliff, Buson's *hokku* enacts earlier representations of Red Cliff, including Su Shi's song lyric (*ci*) "To the Tune, 'Recalling Her Charms,' Cherishing the Past at Red Cliff." In the song, the speaker compares the scene at Red Cliff to a painting:

Jagged rocks break the clouds,	亂石崩雲
Tossing waves pound the bank,	驚濤拍岸
Furling up a thousand piles of snow.	捲起千堆雪
The river and mountains are like a painting;	江山如畫
At one moment, how many valiant men were here!	一時多少豪傑 [61]

These lines illustrate how poetry, like a painting, encapsulates the relationships between time and space, and between historical event and representation. Up above, the rocks on the mountain cliff break apart the sea of clouds; down below, the waves beat upon the rock at the bank of the river in winter and disturb the thousand piles of snow that have accumulated over the season. Su Shi's use of the verb "to furl up" (*juan qi*) evokes a courtesan furling the blinds, about to view the scene beyond her chamber window, or a literatus furling a scroll with a landscape painted upon it. The landscape bears markers of time: the waves furl and push upwards the piles of snow that have blanketed the rock face. Once the rock face is bare, the speaker exclaims: "The river and mountains are like a painting." The metaphor enables him to place the landscape he beholds in history with the exclamation that "at one moment" (*yi shi*), the landscape was once filled by valiant men.[62]

By taking elements from one medium and rearranging them into a distinct aesthetic representation, Buson not only created new lyric forms in the literati tradition but also revealed the kinship between *bunjin* forms, speaking to W.J.T. Mitchell's idea that all media are mixed because one medium invariably stirs our imagination of another.[63] Buson's *hokku* represents scattered leaves, a sere stream, and rocks. The reader thus imagines a barren landscape, but the inscription's intertextuality between *haikai* and *kanshi* invokes a polyphony of voices that fill the barren landscape with sound from the Japanese and Chinese traditions.

This interplay between forms and genres demonstrates how Buson's *haikai* aspire toward a state of becoming. The *hokku* and *haiga* emerge as their own representations of Red Cliff and Ashino, standing in for Red Cliff and Ashino, imagining them blended as one. Such representation speaks to Edward Casey's claim that a painting is an original to itself: "A painting that represents something at once *stands for* and *stands in for* that which it represents."[64] Casey argues that a painted landscape stands in for the natural landscape, transmuting it: "The topos of the topic, the place of the landscape, is taken up in the representation that both stands for this place and stands in for it. In this way, place is at once signified and reinstated, reinstated-as-signified, *assigned* in a painting that represents it. Place is not replicated but transmuted in the work."[65]

In Buson's *haiga*, the rocks, in their impressionistic manner, sit on the page, "protruding" out of the poems and the histories into a new landscape where they gain new meaning. Part of this new meaning comes from being autonomous living objects; the other part is their continuous but varied relationship with tradition, made possible by the visual language of the *haibun* inscription, which places the rocks amid different representations from poetry and painting.

I have shown how the visual language of the inscription mediates the image's connection to multiple moments in the literati tradition. Supplementing the visual performance in the *haiga*, the *hokku* evokes a variant of itself as a line of poetry in Chinese. This variant *hokku* exemplifies how the visual and sonic affordances of Buson's poetry challenge the boundaries of the *haikai* genre by blending it with *kanshi*:[66]

ryū	*san*	*sei*	*sui*	*ko*	*seki*	*sho*	*sho*
柳	散	清	水	涸	石	処	処
●	●	○	●	●	●	●	●

Although the *hokku* can be read aloud in Japanese as *yanagi chiri / shi-mizu kare ishi / tokoro-dokoro*, it can also be read aloud using the Chinese readings of the graphs that compose the verse, as shown above.[67] The form of Buson's variant *hokku* resembles the way *haikai* poets in the late seventeenth century experimented by infusing their poetry with Chinese elements, creating what has come to be referred to as a "Chinese-style *haikai*."[68] The Chinese meter of Buson's verse (○ = level tone; ● = oblique tone) matches the meter of an ancient-style poem (*koshi*), a rhapsody (*fu*), or a song lyric (*ci*). In these genres of Chinese poetry, tones are less regulated and oblique tones are more prominent. In this way, the Chinese form of Buson's *hokku* opens more possibilities for reading it alongside earlier experiments in *haikai* and other poetic genres in the literati tradition.

By blurring the lines between *kanshi* and *haikai*, the variant *hokku* echoes the visual ambiguity of the rocks in the *haiga* through its sonic affordances. The end of the *hokku* marks the end of the inscription: an onomatopoeia that gives sound to objects moving "here and there" in time and space: *sho-sho* (in *kanshi*) and *tokoro-dokoro* (in *haikai*). This sound evokes the image of rocks in the painting, giving them a new sonic dimension: as the rocks appear strewn "here and there" on the page, their sound moving here and there in time and space can be heard through the polyphony of Su Shi's rhapsodies and song lyric on Red Cliff, Bashō's and Saigyō's willow poems at Ashino, and other poetic and visual representations from the Chinese and Japanese traditions.

REPETITION AND TAUTOLOGY

The remainder of this chapter examines how Buson experimented with literary form in order to represent the feeling of longing through imagery from multiple poetic genres. His poem "Lyric on Spring Endings" (Shunbo no kotoba)[69] combines *haikai* and *kanshi*, using repetition to perform and ironize the poetic conventions that express longing in the literati tradition.

"Lyric on Spring Endings" is anthologized with other poems under the generic title of *haishi* because it combines a *kanshi* quatrain with a *hokku*. The protean form of the *haishi* genre exemplifies the cross-pollination of genres during the Edo period.[70] The *kanshi* portion has been described as the prelude (*maegaki*) to the *hokku*, which dates to 1769.

The poem uses tautology to perform the puns of *haikai* practice and to explore the relationship between repetition and lyric time. I show how the repetition afforded by tautology suspends the fulfillment of meaning, suggesting the endless possibilities of interstitial experience at the penultimate moment of sunset:

> The man behind follows the man in front;
> A hundred paces, still a hundred paces.
> Down the bank, up the bank and back again;
> Just about to set, the sun yet to set.

> Treading on the tail feathers
> Of a copper pheasant,
> In the spring sunset.

kōjin wa zenjin o ou	後人逐前人
hyappo nao hyappo	百歩尚百歩
tsutsumi o kudarite, mata tsutsumi ni noboru	下堤還上堤
kuren to hosshite, hi imada kurezu	欲暮日未暮
yamadori no / oo fumu haru no / irihi kana	山鳥の尾を踏む春の入日哉[71]

The first four lines all tarry in the same time and space, as if the speaker's lyric mind were spinning on a wheel. In line 1, a man and the man whom he follows are equidistant; in line 2, the adverb *nao* (still) indicates that every step taken by the man behind does not change the distance between him and the man in front.[72] In line 3, the same thought continues: they both descend the embankment, they both ascend the embankment, and that process repeats, indicated by the adverb *mata* (back again). In Line 4 the speaker then draws attention to another natural being in a state of imminent movement: the evening sun about to set (*kuren to hosshite*) that has not yet set (*imada kurezu*). The four lines repeat the same idea, echoing each other, but to what end? The conclusion seems to be that there is no end—that the man chasing the other man and the sunset trying to set are both caught in temporal and spatial suspension.

The form of the poem produces repetition and tautology that mirrors the action (or non-action) in the content of the poem. On a lexical level, each line features the repetition of words: man; hundred paces; bank; set. Lines 2 and 4 mirror one another in the way they place words in opposition: front, back; up, down:

後人逐前人   ●○●○○
百步尚百步   ●●●●●
下堤還上堤   ●○○●○
欲暮日未暮   ●●●●●

These are the techniques by which the poem's form makes its repetition visual, heightened by the opposition of words from line to line. This mirroring also registers on the prosodic level in the Chinese meter. The *kanshi* is a pentasyllabic ancient-style poem (*gogon koshi*)—a genre characterized by its loose constraints regarding lineation and prosody. Although the rules of prosody—the balance between "level" (*hyō*) and "oblique" (*soku*) tones—are loose, the last word of every other line must rhyme, as with *ho* in line 2 and *bo* in line 4 in the Chinese reading of the poem. Lines 2 and 4 also "rhyme" as oblique tones, whereas lines 1 and 3 are a mixture of level and oblique. In this way, the poem displays repetition semantically, syntactically, visually, and prosodically.

The *hokku* that follows the *kanshi* alludes to a *waka* attributed to Kakinomoto no Hitomaro (660–724 CE) in *Collection of Ten Thousand Leaves* (759 CE; Man'yōshū). Buson calls upon the longing represented in Hitomaro's poem, which exemplifies the never-ending feeling of time in poems on the separation of lovers:[73]

Am I to sleep alone
This long night, long
Like drooping tails,
Tail feathers of copper pheasants
Resting mountains apart?

ashihiki no / yamadori no o no / shidari o no / naganaga shi yo o / hitori kamo nemu
葦引の山鳥の尾のしだり尾のながながし夜をひとりかも寝む [74]

The image of tail feathers from a copper pheasant (lit. mountain bird) in Hitomaro's autumn poem reappears in Buson's spring *hokku*. "Copper pheasant tail feathers" (*yamadori no o*) is an example of a *jokotoba*, or "preface word"—a poetic device in the family of *makurakotoba* (lit. pillow words), epithets that allude to earlier poems in the tradition. Hitomaro's poem uses the image of the copper pheasant's long tail feathers as a metaphor for the long autumn nights the speaker must sleep through alone and as an image in a line of repetition: the word *ashihiki* (an epithet evoking the expanse of a mountain), the noun *o* (tail), and the adjective *naga* (long). By alluding to Hitomaro's poem, Buson evokes the longing Hitomaro's speaker must endure over the course of the long night, only this time in spring.

When Buson combines the *kanshi* and the *hokku* to form one composite poem, he refigures the lonesome longing in Hitomaro's *waka* into an ironic comment on the circularity of time and feeling at sundown. The pathetic feelings in Hitomaro's poem evoke the conceit of endless longing and unfulfillment in poems on separated lovers, a conceit that is dramatized by the repetition and tautology in Buson's quatrain. "Lyric on Spring Endings" thereby transforms a conventional poetic conceit into a comment about the suspension of time and feeling itself when a poet finds himself at the penultimate moment before spring sunset.

By evoking sorrow through the allusion to Hitomaro, Buson also refigures the temporal and spatial dimensions of longing into a visual metaphor that confounds perception. Like the above *hokku* that showed how the setting sun seen through the pines and oaks produces the optical illusion of plum blossoms, the *hokku* here also tricks the eye: the poem uses tail feathers as a visual metaphor for the sun setting on a mountain path. The reader may imagine the speaker is walking and, as the sun sets, shadows stretch upon the ground in the form of copper pheasant tail feathers. The sunset in the *hokku* follows the sunset in the prelude poem; the shadows figured as pheasant feathers in the *hokku* add a new visual dimension to the earlier sunset. The *hokku* refigures the liminal suspension generated by the repetitiveness and redundancy of the *kanshi* into a trompe l'oeil of tail feathers and sunset shadows.[75]

In this poem, Buson uses repetition, tautology, and the blending of genres (*kanshi* and *hokku*) to create a composite poetic form that represents perception and feeling at sundown. While repetition and tautology also evoke the playfulness and humor of *haikai* practice, on a meta level they suggest the idea that poetic form need not find an ending but rather can be content suspended in the time (and space) of imminence and interstitial experience. The longing and un-fulfillment evoked through allusion to Hitomaro's poem also imbues Buson's poem with irony about its claim (or non-claim) on time. As "Lyric on Spring Endings" tarries in the eternal present, where action (or non-action) recurs in ceaseless penultimateness, what begins as a pleasurable evocation of the beauty of sunset becomes an anxious entrapment in its endlessness.

FORM AND LONGING

I conclude this chapter with yet another new and experimental lyric form that Buson created by blending the *haikai* and *kanshi* genres. In addition to "Lyric on Spring Endings," Buson composed other *haishi*, including "Song of the Yodo River" (1774–1775; Denga no uta) and "Song of Spring Wind on the Riverbank at Kema" (1775; Shunpū batei kyoku), which have also been called ballads. Buson was not alone in carrying out these experiments in lyric: *haishi* and poems of the unconventional sort emerged in the eighteenth century during the height of pleasure quarter (*yūkaku*) culture in Edo when songs about romances with courtesans were in vogue.[76] The revival of the song lyric (*ci*) genre in late imperial China surely had some influence on the development of these lyric experiments in the eighteenth century. In content, these unconventional poems echoed the sentiments of popular song; in form, they explored new frontiers in lyric expression.

One of Buson's compositions is a *haishi* entitled "Mourning for Hokuju Rōsen" (1777?; Hokuju Rōsen o itamu). This poem is often discussed alongside the two aforementioned *haishi* ballads and is anthologized in the same motley group of poems as "Lyric on Spring Endings." "Mourning for Hokuju Rōsen," however, is an elegy in "free verse"—a poem unregulated by meter. Its language is vernacular and its structure blends forms beyond generic distinction.[77] Buson composed it for his mentor and friend Hayami Shinga (1671–1745), who died at age 75 when Buson was 30.[78] Shinga was a sake brewer and *haikai* poet who studied under Kikaku, a pupil of Bashō. Shinga adopted the nom de plume "Hokuju" (lit. northern longevity) upon retirement. In the title, Buson addresses him with the honorific "Rōsen," which means "the venerable immortal." Some scholars speculate that Buson composed the poem in 1777, but it was not published until 1793, a decade after his death.[79] The poem mourns the death of a beloved friend regarded with the highest esteem. Buson mediates feelings of grief and the process of grieving through the diverse imagery drawn from the *haikai* and *kanshi* traditions as well as through the rhythm and repetition afforded by elegy's protean poetic form:

Mourning for Hokuju Rōsen

You departed this morning; my heart this evening scattered in a
    thousand pieces,
Why are you so far away?

Longing for you, I walked to the hills and roamed;
Why are the hills so sad?

5   The dandelions bloomed yellow, the shepherd's purse white;
There is no one to share the view.

Is there a pheasant? I hear it crow and crow;
I had a friend. He lived across the river.

Poof—a Protean disperses into smoke, the west wind blows
10   *So hard on the bamboo fields and the sedge plains,*
There is nowhere to take refuge.

I had a friend. He lived across the river. Today,
no pheasant crows hororo.

You departed this morning; my heart this evening scattered in a
    thousand pieces,
15   Why are you so far away?

In my humble hut, by the Buddha[80] I light no candles,
I offer no flowers; in silence with a heavy heart, standing still
    tonight,
All the more reverent.

hokuju rōsen o itamu
kimi ashita ni sarinu yūbe no kokoro chiji ni

nanzo haruka naru
kimi o omōte okanobe ni yukitsu asobu
okanobe nanzo kaku kanashiki
tanpopo no ki ni nazuna no shirō sakitaru
miru hito zo naki
kigisu no aru ka hitanaki ni naku o kikeba
tomo ariki kawa o hedatete suminiki
hege no keburi no hato uchichireba nishi fuku kaze no
hageshikute ozasahara masugehara
nogaru beki kata zo naki
tomo ariki kawa o hedatete suminiki kyō wa
hororo tomo nakanu
kimi ashita ni sarinu yūbe no kokoro chiji ni
nanzo haruka naru
waga io no amida butsu tomoshibi mo monosezu
hana mo mairasezu sugosugo to tatazumeru koyoi wa
koto ni tōtoki

北壽老仙をいたむ
君あしたに去ぬゆふべのこゝろ千々に
何ぞはるかなる
君をおもふて岡のべに行つ遊ぶ
をかのべ何ぞかくかなしき
蒲公の黄に薺のしろう咲たる
見る人ぞなき
雉子のあるかひたなきに鳴を聞ば
友ありき河をへだてゝ住にき
へげのけぶりのはと打ちれば西吹風の
はげしくて小竹原眞すげはら
のがるべきかたぞなき
友ありき河をへだてゝ住にきけふは
ほろゝともなかぬ
君あしたに去ぬゆふべのこゝろ千々に
何ぞはるかなる
我庵のあみだ仏ともし火もものせず
花もまいらせずすごすごとイめる今宵は
ことにたうとき 81

The poem opens with the reality that Shinga is gone and the speaker's heart is in disarray. The speaker walks to the hills where he finds signs of spring in the dandelions and shepherd's purse blossoms. This is where Buson would spend time with his friend Shinga; while thinking of him, the speaker suddenly hears the call of what sounds like a pheasant. The poem shifts voice and embarks on a monologue by a pheasant lamenting the death of a friend.[82] Then the poem shifts back to the human speaker's voice, as marked by the repetition of the first line. The poem concludes with a scene of silent vigil in darkness.

The events that unfold in "Mourning for Hokujū Rōsen" are clear, but the treatment of emotion in time and space, the problem of voice and lyric address, and the use of rhythm and repetition raise questions about the boundaries of lyric containment, the relationship between sound and lyric form, and the possibility for lyric to give form to longing.

The rupture that opens the poem is echoed in images that mediate feelings of grief in temporal and spatial ways. The first line frames the trauma of loss in one day: the speaker mourns from the moment in the morning when he learns of Shinga's death to the moment around twilight when he realizes that his heart is in a state of disarray, "scattered in a thousand pieces." The adjectival noun *chiji* describes the speaker's heart (and mind) as "*shattered* into a thousand pieces," as other translators have interpreted, yet the particle *ni* makes it an adverb, indicating that these pieces have also moved in myriad directions, hence "scattered." The original term *chiji* literally means "thousands and thousands," the repetition of which highlights the great number of pieces as well as the many places to which these pieces have scattered. *Chiji* also refers to the manifold forms the heart and mind can take in a contemplative state, a spatial metaphor to describe the protean nature of the heart during times of sorrow as well as the boundless depths of the poetic imagination.

The second line echoes the spatial meanings of *chiji ni*, but also gives its meanings of unlimited distance and variation a temporal dimension. The line opens with *nanzo*, a classical interrogative meaning "why," asking why Shinga is *haruka*, which means "distant" and "far away," but also "dark and indistinct." Although in my translation, the question "Why are you so far away?" marks the subject as the deceased, which is how most critics have interpreted the line, the subject may continue from the first line in enjambment. This means that line 2 can be read as "Why [does my heart scatter] so far away [searching for you]?" With both readings in mind, the question refers to the vast distance that separates life and death in addition to the distance and time of longing evoked by *chiji ni* in the first line, and the darkness and obscurity of the directions to which the pieces of the speaker's mind and heart have scattered in the search for the deceased.

The apostrophes that punctuate the poem question the role of voice and lyric address and show how the poem is about voices summoning the dead by incantation. The apostrophe to Shinga "Why are you so far away?" is echoed in the question the speaker asks of the hills: "Why are the hills so sad?" Above, I discussed lyric address in the second of Buson's death verses where the speaker poses a question to the warbler. In that *hokku* the dialogue is between the speaker and warbler, and I argued that the apostrophe turns back on the speaker. The apostrophes in "Mourning for Hokuju Rōsen" are addresses to Shinga, whom the reader knows is absent, displacing the irreversible structure of time when a person dies by making the absent present again in speech, in discourse. In his study of Anglo-European lyric, Jonathan Culler writes: "Apostrophes displace this irreversible structure by removing it from linear time and locating it in a discursive time." He argues that apostrophes in elegies allow for more fluid movements in time because the elegy "replaces an irreversible temporal disjunction, the movement from life to death, with a reversible alternation between mourning and consolation, evocations of presence and absence."[83] So by asking "Why are you so far?" and "Why are the hills so sad?" the speaker summons Shinga back to life to converse with him, a move that contradicts the opening statement that Shinga is gone.

The monologue performed by the pheasant reifies the relationship between the speaker and Shinga through fiction and metaphor. Once the speaker reaches the spot on the hills where he and Shinga together once admired the white and yellow blossoms, he thinks he hears the incessant call (*hitanaki ni naku*) of a pheasant. In my translation, I use the verb "crow," which refers to the loud and passionate cry of a cock pheasant, often heard during mating season in spring. This cry, although illusory, answers the apostrophe that opens the elegy, which is the voice of a woman, as suggested by the second-person pronoun *kimi* (you). In traditional Chinese and Japanese poetry, women speakers use *kimi* to refer to their lovers;[84] it was also common for a male literatus to don the voice of a woman to articulate his difficult-to-articulate feelings of love for another man, in this case, his beloved mentor.

It is no surprise that Buson, as a literatus, chose to figure his relation-ship with his mentor as a romance between a hen and a cockerel. In tradi-tional Chinese painting, pheasants are associated with Confucian virtues. Hou-mei Sung observes that pheasants became an integral part of the bird-painting genre, especially by the Song dynasty. Pheasants are often depicted together with orioles (warblers) to symbolize friendship between literati. Sung writes that by the Yuan dynasty, the pheasant's beautiful feathers were associated with literati talent.[85] Of the two pheasants, the cockerel has the beautiful and colorful feathers, so it makes sense that Shinga as mentor would be figured as the colorful cockerel and that Buson, in subordinate deference, figures himself as the drab hen.

When the speaker hears what sounds like a pheasant (*kigisu no aru ka*), the poem presents a monologue in which a hen pheasant laments the dis-appearance of a friend. The hen, or the female voice of the speaker, uses metaphor to describe the fugitive nature of life: she imagines a "Protean" (*hege* or *henge*) transforming into smoke: Proteans are creatures that change form and are found throughout Edo literature on the supernatu-ral.[86] Then suddenly the wind blows strong upon the spring landscape, and before the Protean in smoke form can take shelter, he is blown away. Echoing the cock pheasant's passionate and repetitive call, the hen repeats the line with which she began her recollection, ending her monologue with the reality that, despite what the speaker thinks he had heard while roaming on the hill, "Today / No pheasant crows *hororo*."

The onomatopoeia *hororo* references a poem by Taira no Sadafun (872?–923 CE), anthologized in *Collection of Poems New and Old* (905 CE; Kokinshū):

On the spring moor,
Among the tall leaves of grass,
Longing for his mate,
A pheasant takes off,
Crowing *hororo*.

haru no no no / shigeki kusaba no / tsumagoi ni / tobitatsu kiji no / hororo to zo naku
春の野のしげき草ばの妻恋ひにとびたつ雉子のほろろとぞなく[87]

Sadafun's poem represents a spring scene in which a cock pheasant flies to find his mate (*tsumagoi ni tobitatsu*). As the cockerel lifts off, he crows *hororo*, a sound of passion and affection. Unlike the speaker in Sadafun's poem, the speaking subjects in Buson's elegy—the human speaker and the hen—are unable to hear with certainty either *hororo* or the feelings it evokes. Like the Protean that poofs into smoke and vanishes in the wind, sound in the fiction of the poem is contingent on illusion and imagination.

On the level of form, however, *hororo* and the sounds of passion, excitement, and affection are audible in repetition. In tune with other elegiac poems in the tradition—from poetry in *Man'yōshū* to the chorus and dialogue in Noh plays from the medieval period—Buson's elegy deploys repetition to showcase a lyric performance that blends pain and pleasure, as the lyric mind mourns a loss to a beat. This beat produces a rhythm that mediates feeling without putting a stamp on what those feelings necessarily are. The repetition of lines 1–2 in lines 14–15 in the poem echoes the repetition of lines 8 and 12 in the hen's monologue. The only difference in the hen's speech is the addition of "Today / No pheasant crows *hororo*" (*kyō wa / hororo tomo nakanu*). This difference highlights the fact that *hororo* is not audible in the fiction of the poem, yet on a meta-formal level the sound resonates in the repetition and rhythm of the entire poem: a pheasant's call that recurs again and again.

Rhythm also mediates the relationship between poet and reader, and the connection to divine experience. Gary Ebersole has shown that the repetition in *Man'yōshū* poems serves a sacred and ceremonial purpose in death rituals.[88] The incantatory power of repetition in Buson's elegy resembles that of an ancient ritual lament—with the exception that the incantation in Buson's elegy does not end. The poetic form of the elegy allows Buson, simultaneously and endlessly, to grieve, mourn, and summon the deceased back to life: this plays out in the speaker's apostrophes and in the fiction between the hen and cockerel, whose presence manifests in an illusory sound caught by the ear of the human speaker as well as in an illusory imaginary image of a Protean conjured in the hen's memory and imagination. Reading the elegy aloud performs these incantatory acts: the repetition of lines and the repetition of sounds (such as *ki* and *no*) create a rhythm, producing a somatic feeling beyond representation in language, which is possible only in sound. Culler writes that in the history of lyric, free verse forms enabled poets to escape the shackles of classical meter and enter a direct relationship with the divine.[89] He argues that "rhythm is an event without representation" because it suggests something else, an experience beyond the poem itself.[90] In the process of reading, the reader becomes aware of rhythm, pulse, and the poem's something-else-ness that creates empathy for the speaker in communion with the divine.

The conclusion of the elegy contradicts the sound made audible by the repetition and rhythm in the form of the poem, and yet, at the same time, the ending echoes the silence that pervades the content of the poem. After the repetitions, the speaker finds himself in his humble hut before an image of the (Amida) Buddha. He notes that he does *not* perform any prescribed forms of ritual: he lights no candles, and he offers no flowers, (non)acts that intensify the gravity of loss because material and ritual objects seem to have no use. He offers only stillness and reverence. The onomatopoeic adverb *sugosugo to* (here, "in silence with heart heavy") speaks to the anxiety, weightiness, and stillness of the moment endured in crestfallen silence. *Sugosugo to* describes the manner in which the speaker stands still (*tatazumeru*) in the wake of the incantatory charm from the earlier repetition and rhythm. The term also refers to the disappointment one feels immediately after expectations of excitement and pleasure go unfulfilled. If the repetition is the poem's performance, once it stops, the scene grows more silent than before, and the speaker returns home feeling unfulfilled.

The poem ends, however, with a declaration that tonight will be "all the more reverent" (*koyoi wa / koto ni tōtoki*), which adds a layer of profound admiration and respect to the "in silence with heart heavy" with which the speaker stands still. This stillness in reverence extends the eternal and divine moment—the awesome feeling that earlier resonated in the nerves and tensions between the words that recur and the images that repeat. Like *tōtoki*, the word "reverence" also means the quality that inspires a profound sense of awe, the feelings that strike a person when confronting the divine or the sublime. In this way, the poem ends ambiguously: both in deferential silence and reverential awe, as if the song and dance in the incantation and rhythm have summoned a presence from absence. The poem tarries in the moment of the *as if*, resisting closure.

Buson was experimenting in a lyric form in order to transcend the boundaries of traditional poetic genres, while at the same time making use of the artifice afforded by the literati repertoire. Unlike in his *hokku*, painterly landscapes in the elegy are figured as places of absence: the hill marks the spot where the speaker and friend once enjoyed each other's company; the plains of bamboo and sedge mark the spot where the Protean disappears. While the blossoms blooming yellow and white evoke how colors emerge brightly and prominently in Buson's *hokku*, their role here is static and their beauty goes unappreciated. As the speaker laments, "there is no one to share the view"; taken more literally, "there is no one to view them." Buson may have deprived the elegy of color to bolster its somber theme, letting the landscape of vision be overtaken by a landscape of feeling. In this way, the elegy seamlessly blends earlier genres, themes, and techniques without giving weight to one element or the other.

The tensions in the elegy lie less in content and more in form: the elegy's use of displacement in time and space, the complexities of voice and gender, and the incantatory power of rhythm and repetition. This contradiction between form and content exemplifies the dissonance in lyric poetry and reveals a larger concern poets face when mediating feelings of longing through lyric form. In his essay on longing and form, György Lukács (1885–1971) presents a paradox concerning the poetry of longing: he asks whether longing can have a form; how—if its fulfillment is form itself—can longing be longing once it has been fulfilled?

> Longing is always sentimental—but is there such a thing as a sentimental form? Form means getting the better of sentimentality; in form there is no more longing and no more loneliness; to achieve form is to achieve the greatest possible fulfillment. Yet the forms of poetry are temporal, so that the fulfillment must have a 'before' and an 'after'; it is not being but becoming. And becoming presupposes dissonance… Poetry cannot live without dissonance because movement is its very essence, and the movement can only proceed from disharmony to harmony and back again the other way.[91]

Lukács argues that dissonance cannot happen in painting since it is a form outside of temporality, and so dissonance must come to resolution—otherwise it is incomplete.[92] Even in their ekphrastic representations of the natural world in *bunjin* painting, Buson's *haikai* leave room for the imagination to roam. They are forms in the process of "becoming," dependent on the reader and his knowledge of the poetic tradition to fill in the gaps. Similarly, Buson's elegy aspires toward formlessness by negating conventions and by showing the emergence of an unknown form.

What does the elegy achieve, then, with its form? In the same essay Lukács describes the idea of German longing as so strong that it "destroys all form," that it is so powerful that "one cannot express it except by stammering."[93] He asks "whether this formlessness of longing is really proof of its strength or, rather, of an inner softness, a yieldingness, a never-endingness."

There is an analogy to Buson's poem: as the elegy tries to contain the trauma of loss, it also contains the movement, pulses, and variations of the feelings loss engenders, like the word *chiji ni*. These pulses are the stammers of the poet's voice and thought: the destabilization of voice and containment as the poetic language rides the backs of rhythm and repetition in place of the pheasant's crow *hororo*, only to end in silence and stillness that gives presence to an ambiguous feeling evoking something between reverence and sublimity.

This chapter has examined how Buson displayed the colors of his *bunjin* mind by creating *haikai* forms that represent feelings of anxiety and longing. The next chapter turns to the lyricism of Ema Saikō (1787–1861), a woman *bunjin* who experimented with the *kanshi* genre in the early nineteenth century.

NOTES

1. See Crowley, *Haikai Poet Yosa Buson*.
2. For more on Buson as a *bunjin* see Ikezawa, *Edo bunjin ron*, 353–381; Yokota, "Buson as Bunjin."
3. Marcon, *The Knowledge of Nature*, x.
4. Translations are mine unless otherwise noted. Yosa Buson, *Buson zenshū*, 1: 93. From here on, *BZ*.
5. *BZ*, 1: 100.
6. Ibid.
7. Backus, "What Goes Into a Haiku," 739.
8. In his preface to *Correct Use of Haikai Topics* (1782; Haidai seimei), a dictionary compiled by Yamamoto Rokyō, Buson discussed *sarikirai*, a rule in *renku* that forbids repetition: "If the occasion warrants it, breaking the rules should become the rule.... A *haikai* rule is like the wind and the rain, and the hot and the cold of the four seasons: change has no limit." *BZ*, 4: 209–210.
9. Buson composed a *hokku* on red plum blossoms that mocks the literati tradition by pairing red plum petals with horse dung:

    > Red plum petals
    > Fallen, might be shoots of fire
    > On the horse dung.
    > 紅梅の落花燃ゆらむ馬の糞

    BZ, 1: 510. Backus, "What Goes Into a Haiku," 762. Backus's translation reproduces the pun in the verb *moyu*, which can mean "to put forth shoots," or "to burn in flames."

10. *BZ*, 1: 274.
11. Jullien, *The Great Image*, 194.
12. The brilliance and vividness of the colors in the Buson poems examined in this section also seem to anticipate the way color and form are figured in modern European painting. In his discussion about form and color in Chinese painting, Jullien compares the use of color in the European tradition, distinguishing classical painting from modern. He observes that the classic idea of painting "submits form to color," while "the moderns move in the opposition direction…liberating color from form and even giving precedence to color," like in paintings by Kandinsky, Picasso, and Matisse. Jullien, *The Great Image*, 196. On a visual level, Buson's *hokku* juxtaposes colors in order to suggest their blending into new colors. The fragrance of the ink adds an olfactory dimension to the swatches of black and white, but in the end the poem gives precedence to vision over smell.
13. *BZ*, 1: 511.
14. *BZ*, 1: 570.
15. One commentary: "A colorful scene that looks more like an oil painting than a nanga." Ueda, *The Path of the Flowering Thorn*, 162. Scholars Teruoka Yasutaka and Kawashima Tsuyu have described the poem as a "topographical view of early summer" (*fukan seru shoka no fūkei*). See *Buson-shū Issa-shū*, 122. Other scholars believe the poem is showing depth and perspective, playing with the near (the young leaves) and the far (the stream and barley), which is different from *nanga*. *Yosa Buson shū*, 291. From here on *YBS*.
16. Takeuchi, *Taiga's True Views*, 144.
17. As Melinda Takeuchi has shown, the meaning of "spirit-resonance" (*kiin* 氣韻) varied among Edo literati: for Tosa Mitsuoki (1617–1691), she writes that spirit-resonance "originates in the painter": "[spirit-resonance] means that the painter, as he sets out to work, lets the spirit of his soul circulate through his body. When his soul is small and his spirit insufficient, his brushwork will be stunted, feeble, and always unsatisfactory." For Hayashi Moriatsu (early eighteenth century), it "resides in the forms": "to give vent, just as if projecting one's voice, to the mysterious life-force [*ki*] that resides in the 10,000 things…and to cause this vigor of living things to flow forth just as it appears before the eyes." For Gyokushū (early nineteenth century), the term was more liberal, and that "spirit-resonance could reside in the artist, the scene, and the painting." Takeuchi, *Taiga's True Views*, 138–9.
18. Yamashita, *Shiro no shijin: Buson shinron*. Yamashita catalogues numerous *hokku* in which white appears, and examines their different symbolic and affective meanings, including "pure elegance," "visual impact," "value," "wit," "love," "longing," and "ambiguity of meaning." Yamashita, *Yamashita Kazumi chosakushū*, 3: 389–416. From Yamashita's

extensive survey, it is sensible to say that white figures in a variety of ways and has many functions in Buson's *haikai*.

19. For more on poems Buson composed in the year of his death, see Zolbrod, "Death of a Poet-Painter."

20. Stevens, *Opus Posthumous*, 187.

21. *BZ*, 1: 524.

22. For a summary of the rules of *renku* see Jonsson, *Haikai Poetics*, 18–24.

23. Buson's fondness for Wang Wei may be evidence of Tang poetry's popularity during the eighteenth century after the death of Ogyū Sorai (1666–1728). Sorai imparted his passion for Ming Ancient Phraseology to his disciple Hattori Nankaku (1683–1759), under whom Buson studied classical Chinese. In 1724 Nankaku published *Selections of Tang Poetry* (J. Tōshisen; Ch. Tangshi xuan), a Ming dynasty anthology of Tang poetry annotated by Li Panlong (1514–1570). The anthology was widely read among Edo *bunjin*, fostering a community that embraced ideals of elegance, an aesthetic freedom from the reins of Edo Confucian order. Flueckiger, *Imagining Harmony*, 123.

24. Narushima Yukio agreed with Takahashi Shōji's argument that *mukashi* (long ago) does not refer to Wang Wei, but to Buson's past idealization of Wang Wei. Narushima, *Buson to kanshi*, 59. Narushima's reading gives the *hokku* more autonomy as a poem that refers to Buson's subjective understanding of the past.

25. Casey, *Representing Place*, 116.

26. In the "spring" section of their Buson collection, Fujita Shin'ichi and Kiyoto Noriko list forty-four *hokku* in which *uguisu* (warblers) appear. Of the forty-four warblers, thirty-two are represented with direct reference to their song. *Buson zenkushū*, 11–18.

27. Ogata and Morita in *BZ* categorize the warbler in the second *hokku* as the *kigo* for spring. Fujita and Kiyoto believe it is winter, grouping the poem with the first *hokku*.

28. Jonsson, 27.

29. In a preface to *Ya-kana-shō*, a work on *kireji* by waka poet and fiction writer Ueda Akinari (1734–1809), Buson writes that the insertion of a *kireji* does not necessarily break the continuity of a verse: "A *kireiji* is something which is not when it is, and is when it is not. There are poems with *kireji* that are not cut, and poems with no *kireji* that are cut." Jonsson, *Haikai Poetics*, 27.

30. The address enhances the "now-ness" of the poem, making it a lyric event. As Jonathan Culler has observed, "Fiction is about what happened next; lyric is about what happens now." Culler, *Theory of the Lyric*, 226. In his discussion of lyric address in the Anglo-European tradition, Culler writes that apostrophe enables the poet to develop a relationship with the

addressee: "apostrophe treats that bringing together of subject and object as an act of will, something accomplished poetically in the act of address." Culler, 223. This applies to Buson as well: by addressing the warbler through apostrophe, the speaker constitutes it as another subject, with whom he can develop a relationship.

31. Buson's address to the warbler in the form of a lyric speaks to Allen Grossman's observations about the triangular relationship between poet, object, and reader in poetry: "In the most primitive terms, the presence of a poem involves a triadic state of affairs, in which there is a self, and the beloved of that self which always has a transcendental character ascribed to it, and a third—the third being the audience, the ratifier, the witness, and the inheritor of the drama of loving relationship to which the poem gives access." Grossman, *The Sighted Singer*, 13.

32. This reading makes less sense considering the context of the poem. There is the subject (the warbler), and there is the object of rustling (the frost on the bush), which is also the place where the subject resides. "Why" sounds like the right question. This is supported by the accusatory tone of the line, which suggests that the speaker is slightly bothered by the sound he hears, and he wants to know why the warbler is doing what it is doing.

33. My interpretation rests on three assumptions: the verb *akuru* means "to dawn" in the simple future tense, meaning "it will dawn"; the particle *ni* marks *shiraume* as the indirect object of *akuru*, which means that night will dawn, but also *on* the plum; and the adverb *bakari to* means "now and only," supported by the predicate *narinikeri*, which registers the subject's emphatic awareness of the now-and-only-ness of the moment.

34. In 1768, Buson composed a *hokku* that gives sound to darkness:

> In an ancient well—
> A fish jumps for mosquitos
> And makes a dark splash.
> 古井戸や蚊に飛ぶ魚の音くらし

BZ, 1: 40.

35. Jullien, *The Greater Image*, 194.
36. Jullien, *In Praise of Blandness*, 87.
37. Ibid., 95. Mei Yaochen, *Wanlingji*.
38. Jullien, *In Praise of Blandness*, 24. Original emphasis.
39. The last verse's "now-ness" and relationship to time speaks to George Kubler's idea of the in-between moment he calls "actuality": "Actuality is when the lighthouse is dark between flashes: it is the instant between the ticks of the watch: it is a void interval slipping forever through time:

the rupture between past and future: the gap at the poles of the revolving magnetic field, infinitesimally small but ultimately real. It is the inter-chronic pause when nothing is happening. It is the void between events." Kubler, *The Shape of Time*, 15. Nothing is happening in Buson's final verse on white plum blossoms but the feeling of expectancy and waiting.

40. Rosenfield, *Mynah Birds and Flying Rocks*, 61.

41. *BZ*, 6: 444. For the *hokku*, also see *BZ*, 1: 13. The version of the *hokku* in *YBS* notes that the last measure reads "*tokoro-doko*," which leaves out the *ji-amari* (extra syllable) that sometimes occurs in *haikai* practice.

42. Rosenfield, *Mynah Birds and Flying Rocks*, 49–63.

43. Melinda Takeuchi observes that the encyclopedic way Chinese painting is presented in *The Mustard Seed Garden Manual of Painting* (1679; Jieziyuan huazhuan) inspired the eclectic approach to painting embraced by Edo *bunjin*, including Buson and his contemporary Ike no Taiga. Takeuchi, *Taiga's True Views*, 23. A Japanese version of the *Manual* had circulated by the eighteenth century, and like Taiga, Buson looked to it for inspiration. Takeuchi argues that the images in the *Manual* were meant to be parts of a larger whole, but literati painters in the Edo period treated the parts as wholes in themselves: "Early Japanese literati painters seem to have interpreted such designs, wrenched out of compositional context for the sake of demonstrating brushwork or grouping of form, as pictures in their own right." Takeuchi, 29.

44. This visual language evokes the kind of pairing between text and image in English Romantic poet William Blake's (1757–1827) metal plates, upon which he juxtaposed illustrations with poems. In his study of Blake's visual language, W.J.T. Mitchell explores how a text can make the reader think in images, arguing that "all media are mixed media," and that representation itself is a confluence of mediums, rather than their separation. Mitchell, *Picture Theory*, 5. Since all media are mixed, a work of art inspires the viewer to see in multiple ways. Mitchell argues there is an "iconology of the text," a means of interpreting a text by way of examining the images it evokes in the mind of the reader.

45. The opening commentary on Su Shi's rhapsodies on Red Cliff sets the tone for the entire inscription, imbuing the image of rocks with literary and historical significance. Buson describes every word in Su Shi's rhapsodies as "sublime" (*zetsumyō*), a state of being that evokes exquisiteness, grandeur, beauty, and fear. During his years of exile, Su Shi composed the two *fu* (rhapsodies, or poetic expositions) upon his visit to Red Cliff on the Yangzi River in Huangzhou. Red Cliff is remembered as the site where Han dynasty General Cao Cao and his army fought to reunite China in 208 CE. The battle ended in Cao Cao's defeat, ushering China into an era of disunity known as the Three Kingdoms period.

46. Egan: "The sanguine reassurance that Su finds in the underlying thought of an ongoing human consciousness and community, greater by far than any single life, yet linking separate lives together, as Su is linked to the Red Cliff warriors and later readers are, in turn, linked to Su as a special and memorable resolution of the problem raised so often by encounters with ancient sites in Chinese poetry. It is this evocation of human continuity, in the face of which individual possessiveness is meaningless, that makes the ending of the rhapsody so immensely satisfying." Egan, *Word, Image, and Deed*, 224.

47. For the original Chinese, see Su Shi, *Su Shi quan ji jiao zhu*, 10: 39. From here on *SSQJJZ*.

48. Egan, *Word, Image, and Deed*, 221–250.

49. The Chinese graph that Buson uses for crane is *kaku* 霍 (a variant of *kaku* 鶴), which means "the whoosh of a bird in flight." In Chinese the graph is *huo*, which is onomatopoeia for a bird's swift flight. Buson could have made an error, or he was emphasizing that Su Shi's verse is so sublime that it flashes before the eye.

50. Egan translates the commentary by late imperial poet Yuan Hongdao: "The second rhapsody carries within its narration of events boundless scenic description. As for the ending, even Zizhan [Su Shi] himself would not be able fully to explain its marvelousness." Egan, *Word, Image, and Deed*, 246–7.

51. For a history of the symbolism of the crane in Chinese painting, see Sung, *Decoded Messages*, 39–62.

52. The *hokku* was published several times in different anthologies, featuring different headnotes. For a list, see *BZ* 1:13. Ashino is located in present-day Tochigi Prefecture.

53. Matsuo Bashō, *Bashō bunshū*, 75.

54. The poem is anthologized in *New Collection of Poems Old and New* (1205; Shin Kokinshū). *Shin Kokin wakashū*, 91.

55. In *BZ* the poem is anthologized as a winter poem; in Takai Kitō's *Buson kushū* (1784), the poem is anthologized as an autumn poem.

56. The dissonance and consonance the *hokku* bears in relation to the Su Shi and Saigyō poems mirrors the dynamic relationship between elements in Chinese painting. In his discussion on painting manuals and aesthetic treatises from medieval through late imperial China, François Jullien has observed that Chinese landscapes are worlds bound by dualism. He argues that the elements in Chinese landscapes oppose *and* correspond, giving the sense of totality to the scene depicted in the painting. The Chinese word for landscape is *shanshui* (J. *sansui*), or "mountains and water." The tension between the two elements is what constitutes the Chinese-style landscape paintings Buson practiced: "'Mountains-waters'

symbolizes these dualities that hold the world in tension, and the infinite exchanges that result from them. Hence, far from being conceived as a fragment of land subject to the authority of the gaze and delimited by its horizon, the Chinese landscape puts into play the functional aggregate of opposing yet corresponding elements, and it is that dynamism as a whole, whatever the scale, that the brush will be called on to capture. The Chinese painter, in his most significant painting, figures the process of things as a whole, the entire, infinitely diverse play of its polarities. He does not paint a corner of the world." Jullien, *The Greater Image*, 122. Peter Flueckiger observes that the idea of totality was present in eighteenth-century intellectual discourse: "When Japanese intellectuals of this time looked to ancient cultures as the source of a normative Way, they typically defined the value of such a Way in terms of its ability to structure society as a whole that exceeds the sum of its parts, so that individuals and their relationships take on meaning through their incorporation into a totality that transcends them." Flueckiger, *Imagining Harmony*, 3.

57. In three images Buson's *hokku* distills the tension between Su Shi's two rhapsodies on Red Cliff and provides oppositional balance to Saigyō's summer verse on willows at Ashino.

58. Kamens: "Allusiveness is extremely conspicuous in this tradition,…even when a poem of this tradition makes no explicit allusion through gesture, playful or otherwise, to another particular poem, it nonetheless rather transparently relates itself intertextually to virtually all other poems in the tradition, by replicating familiar formal structures and enacting familiar attitudes; and even when these structures and attitudes are overthrown by something unfamiliar or unorthodox, that seemingly antagonistic relationship is also one that attains significance through intertextuality." Kamens, *Utamakura*, 4.

59. Matsuo Bashō, *Bashō kushū*, 237.

60. Kamens, *Utamakura*, 4.

61. Translation of the *ci* title is by Egan. My translation is based on an alternate version of the *ci* in a recent collection of Su Shi's works. *SSQJJZ*, 9: 391–402.

62. The song lyric unfurls a sequence of images inspired by Su Shi's visit to Red Cliff, which self-reflexively figures the landscape as a painting of history. Buson never visited Red Cliff, but he read and saw representations of it, and his *hokku* condenses those mediations of history into residual images of loss and absence. This process speaks to George Kubler's ideas on how a historian produces historical knowledge. He argues that although an event is made up of a finite number of signals, no individual

has the capacity to interpret all the signals in all their meaning. Therefore, he argues that the historian must condense "the multiplicity and redundancy" of the signals that constitute an event so that his reader can understand the event without experiencing the entirety of the historical moment and "all its instantaneous confusion": "Though finite, the total number of historical signals greatly exceeds the capacity of any individual or group to interpret all the signals in all their meaning. A principal aim of the historian therefore is to condense the multiplicity and the redundancy of his signals by using various schemes of classification that will spare us the tedium of reliving the sequence in all its instantaneous confusion." Kubler, *The Shape of Time*, 20. Like the two rhapsodies and the song lyric, the *hokku* arranges images in remembrance of Red Cliff, infusing the scene with lyric feeling.

63. See note 44.
64. Casey, *Representing Place*, 17.
65. Ibid., 19. Elsewhere, Casey has expressed similar thoughts on the difference between memory and the imagination, that a memory is fallible because it can be discredited, whereas the imagination is true to itself: "Imagining proper is an act of differing significantly from the kind of imagining that may be involved in coming to know or understand something. The reason for this is that in imagining proper we project or entertain possibilities for *their own sake*. More exactly, we posit objects as possibilities *simpliciter*, not as possibilities that might be confirmed or discredited by experience." Casey, "Imagination: Imagining and the Image," 477.
66. The version in *Buson kushū* does not feature the *re れ* in the poem text. *YBS*, 135.
67. Narushima Yukio discusses the "Chinese rhythm" (*kanbunchō*) of the poem and its connection with Su Shi, *nanga*, and *haikai* history. Narushima, *Buson to kanshi*, 225–228.
68. Xie, "From Form to Spirit."
69. In a recent anthology of Buson's prose works, editor Fujita Shin'ichi groups the quatrain and *hokku* together under a title of his own creation: "Lyric on Spring Endings" (Shunbo no kotoba). *Buson bunshū*, 202–203.
70. Buson composed several poems that have posthumously been categorized under the ad hoc genres *haishi*, *washi*, or *haitaishi*—all of which refer to poems that are in between *haikai* and *kanshi*. Eri Yasuhara has observed that *haishi* draws from *kayō* (songs) and *kana-shi* (Chinese poems in Japanese vernacular), both of which grew in popularity during the seventeenth century. Yasuhara, "Buson and *Haishi*," 289–356.

71. *BZ*, 4: 36–37. Ogata and Morita entitle the poem collectively as "Prelude to 'Copper Pheasant'" ("Yamadori no" maegaki). The "copper pheasant" refers to the *hokku*.

72. Fujita takes a literal reading of the poem, but the *kanshi* may also be read as a metaphor for Buson's belatedness, or more broadly as the belatedness of the poetic tradition: *kōjin* can mean "the poet of the present" (lit. the person who has come later) and *zenjin* can mean "the poet of the past" (lit. the person who has come before). By stating that the former is 100 miles away from the latter—a distance that the poem maintains thematically—the poem places the speaker in perpetual and belated opposition to his forebears.

73. "Lyric on Spring Endings" evokes the spring *kigo* "slow-setting sun" or "long day(s)." Buson features that *kigo* in a 1775 *hokku* he composed on the theme of "recollecting the past" (*kaikyū*):

> Long days
> Pile up in the distance
> Of long ago.
> 遅き日のつもりて遠きむかし哉

BZ, 1: 278.

74. *Shūi wakashū*, 226. Ian Hideo Levy has argued that Japanese lyricism started with Hitomaro. Levy, *Hitomaro*.

75. For a colorful illustration of the *yamadori* and other birds in the pheasant family see the entry for *kiji* in *Nihon daihyakka zensho*, 6: 456.

76. For more on early *haishi* experiments, see Yasuhara, "Buson and *Haishi*," 159–197.

77. Ueda has observed that the poem's plain language and free-style structure resembles nineteenth-century Western poetry.

78. Shinga and Buson were apparently quite close. Shinga's son was friends with Buson, and Shinga treated Buson like a second son. Ueda, *The Path of the Flowering Thorn*, 19–20. As H. Mack Horton has observed, communal poetic composition like *haikai* fostered strong relationships between master and disciple, and "death represented a particular crisis to identity and continuity." Horton, *The Rhetoric of Death*, 27.

79. The date of composition is a matter of debate. The editors of *BZ*, Ogata and Morita, as well as Muramatsu Tomotsugu, speculate that Buson composed the poem in 1777, after the publication of "Denga no uta" and "Shunpū batei kyoku." For a summary of the debate, see Yasuhara, "Buson and *Haishi*," 123–125. In 1793, Shinga's son Momohiko at age

eighty-one published *Isonohana*, a collection of poems by his father and others to commemorate the fiftieth anniversary of his father's death. Ueda suggests that the poem was written before 1777. Buson left his signature "the monk Buson," which Ueda claims Buson stopped using after 1757. Ueda argues that the tone of the poem is youthful, and not like the *haishi* Buson was writing in 1777: "It's boldly unconventional form, impassioned tone, and waka-like language all set it apart from the other longer poems Buson composed in or around 1777." Ueda, *The Path of the Flowering Thorn*, 21.

80. This refers to Amida Buddha, the central figure of Pure Land Buddhism. I omit "Amida" for the sake of rhythm and simplicity in the English translation.

81. *BZ*, 4: 26–28.

82. For Muramatsu Tomotsugu's discussion of the poem's structure and complexity of voice, see *Buson shū*, 50–69.

83. Culler, *Theory of the Lyric*, 227.

84. In classical Chinese poetry, *jun* 君 is synonymous with *gong* 公, and evokes the archetype of the abandoned woman in the Yuefu (Music Bureau) tradition. In Japanese poetry as early as *Man'yōshū*, the pronoun *kimi* referred to one's master, and in other early Japanese texts, it is used as an honorary term of address for lords and sovereigns. In the preface to *Collection of Poems Old and New* (905; Kokin wakashū), the pronoun appears in a *waka* in which a woman addresses her absent lover and compares him to the morning frost:

> You and the morning:
> Like the morning frost
> That comes and goes,
> By the time I long for you,
> You have melted away.
> 君に今朝朝の霜のおきて去なば恋しきごとにきえやわたらむ

Kokin wakashū, 7. By the medieval period, *kimi* could refer to a courtesan (*yūjo*), and this usage continued through Edo. By the Edo period, the use of *kimi* became more fluid: it was used among men in the *bushi* (warrior) class to refer to others of equal social standing. In the case of Buson's "Mourning for Hokuju Rōsen," biography and the poetic tradition help delimit the meaning of *kimi* in the way that I have argued; however, these other possibilities may be at play as well, enriching and further blurring the boundaries of gender and voice.

85. Sung, *Decoded Messages*, 81–90.
86. There is much debate surrounding the term *hege* (originally *henge* but with an elided syllabic nasal). Eri Yasuhara, Makoto Ueda, and Cheryl Crowley read it as an adjective modifying *keburi* (smoke): "Mysterious smoke," "Ghostly smoke," and "Eerie smoke," respectively. For a discussion of the debate, see Yasuhara, "Buson and *Haishi*," 113–116. Buson composed a *hokku* using the word *henge*:

> Bestowed a house
> Where a Protean resides
> During winter slumber.
> 変化住屋敷もらひて冬籠

BZ, 1: 79. Considering the amount of supernatural literature published in Buson's lifetime, especially by contemporary Ueda Akinari, it makes sense to treat *hege* (*henge*) as a noun referring to creatures that have the ability to change shape at will. In English, the noun "Protean" (from Proteus in Greek mythology) is the only neutral word that captures the meaning of a being that transforms.

87. *Kokin wakashū*, 314. Editors Kojima Noriyuki and Arai Eizō note that the *hororo* is associated with *horohoro*, the onomatopoeia for falling tears. This resonates with the verb *naku*, which means "to cry" in both senses of the word: to make a loud call, and to shed tears. Buson's use of *naku* in the elegy also plays with the double-entendre, but I have avoided using the verb "to cry" in my translation to preserve the detachment from sentimentality and the concomitant evocation of mournful tears. A survey of his paintings and poetry will show that Buson's ethics toward nature betray a nuanced attitude toward animals: on the one hand, as living beings with their own agency (like a cock pheasant that crows for his mate), and on the other, as poetic figures to represent the subjectivity of the artist.

88. Ebersole, *Ritual Poetry*.
89. Culler, *Theory of the Lyric*, 162.
90. Ibid., 138.
91. Lukács, *Soul and Form*, 124.
92. "If fulfillment is attainable, it has to be attained—it can never be there as something natural and stable. In painting there cannot be dissonance—it would destroy the form of painting, whose realm lies beyond all categories of the temporal process; in painting, dissonance has to be resolved, as it were, *ante rem*, it has to form an indissoluble unity with its resolution." Lukács, *Soul and Form*, 123.
93. Ibid., 111.

REFERENCES

Backus, Robert L. "What Goes Into a Haiku." *Literature East and West* 15, (1972): 735–764.
Casey, Edward. "Imagination: Imagining and the Image." *Philosophy and Phenomenological Research* 31, no. 4 (June 1971): 475–490.
———. *Representing Place: Landscape Painting and Maps.* Minneapolis: Minnesota University Press, 2002.
Crowley, Cheryl. *Haikai Poet Yosa Buson and the Bashō Revival.* Boston: Brill, 2007.
Culler, Jonathan. *Theory of the Lyric.* Cambridge, MA: Harvard University Press, 2015.
Ebersole, Gary. *Ritual Poetry and The Politics of Death in Early Japan.* Princeton, NJ: Princeton University Press, 1989.
Egan, Ronald. *Word, Image, and Deed in the Life of Su Shi.* Cambridge, MA: Harvard University Asia Center, 1994.
Flueckiger, Peter. *Imagining Harmony: Poetry, Empathy, and Community in Mid-Tokugawa Confucianism and Nativism.* Stanford, CA: Stanford University Press, 2011.
Grossman, Allen. *The Sighted Singer.* Baltimore, MD: John Hopkins University Press, 1992.
Horton, H. Mack. *The Rhetoric of Death and Discipleship in Premodern Japan: Sōchō's Death of Sōgi and Kikaku's Death of Master Bashō.* Berkeley: Institute of East Asian Studies, 2019.
Ikezawa Ichirō. *Edo bunjinron: Ōta Nanpo o chūshin ni.* Tokyo: Kyūko shoin, 2000.
Jonsson, Herbert. *Haikai Poetics: The Theory and Aesthetics of Linked Poetry in the Age of Buson.* Saarbrücken: VDM Verlag Dr. Müller, 2008.
Jullien, François. *In Praise of Blandness: Proceeding from Chinese Thought and Aesthetics.* Translated by Paula M. Varsano. New York: Zone Books, 2004.
———. *The Great Image Has No Form, or On the Nonobject through Painting.* Translated by Jane Marie Todd. Chicago: The University of Chicago Press, 2009.
Kamens, Edward. *Utamakura, Allusion, and Intertextuality in Traditional Japanese Poetry.* New Haven, CT: Yale University Press, 1997.
Kokin wakashū. Edited by Kojima Noriyuki and Arai Eizō. Vol. 5, *Shin Nihon koten bungaku taikei.* 102 vols. Tokyo: Iwanami Shoten, 2017.
Kubler, George. *The Shape of Time: Remarks on the History of Things.* New Haven: Yale University Press, 1962.
Levy, Ian Hideo. *Hitomaro and the Birth of Japanese Lyricism.* Princeton, NJ: Princeton University Press, 1984.
Lukács, György. *Soul and Form.* Translated by Anna Bostock. New York: Columbia University Press, 2010.

Marcon, Federico. *The Knowledge of Nature and the Nature of Knowledge in Early Modern Japan.* Chicago: The University of Chicago Press, 2015.

Matsuo Bashō. *Bashō kushū.* Edited by Ōtani Tokuzō, et al. Vol. 45, *Nihon koten bungaku taikei.* 102 vols. Tokyo: Iwanami Shoten, 1962.

———. *Bashō bunshū.* Edited by Sugiura Shōichirō, et al. Vol. 46, *Nihon koten bungaku taikei.* 102 vols. Tokyo: Iwanami Shoten, 1959.

Mei Yaochen, *Wanling ji.* Vol. 46. *Siku Quanshu* (q.v.).

Mitchell, W.J.T. *Picture Theory.* Chicago: The University of Chicago Press, 1994.

Montague, James J. "Proteans of the Wild." *Zanesville Signal,* November 10, 1927.

Narushima Yukio. *Buson to kanshi.* Tokyo: Kashinsha, 2001.

Nihon daihyakka zensho. 27 vols. Tokyo: Shōgakukan, 1985.

Rilke, Rainer Maria. *Letters on Cézanne.* Translated by Joel Agee. New York: North Point Press, 2002.

Rosenfield, John M. *Mynah Birds and Flying Rocks: Word and Image in the Art of Yosa Buson.* Lawrence, KS: Spencer Museum of Art, The University of Kansas, 2003.

Shin Kokin wakashū. Edited by Tanaka Yutaka and Akase Shingo. Vol. 11, *Shin Nihon koten bungaku taikei.* 106 vols. Tokyo: Iwanami Shoten, 2019.

Shūi wakashū. Edited by Komachiya Teruhiko. Vol. 7, *Shin Nihon koten bungaku taikei.* 106 vols. Tokyo: Iwanami Shoten, 1990.

Stevens, Wallace. *Opus Posthumous,* edited by Milton J. Bates. New York: Vintage Books, 1990.

Su Shi. *Su Shi quan ji jiao zhu.* Edited by Zhang Zhilie, Ma Defu, and Zhou Yukai. 20 vols. Shijiazhuang Shi: Hebei ren min chu ban she, 2010.

Sung, Hou-mei. *Decoded Messages: The Symbolic Language of Chinese Animal Painting.* New Haven: Yale University Press, 2009.

Takeuchi, Melinda. *Taiga's True Views: The Language of Landscape Painting in Eighteenth-Century Japan.* Stanford, CA: Stanford University Press, 1992.

Ueda, Makoto. *The Path of the Flowering Thorn: The Life and Poetry of Yosa Buson.* Stanford, CA: Stanford University Press, 1998.

Xie, Kai. "From Form to Spirit: Infusing Chinese Elements in *Haikai*." *Japanese Language and Literature* 56 (April 2022): 118–156.

Yamashita Kazumi. *Shiro no shijin: Buson shinron.* Tokyo: Furansudō, 2009.

———. *Yamashita Kazumi chosakushū.* 10 vols. Tokyo: Ōfū, 2013.

Yasuhara, Eri Fujita. "Buson and *Haishi*: A Study of Free-Form *Haishi* Poetry in Eighteenth Century Japan." PhD diss., University of California, Los Angeles, 1982.

Yokota, Toshiko. "Buson as Bunjin: The Literary Field of Eighteenth-Century Japan." PhD diss., University of California, Los Angeles, 2000.

Yosa Buson. *Buson bunshū.* Edited by Fujita Shin'ichi. Tokyo: Iwanami Shoten, 2016.

————. *Buson shū*. Edited by Muramatsu Tomotsugu. Vol. 17, *Kanshō Nihon no koten*. 18 vols. Tokyo: Shōgaku tosho, 1981.

————. *Buson-shū Issa-shū*. Edited by Teruoka Yasuo and Kawashima Tsuyu. Vol. 58, *Nihon koten bungaku taikei*. 102 vols. Tokyo: Iwanami Shoten, 1959.

————. *Buson zenkushū*. Edited by Fujita Shin'ichi and Kiyoto Noriko. Tokyo: Ōfū, 2000.

————. *Buson zenshū*. Edited by Ogata Tsutomu, et al. 9 vols. Tokyo: Kodansha, 1992.

————. *Yosa Buson shū*. Edited by Shimizu Takayuki. Vol. 79, *Shinchō nihon koten shūsei*. 82 vols. Tokyo: Shinchōsha, 1979.

Zolbrod, Leon. "Death of a Poet-Painter: Yosa Buson's Last Year, 1783–84." In *Studies on Japanese Culture*, edited by Japan P.E.N. Club. Tokyo: Japan P.E.N. Club, 1973.

CHAPTER 3

Sense and Sensibility in the Poetry of Ema Saikō

Sitting by the window in spring,
Too forlorn to lean on the railing.
—Li Qingzhao, "Spring in the House of Jade"

The Outer—from the Inner
Derives its magnitude—
—Emily Dickinson

I grind the fragrant ink myself.
—Ema Saikō, "Bamboo"

This chapter focuses on how Ema Saikō (1787–1861) made her claim to literati (*bunjin*) culture in the Late Edo period (1750s–1867) by composing Chinese poems (*kanshi*) that expressed a sensuality beyond the reach of poetic convention or topos. I argue that Saikō refigured the tropes of sensual experience as a lyricism that revealed the irony of being a woman *bunjin*.

Saikō was born into an affluent samurai-class (*bushi*) family; her father, Ema Ransai (1747–1838), was a scholar of Dutch learning (*rangaku*) and a physician. At a young age, Saikō acquired skill in Chinese poetry, painting, and calligraphy. She became one of the most highly acclaimed women poet-painters in Japanese literature, known for her Chinese-style

M. Mewhinney, *Form and Feeling in Japanese Literati Culture*, https://doi.org/10.1007/978-3-031-11922-4_3

landscapes (*bunjinga*) and compositions of more than 300 *kanshi*.[1] Saikō
is unique, in part, in the *bunjin* tradition because she was a woman: in the
Japanese tradition, Chinese arts and literature—and by extension literati
culture—were considered the intellectual pursuits of men. During the
Heian period (794–1185), the woman author of *The Tale of Genji*,
Murasaki Shikibu, was well versed in Chinese literature and philosophy,
but social convention prevented her from displaying her knowledge out-
right. By Late Edo, however, the surge of independent artists, the wide
dissemination and translation of books, and the democratization of reading had created the social infrastructure that made it possible for women
like Saikō to pursue the path of a *bunjin*.

Saikō's lyric voice is idiosyncratic. Being a woman *bunjin* involved performing as a woman in *kanshi*, a genre in which poetic personas and the
norms for feminine expression were informed by Confucian ideals. Saikō
followed these conventions of women's poetry by writing in the generic
persona of a *keishū*, a "talented woman of the inner chamber." Her critics,
including her mentor, Confucian scholar and *bunjin* Rai San'yō
(1780–1832), judged her *kanshi* by how well she performed this persona.
But in order to represent the senses and feelings of one individual woman
in this poetic genre, Saikō attempted to transcend the boundaries of such
conventions: she infused the *keishū* persona with an empiricism drawn
from the late imperial Chinese ideal of "true poetry" (*shinshi*)—poetry
that represented individual perceptions and feelings. She also drew from a
pictorial realism derived from the ideal of the "true view" (*shinkei*) in late
eighteenth-century Dutch-style painting (*ranga*). Over the following
pages, I show how Saikō represented her existential self by asserting her
sense and sensibility as a woman *bunjin* writing through the very literary
artifice that entrapped the representation of self in poetic convention.

A ROOM OF ONE'S OWN

In the eighteenth century, visual culture from the Ming dynasty
(1368–1644) gave rise to *materia medica*, the study of the medicinal
properties of natural substances, and specifically plants. By the late eighteenth century in Japan, this empirical science had come to dovetail with
a new discipline called "Dutch learning" (*rangaku*), which introduced
new epistemological models from European art, thought, and science
regarding the representation of how objects truly appeared. As the

daughter of a *rangaku* scholar and physician, Saikō was exposed to this European empiricism and realism from an early age.[2] By the early nineteenth century, Japanese scholars were producing their own compendiums on plants and animals, paralleling the "evidential research" (Ch. *kaozhengxue*) of Chinese scholars in the Qing dynasty (1644–1912) as well as the scientific and philosophical treatises on natural history in early modern Europe. Saikō thus witnessed firsthand the emergence of this new scientific pursuit to "represent the real," or *shashin*, which classified and rendered natural objects with precision and fidelity to real life.[3]

In the context of this rise of empiricism and realist representation, Saikō aspired to represent a "true" or "real" self within the poetic artifice afforded by *kanshi*. During the Edo period, the poetic artifices afforded by *haikai* and *kanshi* allowed poets to communicate concerns of the everyday, including their personal reflections on the aesthetic forms of the literati tradition.[4] In literati culture, this realism was informed by a late imperial Chinese poetics called "natural sensibility" (Ch. *xingling*; J. *seirei*), which promoted spontaneous expression—drawing inspiration from one's inner nature to communicate heart, mind, and soul, and writing about the quotidian as a means to presenting oneself as true and sincere. Mari Nagase has shown that Saikō's *kanshi* reveals the contradictions of this poetics, which, on the one hand, valued truthful self-representation and, on the other, the performance of conventional feminine ideals.[5] In my view, Saikō used these contradictions to her artistic advantage, demonstrating that composing *kanshi* as a woman created a situation made to order for irony. The following three poems each describe a lyric subject who is aware of the aesthetic forms and poetic conventions of the literati tradition and who attempts to make them her own by emphasizing modern ideas of representation based on personal and subjective perception and feeling.

Saikō wrote a pentasyllabic ancient-style poem (*gogon koshi*) entitled "Calligraphy" (Sho), one of the aesthetic forms that comprises the "three excellences" (*sanzetsu*) in literati practice. The poem describes calligraphy as an act of artistic creation that calls upon the words of literati forebears and represents a poet's true nature in the present against the past:

Calligraphy

Where is a good place to write with leisure?
Beneath the window, I clear dust off the ink stone.

A pair of wrists, within dwells a daemon;
All I sense is depletion of mind and spirit.
5   Behold the inscriptions by Cai, Official of Documents,
At Goose Gate of Luoyang, left for hundreds of years.
Deep in the heart we must store the words of the past;
Wielding the brush, we need only make them new.
Writing has always been painting of the heart,
10   Retaining our true nature for thousands of years.
Impossible to imitate writings from the Jin and the Tang,
I find joy just in encountering the words of the ancients.

sho	書
enkan nan no tekisuru tokoro zo	燕間何所適
sōtei ni kenjin o harau	窓底掃研塵
sōwan no naka ni ki ari	雙腕中有鬼
tada ni oboyu seishin o tsuiyasu koto o	徒覺費精神
ishibumi o miru saishōsho	觀碣蔡尚書
kōto ni todomaru koto jūjun	鴻都留十旬
kyōoku suberaku inishie o takuwau beshi	胸臆須貯古
rakuhitsu tada arata naru o yōsu	落筆但要新
yurai kokoro no ga	由來心之畫
senzai tenshin sonsu	千載存天眞
manabigatashi shintō no chō	難學晉唐帖
tada yorokobu kojin ni taisuru o	唯喜對古人 [6]

The opening lines suggest the setting where a *keishū* explores her true nature: the *kei*, or "the inner chamber," a poetic topos used in Chinese poetry to depict the archetype of the "abandoned woman"—a lonely woman who waits (in vain) for her lover to return. The speaker asks "Where is a good place to write with leisure?" and replies "Beneath the window" (*sōtei*), a metonym for the inner chamber represented in *kanshi* as well as for the domestic sphere in Late Edo painting. Imanishi Riko has observed that the window was a place of creative inspiration for Qing dynasty and Edo period literati; it was also a material frame for landscapes and other natural objects in their paintings.[7] Odano Naotake (1749–1780) and other European-style painters of the Akita Ranga school depicted people and objects in the domestic sphere, framing them in circular windows.[8]

In Chinese poetry, the inner chamber (Ch. *gui*) was an idealized space for women; it signified a woman subject.[9] Xiaorong Li has argued that the inner chamber was a real and imaginary place in which late imperial Chinese women constructed new subjectivities. The possibilities of poetic expression and experience in the *gui* changed over time.[10] The *gui* was real for some women, and imaginary for others, but it was a space that traditionally separated women from men.[11] By the Qing dynasty, poets no longer adhered to the "abandoned woman" trope, and breathed new life into this "boudoir" genre. Female subjects were no longer passive women, but rather women of talent who appropriated the *gui* as their own domestic space to talk about their feelings and daily activities.

In the Japanese tradition, the *kei* was purely imaginary.[12] It was thus a figure for the constraints of the boudoir genre that Saikō followed as a woman *kanshi* poet, as well as for the formal containment that was required to represent personal and intimate reflections about the self through a poetic persona. She used this imaginary space to mediate the aesthetic and scientific discourses of her time, and to undertake empirical investigations of the senses, including the parts of the human body that channel creativity.

After positing the image of the window as the perfect place to begin composing calligraphy, the speaker (in line 3) describes the corporeal hinge that mediates the speaker's creative impulse: "A pair of wrists, within dwells a daemon." By figuring the wrist as the conveyor of creativity, Saikō evokes the poetics of "natural sensibility" promoted by Ming dynasty poet Yuan Hongdao (1568–1610): "Whatever the mind-heart [*xin*] wants to express, the wrist [*wan*] can convey it."[13]

With a flick of the wrist, literary inspiration can take the form of a "daemon" (*ki*), an idea that evokes the theory of the imagination in the chapter "Spirit thought" (Shen Si) of Liu Xie's treatise *The Literary Mind Carves Dragons* (Wenxin diaolong) from the Six Dynasties (220–589 CE), one of the bedrocks of the Chinese tradition.[14] Once a writer has attained quietude, a spirit within him or her then wanders throughout tradition, seeking inspiration from writers of the past. This spirit, which is like a daemon, or creative force, resides within the breast of the writer:

When the basic principle of thought is at its keenest, the spirit wanders together with things. The spirit resides within the breast, and our aims and our vital forces control the gate to let it out. The things of the world come in through the ears and eyes, and language has charge of the hinge. When

that hinge permits passage, nothing can hide its face; but when the bolt to
that gate is closed, the spirit is concealed within.
故思理為妙, 神與物游. 神居胸臆, 而志氣統其關鍵. 物沿耳目, 而辭令管其
樞機. 樞機方通, 則物無隱貌; 關鍵將塞, 則神有遁心.[15]

"Spirit thought" is a way of conceptualizing the poetic imagination in
medieval China.[16] Liu Xie describes the pivotal role of language as the
figurative hinge on the door of literary creation. Once the writer focuses
his "aims" (*zhi*) and "vital forces" (*qi*) in language, he controls that passage to creative work. In his treatise, Liu Xie employed an array of biological metaphors that describe literary creation as vitally dependent upon
mental concentration and breath regulation. In this system of thought,
literature is akin to the human body, and literary forms mimic the organic
processes of a living body, such as cycles of breath and heartbeats. Liu Xie
states that the spirit resides within "the breast" (*xiongyi*)—the same word
translated as "deep in the heart" (*kyōoku*) in line 7 of "Calligraphy," where
the writer stores words of the past. The spirit, or daemon, in Saikō's poem,
however, resides within a "pair of wrists" (*sōwan*): the hinges that connect
the writer's hands to her body.

The relationship between daemon and wrist speaks to contemporaneous writings about "divine inspiration" or poetic afflatus in European
Romanticism. In this body of literature, theories of a literary genius were
religious and artistic: "The infusion of the heavenly spirit into the mind or
soul" and "the awareness of an idea or image that stimulated
creativity."[17]

While the initial process of literary creation references Chinese literary
theories as old as the Six Dynasties, Saikō's line 4 representation of the
effects of creation is new and psychological: "All I sense is the depletion of
mind and spirit." The "depletion" (*tsuiyasu*) of "mind and spirit" (*seishin*)
evokes how nineteenth-century French artists who were obsessed by art
and scientific curiosity fell victim to "the ravages of thought."[18] Anka
Mulhstein describes the literary imagination in nineteenth-century French
literature as a malefic force that comes from within. In Saikō's poem the
Chinese graph that represents "daemon" (*ki*) can also mean "demon" or
"demonic spirit," alluding to the demonic possession in nineteenth-
century European literature.[19]

The process of creation in calligraphy that consumes the poet is making
old words new again. Lines 5 and 6 reference the forgotten writings of
Eastern Han dynasty scholar and calligrapher Cai Yong (132–192 CE),

who is remembered for having the Five Classics engraved in stone to serve as models of writing for later generations. The Five Classics include the *Book of Documents* (Shangshū; J. Shōsho). This allusion to Cai illustrates the purpose of calligraphy: to model oneself on the writings of literary forebears, but under the condition that the writer "need only make them new" (*tada arata naru o yōsu*). The key to newness is in how one wields the brush, an echo of the earlier image of the wrists that mediate literary inspiration or demonic possession.

The need to be new speaks to theories of art in early nineteenth-century literati culture. Fellow *bunjin* and painter Uragami Shunkin (1779–1846), one of Saikō's mentors, expressed similar views about newness in his poetic treatise *Poems on Painting* (1842; Rongashi):

> Transformation follows the trend,
> Propensity likewise accords with nature.

henka kiun ni shitagai	變化隨氣運
ikioi mo mata shizen ni yoru	勢亦因自然 [20]

The lines above come from a poem in his second volume of *Poems on Painting*, which presents a history of literati painting, stating that it emerged in the Song dynasty, transforming according to "trends over time" (*kiun*). This "propensity" (*ikioi*) for painting to transform accords with "nature" (*shizen*), which Taketani Chōjirō glosses as "Mother Nature" (*daishizen*) in modern Japanese. In traditional Chinese thought, the laws of nature accord with the Dao, or the Way. By the nineteenth century, the Daoist idea of nature as the spiritual source of all creation had merged with the scientific idea of nature as a disenchanted object that can be empirically observed and understood. The Romantic idea of nature as a tutelary presence is also at play here, since nature was depicted as such in European landscape paintings.[21] With all these meanings coincident, the two lines suggest that form and content are historically contingent.[22]

The ending of Saikō's poem emphasizes the historical contingency of poetry, arguing that calligraphy is "painting of the heart" (*kokoro no ga*) that has represented the "true nature" (*tenshin*) of poets for 1000 years. The final couplet qualifies this argument by claiming that poets of the Jin (265–420 CE) and the Tang (618–907 CE) dynasties are "impossible to imitate" (*manabi gatashi*). The final line—"I find joy just in encountering the words of the ancients"—highlights the oppositional relationship between past and present: the verb *taisuru* (to encounter; to oppose; to face) suggests that calligraphy and poetry are not about imitation but creation, and that tradition is a source from which a poet draws and with which she also contends.

Saikō's choice to distance creativity from works of the Jin and the Tang critiques Early Edo Confucian scholar Ogyū Sorai's (1666–1728) literary movement to return to the classics, by which he meant the poetry of the High Tang. Sorai's neoclassicism was challenged by the poetics of "natural sensibility" embraced by Late Edo *bunjin*, including Yamamoto Hokuzan (1752–1812). Hokuzan's treatise *Thoughts on Composing Poetry* (1783; Sakushi shikō) initiated a major shift in *kanshi* practice: to move away from the elegant and grandiose style of High Tang poetry, and toward a poetics that represented present, everyday feelings.[23]

A response to the empiricism of Saikō's era, "Calligraphy" suggests that a writer ought to represent her "true nature" through a creative and oppositional relationship with her *bunjin* forebears. The speaker's assertion of her present moment vis-à-vis the past reveals her self-awareness as a nineteenth-century *bunjin* and her desire to make a traditional form her own.

Saikō also composed a pentasyllabic ancient-style poem entitled "Painting" (Ga), a second aesthetic form that comprises the "three excellences" in the literati tradition. The poem examines an early notion of realism in Chinese painting, claiming that representation mediated by the poetic imagination has more aesthetic value than verisimilitude. The poem transforms this idea via early nineteenth-century empiricism, arguing that when a viewer discerns the expression of feeling in a painting, sense experience adjudicates between the representation and the real:

Painting

'Saying that to paint is to resemble
Is like seeing through the eyes of children.'
Who dared to utter these words,
But the venerable recluse of East Slope?
5   I take them as my method,
Whenever ink touches paper.
One scroll instantly turns into the Xiaoxiang,
Myriad forms spring forth from the brush tip.
If a painting can picture the center of the heart,
10   What need to worry about praise or criticism?
A representation of hemp or a representation of reeds,
Identification is all in the eye of the beholder.

ga	畫
ga o nashite keiji o ronzu	爲畫論形似
sono ken wa dōji ni tonarisu	其見隣童子
kono go tareka yoku haku	此語誰能吐
tōha rōkyoshi nari	東坂老居士
yo torite motte hō to nasu	余取以爲法
mokkun aruiwa kami ni otoseba	墨君或落紙
shakufuku sunawachi shōshō	尺幅即瀟湘
hyakutai gōtan ni okori	百態毫端起
moshi yoku kyōchū o utsuseba	若能寫胸中
nanzo kanarazushimo yoki o osorenya	何必畏譽毀
asa to nashi mata ashi to nasu	爲麻亦爲芦
shimei subete kare ni makasu	指名総任彼 [24]

Song dynasty literatus Su Shi (1037–1101; pen name Dongpo, or "East Slope") was a model for Japanese literati. The poem opens with a quotation from the first of Su Shi's two-poem set "Written on paintings of flowering branches by Secretary Wang of Yan-ling."[25] The rest of Saikō's poem engages with the idea behind the quotation, namely that "resemblance" (*keiji*) is a simplistic way of viewing the purpose of painting. Su Shi argues that representation is about the poetic imagination: since a child is too young to have mastered the aesthetics and theories of representation in literati painting, when they see a painting of hemp, they see hemp itself, without considering the effort the painter has taken to represent it.[26]

When the speaker asks "Who dared to utter these words?" the tone of her question suggests that Su Shi's claim about painting may not align with the trend of pictorial realism in Late Edo. She nevertheless embraces his words, taking them as her method (*hō to nasu*) whenever ink falls upon the canvas. The "I" (*yo*) in the poem is explicit and highlights the fact that *she*—the female speaker—is the one appropriating Su Shi and using his ideas for her disposal. This self-assertion resonates with Patricia Fister and Kado Reiko's claims that Saikō was a poet who "expressed herself in the way she saw fit."[27] Her speaker displays her self-assertion by appropriating old ideas, repurposing them anew.

Saikō's speaker puts Su Shi's idea to work by applying black ink onto "one scroll," and suddenly Xiaoxiang emerges. This image refers to *Eight Views of Xiaoxiang* (Ch. Xiaoxiang bajing; J. Shōshō hakkei)—the subject

of many paintings and poems in the Song dynasty that represent or evoke
the natural bodies of water of the Xiaoxiang region in Hunan Province,
China. The word "one scroll" (*shakufuku*) is a metonym for the "one-
scroll window" (Ch. *chifu chuang*) in late imperial Chinese literatus Li
Yu's (1611–1680) writings on windows and painting. The window functions as a frame for a painting as if it were a scroll—what Li Yu calls a
"natural painting."[28] The word "one scroll" is also a metonym for the
window in the speaker's imaginary inner chamber that unfurls, displaying
an imagined Chinese landscape.

Line 8 of Saikō's poem connects this idea of the metonymic window to
the painter's brush, arguing that a painting can stand in and stand for the
Xiaoxiang. The adverb *sunawachi* describes the immediacy and spontaneity with which the landscape forms on the scroll. As I discussed in the
previous chapter, Edward Casey has argued that representation in Song
dynasty painting "stands in as" and "stands in for" the object.[29] The evocation here of Xiaoxiang as a spontaneous landscape speaks to this idea, as
Song painting offered a truth based on the poet's representation of a scene
through the imagination. Recalling the idea that the imagination is mediated by the wrist in the earlier poem "Calligraphy," the brush in "Painting"
now becomes the hinge that opens the gate for the daemon to manifest
once ink touches paper, allowing myriad forms to emerge.

The poem concludes by suggesting that the aesthetic value of a painting is not its fidelity to the painted object itself but the painting's fidelity
to the representation of the object as mediated by the sense and feeling of
the artist: "If a painting can picture the center of the heart, / What need
to worry about praise or criticism?" Late Edo artists were experimenting
with a new scientific gaze, creating representations that aspired to be "true
to life." By "picturing the center of the heart" the speaker suggests that
this scientific gaze leads to an understanding of the "outer"—the external
surface of things—through a close examination of the "inner"—the workings of sense and feeling. Timon Screech has described the scientific gaze
as an "anatomizing stare": "Invisible workings were sought out for inspec-
tion, whether of human beings, animals, particles, or larger abstract systems. It was proposed as axiomatic that a full reevaluation of the significance
of internal workings was necessary for the new comprehension of external
empirical wholes."[30]

Saikō ends the poem with the notion that the comprehension of an
external empirical whole falls upon the viewer. The speaker argues that the
distinction between the representation and the real is subjective, that the

classification of the painted object as "hemp" or "reeds" is a judgment that is "entirely" (*subete*) up to "the viewer" (*kare*). Here the speaker opens a space for democratic interpretation, celebrating the visual perception and subjective discernment of the viewer, which adjudicates between the representation and the real.

While the poem "Painting" leaves the judgment of verisimilitude as a matter of subjective discernment, the poem's presentation of self within a poetic persona raises a question. In a heptasyllabic quatrain (*shichigon zekku*) entitled "Myself Singing," Saikō describes the problem of self-presentation in a genre that requires a woman *kanshi* poet to assume the poetic persona of a *keishū*. The poem investigates whether the presentation of a true self is occluded by poetic convention:

Myself Singing

Several scrolls of wisteria parchment cover the table in piles;
In picturing bamboo, feelings of the heart never burn to ash.
How can the public eye know me and my mind,
When they see a painter of the inner chamber?

mizukara utau	自咏
sentō ikufuku manshō ni uzutakashi	剡藤幾幅滿牀堆
take o utsushite jōkai nao imada kai narazu	寫竹情懷猶未灰
segan nanzo shiran ware no kokoro	世眼何知我儂意
mite keikō no gashi to nashikitaru	看爲閨閣畫師來 [31]

This quatrain critiques the epistemology of Late Edo empiricism: "seeing is knowing." The speaker criticizes the "public eye" (*segan*) for seeing her as "a painter of the inner chamber," questioning the correlation between true self-presentation and the artifice of the poetic persona. When she exclaims "How can the public eye know me and my mind?" the painter asks her audience to consider how their perception of a painting allows them access to the person and the creative mind behind the brush. And, in analogous terms for poetry, how can a female poet write about herself if the reader only sees the mask of genre and convention?[32]

The first two lines of the quatrain offer a provisional solution by imbuing the poetic topos of the *keishū* persona with irony. The "wisteria parchment" (*sentō*) evokes the conventionally ornate and sensual space of the inner chamber and its affordances for creativity, as described in "Calligraphy" and "Painting." The scrolls covering the table in piles suggest that, rather than conventionally wallowing in the sorrow of unfulfilled sexual desires, the painter has sublimated her feelings into lyrical paintings, including representations of bamboo. In the phrase "picturing bamboo" (*take o utsushite*), the verb *utsusu* (or *sha*) evokes the act of representation described by the word *shashin*, or "to represent the real." Here the object of representation is not the real, but "bamboo" (*take*), followed by the image of "feelings of the heart" (*jōkai*). By claiming that her inner feelings will "never burn to ash," the speaker suggests that the representation of bamboo mediates personal feelings, giving them a form in painting.[33]

Saikō's poem suggests that inner feelings are made true by the form that represents them, yet whether such representation allows the viewer to know the painter—to know "me and my mind" (*ware no kokoro*)—remains an open question. The conclusions of all three poems discussed thus far suggest that the discernment of truth and value falls upon the individual: to encounter the tradition and make her own claim to it; to adjudicate between representation and the real; and to discern the painter behind the painting, the poet behind the poem.

A CERTAIN SLANT OF LIGHT

Thus far, Saikō's poems have shown how the inner chamber afforded the poet a room of her own in which to transform the literati tradition by representing empirical perception and subjective experience. The question she raises in "Myself Singing" about whether it is possible to represent her existential self when the presentation of self is invariably entrapped in genre and poetic convention points to a crisis of representation in the age of realism. As the poem suggests, by drawing a connection between the picturing of bamboo and the feelings of the heart, the act of representation is subjective—an act of form-giving that mediates feeling.

Saikō composed two poems in which the speaker conducts her own investigations of sensory perception using objects from the literati repertoire. These poems gave her an opportunity to claim the sensual space of the inner chamber and to indulge in sensual experiences beyond the boudoir.

Saikō is most known by art historians for her ink-wash paintings of bamboo, one of the "Four Gentlemen" (*shikunshi*) in literati painting.[34] The strength and durability of bamboo, a natural object, made it a traditional symbol for Confucian ideals, including uprightness, mental strength, and perseverance. As a Confucian daughter, Saikō likely painted bamboo to represent her admiration for these ideals, but as "Myself Singing" suggests, bamboo is also a figure for personal feelings. In her poetry, Saikō figured bamboo in sensual ways as an object of desire and as a means of exploring the senses. Objects that appear in the poetic topos of the inner chamber include artificial ornaments (e.g., hairpins, glass slippers, trousseaux) and metaphors for unfulfilled sexual desire (e.g., gauze canopies, cold pillows). Saikō's poem "Bamboo," however, turns this tradition around, making bamboo the source of the sensual fulfillment:

Bamboo

When I awake there is no one around, the small cloister is pure;
I grind the fragrant ink myself, the sound is soft and faint.
Tall bamboo does not await the moon outside my chamber window;
Pale shades fall aslant around my hand, taking form.

take	竹
suiki hito naku shōin kiyoshi	睡起無人小院清
shitashiku bokuja o sureba hibiki keikei	親磨墨麝響輕輕
shūkō matazu keisō no tsuki	脩篁不待閨窗月
tan'ei shasha toshite te o megurite shōzu	淡影斜斜繞手生 [35]

The poem is a heptasyllabic quatrain (*shichigon zekku*) that blends two poetic conventions: the boudoir topos and the genre of "poems on things" (J. *eibutsushi*; Ch. *yongwushi*). By tradition, when a poem's title describes a natural object, the poem may be categorized in this genre. Ibi Takashi has observed that the rise in the popularity of "poems on things" coincided with the turn from seventeenth-century neoclassicism to the poetics of "natural sensibility" in the late eighteenth century, paralleling the rise of empiricism and realism.[36]

Line 1 places the speaker in the boudoir: she rises and looks out into the cloister where she sees no one, only sensing that the space is "pure" (*kiyoshi*). The feeling of pureness evokes the literati ideal of attaining a state that is tranquil and free of vulgar concerns. The poem begins with her waking in order to avoid associations with the dreamscape, a locus of boundless sensual experience. The speaker rises, the feeling of pureness is in the air, and she decides to paint, whereupon wakefulness in the inner chamber becomes as dreamy as sleep.

In the tradition of "poems on things," the Chinese poet represented affective responses to the object in view. As Saikō's poem unfolds, the speaker enters into a sensual fantasy about her hand's intimate relationship with the materials that make bamboo take form. Line 2 begins with *shita-shiku*, an adverb indicating an act performed intimately, suggesting that the speaker uses her own hand to grind the ink. Literati had servants to perform the labor of preparing ink, but here the speaker decides to grind the ink herself. This ink is not just any ordinary ink: *bokuja* refers to ink with a pungent scent derived from deer musk. As she grinds the ink, the sound is *keikei*, an onomatopoeia for a soft, pleasant sound that reifies the temporality of grinding, the fragrant ink caressing the stone, back and forth. This moment speaks to Susan Stewart's argument that movement and time are part of the experience of touch: "As touch moves and takes time, pattern becomes apparent, just as following sound, we trace a path for it: we hear and feel sound emerge, discerning its form."[37]

As the softness of sound fills the room, echoing the feeling of pureness in line 1, the poet begins to paint. Line 3 establishes that the speaker is in the inner chamber near the window, where she can see that there is no moonlight illuminating the cloister. By stating that "Tall bamboo does not await the moon" she suggests that bamboo (either not present or invisible in the dark) will take form by the work of some force other than the moonlight, which line 4 suggests is the hand of the artist.

The poem concludes with a complex visual and tactile image that echoes the temporality of the pleasant sound of grinding in line 2 while also introducing a new sense with its own temporal and spatial dimensions: "Pale shades fall aslant" (*tan'ei shasha toshite*). At first reading, it seems the pale shades are either shadows cast by the moonlight or pale rays of moonlight (*tan'ei*).[38] Since line 3 ends with the image of the moon (*tsuki*) and line 4 opens with *tan'ei*, it appears that moonlight is present. But the negation in line 3 asserts that it is not, and thus the reader is held in suspense about what the "pale shades" are referencing. The onomatopoeia *shasha* normally refers to sunlight or moonlight falling obliquely, and thus *shasha* becomes a visual echo of the sound *keikei*. By suggesting that the source of the shade is the ink that the speaker has just ground herself, "taking form" (*shōzu*) around the hand, *keikei* gains a corporeality as a shade—an ink wash of bamboo. As the sound transforms into a shade, the sound "fall[s] aslant," entering a new dimension in time and space.

Concluding the poem with the image of bamboo shades taking form around the hand suggests knowledge of form as mediated by the hand. Henri Focillon writes: "The hand knows that an object has physical bulk, that it is smooth or rough, ...The hand's action defines the cavity of space and the fullness of the objects that occupy it."[39] For the painter in the poem, the form of bamboo is aural, tactile, and visual: it begins as ink heard as a sound, then held in a suspension of thought as moonlight, then taking form on the canvas. The temporality of bamboo's sensual embodiments as performed at the end of the poem speaks to how Susan Stewart describes beholding:

> To experience the roughness or smoothness of an object, to examine its physical position or come to understand its relative temperature or moistness, we must move, turn, take time. Visual perception can immediately organize a field; tactile perception requires temporal comparison. We may say in fact that visual perception becomes a mode of touching when comparisons are made and the eye is 'placed upon' or 'falls upon' relations between phenomena.[40]

The reader's eye falls upon the bamboo as the pale shades fall upon the canvas. But the role of the hand as the mediator—the creator of these shades—is just as oblique; *megurite* is a verb that literally means "to enlace; to encircle; to surround." Other interpretations of this poem have assumed that the shades are coming through the hand, dispelling the uncanny idea that they are falling aslant on their own, like rays of moonlight.[41] This specific verb suggests, however, that the shades are falling aslant *around* the hand with the implication that they are brush strokes that result from the painter's hand moving here and there around the canvas. The meaning of forming an enclosure around the hand is key, since it echoes the theme of confinement in the inner chamber but also comments on the boundaries of form in painting.

This representation of perception and feeling in the inner chamber parallels contemporaneous developments in late imperial Chinese poetry, including the revival of the boudoir genre and of *ci* (song lyric) poetry.[42] Without moving from her bedroom window, the speaker has multiple sensory experiences of bamboo that move from the ear to the eye to the hand. Embracing the sensuality and sensuousness of the boudoir genre, Saikō's poem emphasizes touch as the sense of intense and real feeling. As Stewart writes, "of all the senses, touch is most linked to emotion and feeling."[43]

As a poem in the genre of "poems on things," "Bamboo" blends traditional modes of seeing with an early nineteenth-century scientific gaze. Timon Screech has argued that the dominant mode of viewing an object in Japanese art is "synaptic," meaning that an object's meaning is created by associations "drawing the empirically seen into a web of things previously learnt."[44] In "Bamboo," these associations are affective (pureness), material (cloister, ink, paper), and sensual (sound, touch), all of which resonate with the boudoir topos. The scientific gaze refers to a fixity of looking that separates the object from its environment, viewing it as autonomous and apart from culture. When the bamboo comes to life as a natural object by the end of the poem, it straddles poetic artifice, the uncanny, and the fantastical, on the one hand, and a way of seeing an object autonomously on the other.

By making the painted object jump out of the frame, Saikō echoes the way her female speaker ironizes the boudoir genre in other poems. "Bamboo" un-stills the still life, creating a surreal image in the poetic imagination that ironizes the pictorial realism of early nineteenth-century Japanese painting. As the speaker—a painter—beholds the bamboo taking form on her canvas, the bamboo seems to be looking right back at her, with a mind of its own. In a way hauntingly reminiscent of John Keats's "This Living Hand" (1819), the painter beholds bamboo as much as bamboo—now warm and capable—beholds the painter, and by extension the reader.

Saikō's ending also challenges the idea that seeing is knowing, suggesting that the sense of touch feels more real than the sense of sight. In his discussion of sixteenth-century Italian sculpture, Pablo Maurette has argued that "touch does not deceive, sight does; touch gives us reality as it is; sight deforms and transforms it."[45] Indeed, Saikō composed another heptasyllabic quatrain in which she examined the deception of visual perception and the imaginary flights that it makes possible. "Miscellaneous Poems Written on a Journey to the West" explores the possibilities of visual perception in a painting that plays tricks on the eye through opacity and illusion:

Miscellaneous Poem Written on a Journey to the West

Sea colors vast and indistinct like gazing into the obscure;
Serried masts beyond the trees, blanketed in evening smoke.

Blue, blue tricking the eye—is that sky or water?
I wonder how wind-blown sails could fly by treetops.

saiyū zasshi	西遊雜詩
kaishoku bōbō toshite nozomi akiraka narazu	海色茫茫望不明
renshō ki o hedatete ban'en tairaka nari	連檣隔樹晚煙平
seiran me o mayowasu ten ka mizu ka	青藍迷眼天耶水
kaitei su fūhan shōbyō ni yuku o	怪底風帆松杪行 [46]

The quatrain dates to March 1846, when Saikō traveled to Kyoto with her nephew. Mari Nagase has observed that Saikō's travel poems allowed her to escape the feminine space of the inner chamber.[47] In "Journey to the West," the speaker is away from the boudoir, window, and studio, but she takes her brush and canvas with her: as she beholds the landscape, she paints a picture that merges reality with painterly representation, conjuring the sublime.

The poem opens with the image of sea colors, which we might imagine as shades of blue growing increasingly indistinct, stretching into the vast distance.[48] The onomatopoeia *bōbō*, meaning "vast and indistinct," describes the space of the ocean as well as the heart of the speaker longing for an ineffable object. Saikō concludes line 1 with an affirmation of this spatial and affective image, claiming that the sea colors vast and indistinct are like "gazing into the obscure." This "gaze" (*nozomi*) is hopeful and filled with longing.

Late Edo Confucian scholar and *bunjin* Gotō Shōin (1797–1864) commented that Saikō's poem evokes the early nineteenth-century idea of *shashin*, or "to represent the real":

The poem represents a real view of the tossing sea as perceived by the eye.
nishu nada no ma no atari no shin o utsuseru mono nari   二首灘目寫真 [49]

Shōin describes the scene as a *nada*, or "tossing sea" represented as *shin*, meaning "real" or "true." The poem does this in two ways, he writes: it represents a scene with both the suggestion of pictorial realism and an expression of feeling that mirrors the movement of the tossing seascape. This evokes the Late Edo empiricism informed by the late imperial Chinese poetics of the "blending of feeling and scene" (Ch. *qing jing jiao rong*), showing how the speaker merges her personal state of mind with the scene that she beholds before her.

Following the vast indistinctness and visual obfuscation in Line 1 comes an optical illusion that unfolds across the rest of the poem, producing an effect similar to viewing a two-dimensional painting with a distorting lens, perhaps a zograscope—a late eighteenth-century device used to enhance depth perception of a flat image.[50] Maki Fukuoka examines how this device was used in Late Edo to view one-point linear perspective prints, or *vues d'optique* (*uki-e*). She writes that the zograscope lens was "often opaque and warped, unintentionally calling attention to the mediating mechanism of the lens itself."[51] Line 2 opens with the image of "serried masts" (*renshō*), a synecdoche for vessels on water, which are some distance away from the trees. The depth perspective suggested here is then flattened and contradicted by the blanket of evening smoke stretching horizontally over the landscape.

Late Edo gave rise to *kanshi* that represented sea vessels with verisimilitude.[52] Saikō's poem, however, is more interested in representing opacity and indistinctness: timber masts in a sea of fog. In order to mediate the speaker's feelings about the scene, Saikō relies on the modes of painting, drawing from the techniques of the late eighteenth- and early nineteenth-century Dutch painting that informed Naotake and other painters of the Akita Ranga school. These artists are known for practicing European techniques that allowed them to create complex visual effects in paint such as three-dimensional realism, distant perspective, chiaroscuro, reflections in water, and the use of blues to depict the sky and sea.[53]

Line 3 opens with two blues, *sei* and *ran*, that puzzle perception.[54] The speaker describes this visual confusion as not being able to distinguish sky from water (*ten ka mizu ka*). Blue is contiguous with blue, the one melting into the other. Since "Journey to the West" is a travel poem, the reader assumes that the speaker must be standing at an elevated perspective from where she can see the horizon disappear and simultaneously have a totality of landscape within sight: ship masts, treetops, sky, water, and land. This perspective speaks to Timon Screech's description of the Dutch "turret-gaze" in Japanese painting of the late eighteenth century.[55] Late Edo artist Maruyama Ōkyo (1733–1795), for example, painted scenes in which a person is positioned on the balcony of a tall built structure, gazing upon a natural expanse.

But if Saikō's speaker was imagining a painting, then the movement and opacity would be pure fancy, not the realism described in Shōin's commentary. The poem highlights how these visual experiences are not mutually exclusive: in poetry the real is the fantasy and the fantasy is the real. In line 4, the confusion only continues as the eye is tricked into seeing ship sails moving along on the same level as pine treetops. Both indistinct and imaginative, the scene is also confounding and defamiliarizing, as indicated by the verb *kaitei su*, or "I wonder." The verb describes an inexplicable image—a view that confounds reality. By its end, the poem has come to conjure the sublime in a self-referential way as a painting that makes the reader aware of the lens through which she can see landscape in new, non-linear ways.

The poem brings together the techniques of Late Edo painting and the genre of travel poetry. As a travel poem, "Journey to the West" comments on the experience of perceiving a landscape when the lyric subject is in motion. Travel as a poetic genre has a long history in the Japanese tradition, and is conventionally associated with exile, parting, and danger because the safe return of the traveler was uncertain. By the Edo period, travel was more accessible than ever before. *Haikai* poet Matsuo Bashō's (1644–1694) peripatetic wanderings are a case in point. As Marcia Yonemoto has observed, "from the seventeenth century on, the development of a transportation infrastructure and the growth of the market economy vastly increased physical mobility in Japan."[56] Yonemoto has shown how the proliferation of maps disseminated an awareness of space, and how the developments in transportation fundamentally changed the way people wrote about travel in early modern Japan. Poets were no longer limited to images of the past but could incorporate images of the present, including places to which they had actually traveled.[57]

Composed at a historical moment of increasing mobility, "Journey to the West" evokes the disorienting experience of early modern transport.[58] The anxiety-filled wonder that concludes the poem reveals the uncertainty of the lyric subject during a time of increasing mobility domestically and overseas. This mobility reflects not only the physical movement of the poet but also the ideological movements of the early nineteenth century, including the rise of empiricism and realism in literati culture.

Saikō's poems "Bamboo" and "Journey to the West" describe sensual experience inside and outside the inner chamber. In "Bamboo," the imagination of the object turns on the perceiving subject—the painter beholding bamboo becomes the painter beheld by bamboo. This trick of perception is echoed in "Journey to the West," where the lyric subject confronts a sublime landscape and questions the truth of her empirical perception. These *kanshi* display the sensual wonders afforded by literati poetry and painting, showing how Saikō engaged with the epistemological notion that "seeing is knowing."

THERE IS NO FRIGATE LIKE A BOOK

Saikō also composed poems in which her female speaker traveled beyond the confines of the inner chamber just by reading beside a window. "Calligraphy" shows how the window could be a comfortable place in which to exercise creativity in the *bunjin* form of calligraphy. Windows in Late Edo painting were frames of perception, portals to the everyday lives of literati men and women.[59] In *ukiyo-e* painting (paintings of the "floating world"), women were often depicted reading by a window.[60] Saikō's poetry reveals windows as metonyms for the poetic topos of the inner chamber and for the creative practice that constituted the poet's daily life. Her poems on reading participated in the flourishing book culture of the Edo period, evoking the depictions of women reading by the window in visual culture and embodying a reader's sensual experience of finding sympathy and empathy for the authors of fiction and their fictional characters.

As a literata, Saikō had access to books from both the Chinese and Japanese traditions. Chinese vernacular novels circulated widely in translation, and influenced popular genres of Japanese prose, such as *gesaku* (playful writing), *sharebon* (pleasure quarter fiction), and *yomihon* (reading books). As P. F. Kornicki and others have detailed, aristocratic women during the Edo period read a variety of books, especially didactic texts and volumes written for women.[61] Saikō was not an aristocrat, but an affluent samurai woman who had access to a variety of books: she read works in Japanese, including Murasaki Shikibu's *The Tale of Genji* (eleventh century; Genji monogatari). Artists in the late medieval and early modern periods represented *Genji* on folding screens and in *ukiyo-e* paintings, both of which were consumed by the warrior class.[62] Saikō composed poems on reading works in classical Chinese, or *kanbun*, for example Sima Qian's (145?–90? BCE) *Records of the Grand Historian* (Shiji) and Rai San'yō's *Unofficial History of Japan* (1827; Nihon gaishi). Mari Nagase has argued that such poems on historical texts afforded Saikō a means to write herself out of the conventions of poetry composed by women.[63]

Composing Chinese poems on *The Tale of Genji* was another way Saikō wrote herself out of the inner chamber, since the topos is not exclusively Chinese. She began by composing a series of quatrains on selected chapters. In 1834, she composed a longer poem: a heptasyllabic ancient-style poem (*shichigon koshi*) entitled "Reading Murasaki Shikibu's *The Tale of Genji*" (Shishi o yomu) that represents her experience of reading the novel:

Reading Murasaki Shikibu's *The Tale of Genji*

Who wields a red brush and depicts the truth of human emotion,
Intoxicating the hearts and minds of readers for a thousand years?
Discerning the nuances of its beauty, sure enough, she is a woman;
Her elegant sensibilities naturally differ from those of a man.

5 Spring rain falling, he trims the lamp, and ranks a hundred blossoms,
Whereupon his tales of cherishing scent and pitying jade begin.
At dusk he crosses the Milky Way on the bridge of magpie wings;
By dawn he entrusts the blue bird to deliver a letter of immortal love.
The gourd vine flower by the gated villa, traced by the waning moon;
10 The molted cicada's shell, a sheer gown, in the half-light of the torch.
Summer insects burn on their own, throwing themselves into the flame;
Spring butterflies dance about madly, their wings wooing the blossoms.
A mischievous cat lifts the green brocaded blinds;
Chang'e is indistinct, hidden in a palace on the moon.
15 Romances lasting as long as cloud and rain broke their hearts into pieces;
When all but cold embers remained of the flame, in secret they shed tears.

Fifty-four chapters comprising tens of thousands of words,
And in the end, nothing departs from the word "emotion."
In emotion there is joy and pleasure, pain and sadness;
20 Above all, the emotion most resonant is longing for the other.
Do not condemn the entire work for straying into indecency;
The intent is to speak all there is to speak of human emotion.

At my little window I hold up a lamp, the night is desolate and still;
I, too, will attempt to plumb the profundity of mind and heart.

shishi o yomu	讀紫史
tareka tōkan o torite jōji o utsusu	誰執彤管寫情事
senzai dokusha kokoro yoeru ga gotoshi	千載讀者心如醉
myōsho o bunseki suru wa hatashite joji	分析妙處果女兒
onozukara jōfu to fūkai kotonaru	自與丈夫風懷異
shun'u tō o kirite hyakka o hinsu	春雨剪燈品百花
kō o oshimi gyoku o awaremu wa kore yori hajimaru	惜香憐玉自此始

ginkan kure ni wataru ujaku no hashi	銀漢暮渡烏鵲橋
senshin akatsuki ni okuru seichō no tsukai	仙信曉遞青鳥使
koka monkō tsuki ikkon	瓜花門巷月一痕
senzei ishō tō hansui	蟬蛻衣裳燈半穗
kachū mizukara yaku hono'o ni tōzuru mi	夏蟲自焚投焰身
shunchō kuruimau hana o kouru tsubasa	春蝶狂舞戀花翅
rido burai ni shite shōren agaru	貍奴無賴緗簾揚
kōga iki toshite getsuden okubukashi	嫦娥依稀月殿邃
yūun teiu sundan no chō	尤雲殢雨寸斷腸
reikai zanshoku hisoka ni namida o taru	冷灰殘燭偷垂淚
gojūshihen senmangen	五十四篇千萬言
hikkyō idezu jō no ichiji yori	畢竟不出情一字
jō ni kanraku ari hishō ari	情有歡樂有悲傷
nakanzuku shōjō naru wa kore sōshi	就中鍾情是相思
togamuru nakare tsūhen koto in ni wataru to	勿罪通篇事涉淫
kiwamete jōchi o tokiidashitsukusan to hossu	極欲説出盡情地
shōsō tō o kakagereba yoru sekiryō	小窓挑燈夜寂寥
ware mo mata shin'i o satoran togisu	吾儂亦擬解深意 [64]

A literal interpretation of the title of Saikō's poem describes the author Murasaki Shikibu as a "historian" and *Genji* as a "Murasaki history" (Shishi). This title evokes the early idea in the Chinese tradition of fiction as a history or biography of historical figures. As her poem unfurls, Saikō shows that *Genji* is less of a historical record of people than a history of feelings, mediated by the relationships between characters in a work of fiction whose essence is the representation of emotion.

The poem represents the novel's structure of feeling, which in the words of National learning (*kokugaku*) scholar Motoori Norinaga (1730–1801) is *mono no aware* (lit. the pathos of things), or "sympathy or empathy for others." The word in Saikō's poem that addresses this structure of feeling is *jō*, translated above as "emotion." I propose that this term resonates with—though is not a substitute for—Norinaga's theory of *mono no aware* as the essence of the novel. The word *jō* appears in Norinaga's essays on *mono no aware*, and is glossed as *kokoro*, or "heart and mind." The following examination demonstrates how the poem transports the reader to moments in the novel through allusion, creating a montage of images from *Genji*. Through these images, which are followed by commentary about the essence of the novel, the poem represents how Murasaki depicts the empathetic and sympathetic relationships between characters and, in the end, how the reader participates in an affective loop of author, character, and reader.

The speaker opens by suggesting, in the first two lines, that a woman author has the ability to represent emotions with verisimilitude. The word *jōji* (the truth of human emotion) refers to the romances between characters in the novel that could happen as emotional situations in real life—a realism that has enraptured readers for centuries. *Genji* is a novel set in the Heian period (794–1185) that tells, among other things, the tale of Prince Genji's dalliances with women of the court, which end in sadness and longing. Rather than supporting the Confucian discourse that condemned *Genji* for being vulgar and indecent, Saikō's poem echoes Norinaga's claims that *Genji* is about the sensitivity to human emotions that is stirred by depictions of courtship.[65]

Lines 3 and 4 further develop this idea of realism by claiming that Murasaki, as a woman, is more able to "discern" the beautiful nuances of emotional truth. This meaning of *bunseki* derives from early nineteenth-century science, where the term referred to biological or chemical "analysis" of the constituent elements of an object. By using it here to describe the way Murasaki discerns human character and represents emotion in an eleventh-century novel, Saikō treats *Genji* as a modern literary work that analyzes emotion scientifically, paralleling William Wordsworth's 1800 pronouncement that poetry is the "history or science of feelings."

The opening lines of the poem describe a process of reading that begins with the reader establishing a rapport with the novel's author. As a woman, Saikō's speaker shares the same gender and identity as Murasaki. Lines 5 to 16 elaborate on the "elegant sensibilities" (*fūkai*) that are unique to the creative brush of a woman author, and list allusions to scenes from the novel. Line 5 represents a scene from the second chapter "Hahakigi" (Broom cypress), in which Genji, his brother-in-law Tō no Chūjō (one of the Middle Captains serving the Office of the Chamberlain), and other men have an intimate conversation about women during which they discuss the politics of courtship and how to find a suitable woman to marry. Spring rain falls outside; the men chat inside by the candlelight, "ranking one hundred blossoms" (*hyakka o hinsu*)—a metaphor for women. The whole chapter is about the perception and status of women—from looks to pedigree—and how these affect romantic companionship.

Line 6 comments on how Genji's "tales of cherishing scent and pitying jade," a metaphor for his dalliances with women, invite the reader to sympathize with the novel's characters. The poem moves freely into and out of allusions that represent the experience of reading. The novel itself is replete with allusions to poetry, philosophy, and myth, including the legend of the oxherd (Hikoboshi) and the weaver maiden (Orihime) in the couplet formed by lines 7 and 8: the two lovers are separated by the Milky Way and reunite by crossing a bridge formed by the wings of magpies on the seventh day of the seventh lunar month, which is now the Tanabata festival. The allusion summarizes the drama of romance depicted in the novel: Genji consummates his romances in the evening; by morning he has fled, whereupon he sends his messenger boy to deliver poems to the woman with whom he spent the night. Lines 9 and 10 allude to two women who have liaisons with Genji: Yūgao (The Lady of the Evening Faces) and Utsusemi (The Lady of the Cicada Shell); lines 11 and 12 allude to the untoward romantic advances suffered by Tamakazura (Tō no Chūjō's daughter) in the "Butterflies" and "Fireflies" chapters. The allusions in lines 13 and 14 speak to the method by which the heart and emotions of characters are revealed to the reader: some are exposed like those of the Third Princess (Onna San no Miya)—after a cat raises the blinds, Kashiwagi is given a glimpse of her beauty—and some (perhaps Oborozukiyo) are hidden like those of Chang'e, the moon goddess in Chinese mythology. Through these allusions the speaker revisits the complexity of romance and courtship in *Genji*, empathizing with the novel's characters, especially the women.

Following these representations of iconic episodes that invite the reader's empathy, the speaker makes her claim that the essence of the novel is *jō*, or "emotion," referencing Norinaga's theory of *mono no aware* and the history of *jō* in the Chinese tradition. In Chinese, *jō* is *qing*, a word that has inspired centuries of intellectual debate on its meanings and usages. David Schaberg has examined the term's morally inflected meaning in early China, defining it as "any truth—objective or emotional—that is subject to hiding and that is brought into the open through human exposition. Whether they are psychological constants, social or natural dynamics, or personal responses to situations, *qing* are the sorts of things that might remain hidden or unknown, and that require discovery to be called *qing*."[66] Schaberg's discussion does not exclude the word's later connotations of "lyrical feeling," which continue through the Ming and Qing dynasties as the theme of sentimental vernacular fiction in vogue during the Edo period. His argument that *qing* is something hidden that requires discovery is echoed in Norinaga's discussion of Murasaki's larger purpose in writing *Genji*:

> All the things one sees and hear and experiences in this life...when one is deeply moved and struck by them, they cannot simply be shut away in one's heart. We wish to tell someone or write them down and show them to someone. This sets our hearts at ease as nothing else does, and when the listener or reader is moved to feel as we have felt, our relief is even greater.[67]

Writers write to be read and heard. Norinaga's recapitulations of Murasaki's theory of fiction as a way to record human experiences so that they can be discovered by the reader are reiterated in lines 17 to 22 of Saikō's poem, which argue that the entire novel is about emotion, or jō. Norinaga highlights the importance of the listener, speaking to the idea of poetry as feelings overheard that, once heard, allow the listener to understand.[68] In writing a poem about reading Genji, Saikō echoes Norinaga echoing Murasaki, who believed both that writing is about communicating human experiences, and that the task of understanding falls to the reader.

The poem concludes by describing the role of the reader through a self-reflexive comment on the poem as a whole. Line 20 claims that the most resonant emotion in Genji is "longing for the other" (sōshi).[69] In Chinese poetry, sōshi (Ch. xiangsi) is used in situations where one person longs for another person. This sentiment is echoed in the hundreds of poems that comprise "the tens of thousands of words" of Genji, which may be beyond the pale according to Confucian norms of moral decency, but as the speaker states, "The intent is to speak all there is to speak of human emotion." Norinaga uses similar language when he argues that all the emotions are found in situations of romantic "love" (koi):

> Virtually every sort of emotion experienced by the human heart is to be found in love. And so, this tale having been created in order to inventory the full range of life's emotional experiences, thereby moving the reader deeply, the manifold nuances of feeling in the human heart, the savor of the extreme depths of emotion, could hardly be expressed without touching on the subject of love.[70]

While Norinaga concentrates on "love" as the emotion or state of being that has it all—a claim he also makes about mono no aware in Genji— Saikō's poem argues that the strongest emotion is "longing for the other" (sōshi). These emotions are not mutually exclusive. Feelings of longing abound in Genji since all the relationships end in separation, and in most cases the woman is portrayed as both longing and misunderstood. Longing is also the primary emotion in Chinese poetry about women of the inner chamber.

The poem concludes with a scene of the speaker/reader by the window, reading *Genji* by candlelight, that mirrors the first description of Prince Genji in line 5. As Genji and his male associates "rank one hundred blossoms," the speaker finds herself doing the same, but alone and from her own perspective. The longing in line 20 recurs in the image of night "desolate and still" (*sekiryō*) in the penultimate line, as the speaker's own lonesome persona as a woman of the inner chamber joins Murasaki and the characters of the novel. This empathetic and sympathetic union, made possible by reading, is polyperspectival and intersubjective: as a writer, the speaker becomes Murasaki-as-author; as an abandoned woman, she becomes Yūgao and Utsusemi; and as a reader she becomes Genji, who reads and responds to the feelings of the women he courts.

The final line reveals the speaker's own individuated experience of reading, followed by the affirmation that she has composed a poem to record her experience. As Virginia Woolf wrote: "Perhaps the quickest way to understand the elements of what a novelist is doing is not to read, but to write; to make your own experiment with the dangers and difficulties of words."[71] To understand the novelist Murasaki, Saikō conducts her own experiment: she attempts to probe the depths of sense and feeling by offering her own interpretation of *Genji* in the form of a poem and recreating the affective loop between author, character, and reader.

A Formal Feeling Comes

Saikō's poem on reading *Genji* points to a feeling that invites the sympathy of the reader: longing. Now I turn to her poems that represent longing in the inner chamber. By setting her poetry within the context of this poetic topos, Saikō wrote herself into the genre of "the boudoir plaint" (J. *keien*; Ch. *gui yuan*), which depicted the archetype of the abandoned woman who, forlorn and sentimental, wallows in lonesome sorrow. Saikō performed the boudoir plaint while also displaying her awareness of the genre in one heptasyllabic ancient-style poem (*shichigon koshi*) and in one heptasyllabic regulated verse (*shichigon risshi*).[72] The two poems evoke the feelings of grief and longing found in spring and autumn poems from the Chinese lyric tradition, yet also display Saikō's transformation of this genre: the speaker's heightened awareness of sense and feeling refigure loneliness into an ironic affirmation of solitude.

Spring Lyric

Days long by the golden needle, sensing faint fatigue;
Outside the window weeps a willow finer than silk thread.
Proud and pained, the heart pulses and pounds, never to cross the threshold;
Myself knows when idle grief wells from within, and brims over my face.
5   Wanting to dispel a longing for sleep, a constant longing for tea;
By the pitiful cold hearth, quiet in the cloister grows deep and deeper.
In a low voice I summon the young maid several times,
Only to startle the pair of swallows roosting in the eaves.

shunshi	春詞
hi nagaku shite kinshin biken o oboyu	日永金針覺微倦
sōzen no suiryū ito yori mo hososhi	窓前垂柳細於線
kyōshin myakumyaku shikii o idezu	矜心脈脈不出閾
mizukara shiru kanshū noborite omote ni mitsuru o	自知閑愁上滿面
suishi o yaburan to hosshite shikiri ni cha o omou	欲破睡思頻思茶
ayaniku no reiro shinshin no in	生憎冷爐深深院
teisei ikudo ka kanji o yobu	低聲幾度喚鬟兒
osoraku wa chōryō sōshoku no tsubame o odorokasan	恐驚彫梁雙宿燕[73]

Through its representation of sleepiness and languor, the poem converses with the vast corpus of writing on illness by late imperial Chinese women, including poems on fatigue and sleep disorders. Grace Fong has observed that late imperial Chinese women poets used illness as a mode for autobiographical reflection and aesthetic creation, enabling them to construct an alternative space and temporality of being.[74] Fong has shown how their poems on illness privileged poetic evocations of sensory perception and bodily sensation.

In "Spring Lyric" Saikō figures time as long and listless, like poems in the *ci* (song lyric) genre and in ancient poems from the Chinese Yuefu (Music Bureau), a style of Chinese poetry that emerged in the Western Han dynasty (206 BCE–9 CE) that was sung to popular folk tunes. Yuefu poetry and the song lyric featured the trope of the abandoned woman and came back in full swing in late imperial China. By writing in these lyric traditions, Saikō employs the conventional languor and depression of boudoir poetry in a way that articulates a heightened awareness of sensory perception and bodily sensation in the present. She figures the temporality of longing as the interstitial experience between antipodes: inside and outside, motion and stillness, sleep and wakefulness, hot and cold, heard and unheard.

The poem opens with an awareness of time inside and outside the inner chamber. The golden needle is a metonym for sewing and a synecdoche for the hand of a clock. Boudoir poetry conventionally features ornate objects that denote the passing of time.[75] Either sewing all day long or watching time pass on the clock, the speaker in line 1 displays her awareness of the sluggishness of time in spring. The subject of "sensing faint fatigue" (*biken o oboyu*) is both the golden needle and the speaker. By the end of line 1, her consciousness hangs by a thread, a notion developed in line 2, wherein she looks outside her window and sees a weeping willow "finer than silk thread" (*ito yori mo hososhi*). Like the image of the golden needle, the willow branch drooping outside evokes the springtime lassitude of boudoir poetry. The comparison to silk thread at the end of the line shows how the inside and the outside are fused together, suggesting that fatigue spills over beyond the confines of the inner chamber.

The speaker then reveals an awareness of the magnitude of her feelings. Line 3 opens with the word *kyōshin*, which Edo literature scholar Kado Reiko interprets as "heart of restraint." *Kyō* has many meanings, including "sensitive," "pained," and "proud"; here, the heart is *myaku myaku*, an onomatopoeia with at least as many meanings, from "hidden" to "pulsating." The line suggests that the speaker is content with being confined in the inner chamber, and yet her heart is simultaneously pained by such confinement. The line's end—"never to cross the threshold" (*shikii o idezu*)—may be the reason her proud and pained heart pounds. Saikō was not a "kept woman" and does not appear to have felt confined as did many of her Chinese contemporaries composing boudoir poetry. Her speaker acknowledges the genre of the boudoir plaint but makes it her own by asserting a willfulness to stay inside. Line 4 echoes this determination by claiming that, while her heart may be hidden away inside, pulsating with grief, she knows when that grief appears from nowhere, rises up from within, and manifests itself, writ large on her face. This self-awareness speaks to Kado's interpretation of self-restraint, here a kind that does not rein in emotion as much as it evinces a keen awareness of how grief can overwhelm the heart and mind.

Rather than abandoning herself to languor and longing, the speaker tries to find relief, that, ironically, only prolongs her longing. In order to dispel her longing for sleep, she longs for tea. To place both longings in tension with each other, the poet repeats the Chinese graph for "longing"

(J. *shi* and *omou*). Such repetition was used in ancient-style verse to express intense feeling and lyricism. In Saikō's poem, the tension between these two longings is both negated and echoed by the images in line 6: the hearth is cold, so she cannot prepare tea; the cloister falls "deeper and deeper" (*shinshin*) into silence. The repetition of *shin* (deep; to deepen) echoes the longing in the previous line, giving it a temporality, as the ono-matopoeia *shinshin* suggests that the night is deepening. As time passes, the speaker's longing endures as long as she can stay awake.

After failed attempts to make tea on her own, the speaker seeks help that results comically in a misdirected address. In line 7 she summons her maid (*kanji*) for assistance (perhaps with making tea), but instead wakes up the swallows roosting in the eaves of the house. The earlier lines convey the speaker's self-awareness of her grief, how it manifests, and her attempts to find respite from it. The poem does not feature another person until the end, and even when that person is mentioned, the speaker's attempt to communicate with her fails. The only living beings that take notice of her speech are a pair of swallows, likely a male and female roosting together. A pair of swallows (J. *sōen*; Ch. *shuangyan*) is a conventional symbol of mar-riage or companionship between a man and a woman in Chinese poetry.[76] By ending with the image of swallows, the poem turns back on itself, highlighting the single status of the lyric subject, who is without compan-ionship. But rather than wishing to be like the pair of swallows—as con-vention would expect—the speaker concludes with the misdirected address, and goes nowhere conventional: what begins as loneliness in the inner chamber turns into solitude on a long spring day.

Saikō composed another poem on longing set in autumn. Spring and autumn are the most affective seasons in Chinese poetry because they are both considered seasons of change and transience. Longing in spring poems is associated with the long span of the day; longing in autumn poems is associated with cold, decay, and loneliness as winter draws near. In her poem "Sleepless on a Bright Moon Night," Saikō plays with the trope of the moon as the friend of the solitary poet. In the company of the moon, the poet may indulge in toasting with wine, shadow play, and danc-ing—like in the poems of High Tang poet Li Bai (701–762 CE). However, Saikō's speaker suffers from insomnia and consequently suffers from hypersensitivity to the sights and sounds of night:

Sleepless on a Bright Moon Night

Autumn nights are like streams—ever waking me from dream,

A crow in the woodland trees cawing two, three times.
The water clock drips barely faint, my robe getting colder;
The rest of the flame almost dark, I notice light on the window.
5   A couplet at random comes to mind amid the tranquil silence,
Myriad sensations spring forth, spilling from my pillow.
Tossing and turning unable to sleep, I long for old friends;
Just then, I glimpse the clear moon descending the roof.

gesseki inezu	月夕不寢
shūshō mizu no gotoku yume shikiri ni odoroku	秋宵如水夢頻驚
rinju ni karasu naku ryōsan sei	林樹鴉鳴兩三聲
kōrō yaya mare ni shite hi no rei o soe	更漏稍稀添被冷
zantō yōyaku kurakushite mado no akaruki o oboyu	殘燈漸暗覺窗明
ichiren tamatama kanchū ni oite etari	一聯偶向閑中得
bankan subete chinjō yori shōzu	萬感渾從枕上生
tenten shite nemurazu kyūyū o omou	展轉不眠思舊友
atakamo miru rakugetsu okuryō ni kiyoki o	恰看落月屋梁清 ⁷⁷

The title of the poem indicates that the season is autumn, which by convention is associated with melancholy and fleetingness. A "bright moon night" (*gesseki*) can refer to the fifteenth day of the eighth lunar month, on which the moon is bright. In the Chinese tradition, the moon's radiance is an invitation for reflection.[78] In Chinese poetry, the moon mediates feelings between the poet and beloveds across distances; in Saikō's poem, the moon makes a brief appearance before it eventually disappears, leaving the speaker without the means to mediate her longing.

The metaphor that opens the poem indicates that the season is autumn and describes the speaker thinking about the season as a sleep-disturbing rush of water, "ever" (*shikiri ni*) waking her. The reader can assume that the rest of the poem describes what the speaker perceives while awake. Disruptive sounds recur in line 2 with the caws of crows in the trees, which she hears "two, three times." The cawing of crows indexes the conventional lexicon in poems by Chinese women who describe a heightened auditory sense due to insomnia.[79] Although the cawing links the poem to a set of conventional tropes, the speaker counts the caws, heightening the auditory sensation. The numbers give the images in the previous line palpability and immediacy, actualizing the ceaseless flow of the stream.

As the poem unfolds, its images complement and contrast each other, producing a tension—a push-and-pull effect—in the poetic imagination. Following the numbers comes the image of the water clock, or clepsydra, an image Saikō used in poems to represent the sluggishness of time. The clepsydra is an ancient time-measuring device activated by the flow of water. The fluid stream in line 1 here takes form as drops telling time: like the caws of the crow, the drops suggest a sense of quantity or measurability. But the fact that they are barely audible stands in contrast to the loud caws of the previous line. As the night deepens, the speaker feels colder, a coldness that also registers in what she sees. Just as the flowing stream and the crow caws become recurring drops of the water clock, the candlelight is about to go dark, only to be replaced by moonlight. The movement from one image to another reveals the poet's shifts back and forth between degrees of fullness and emptiness, presence and absence.

Just when the moon makes its appearance as a shaft of light on her window, a creative inspiration is called forth. The couplet formed by lines 5 and 6 self-reflexively comments on its form: "A couplet at random comes to mind." The couplet generates "myriad sensations" (*bankan*) springing forth from the pillow where the speaker's head lies. The water imagery evoked by the Chinese graph *kon*, or "spilling all over," echoes the stream and the water clock drops, as if these external sights and sounds have been internalized by the speaker, assimilated into her sensorium, and are now sensations gushing forth from the pillow and spilling everywhere.

With myriad sensations all around, the speaker tosses and turns. Unable to sleep, she starts "longing for old friends" (*kyūyū o omou*). The poem's title suggests that the moon will stay out in the sky to comfort the speaker and mediate her connection with old friends. But the final line pulls the rug from under her feet, concluding with the moon's disappearing act: "Just then, I glimpse the clear moon descending the roof." Saikō sets up the poem to offer a virtual reunion with beloveds through the conventional connection of the moon; instead, she ironizes this convention, concluding with the affirmation of her loneliness unresolved as the moon makes a clean exit from the scene. This final image leaves the scene on the roof "pure" (*kiyoki*), an adjective that refers to the "clear moon (light)" and also to the speaker's refiguration of longing and loneliness as a pure, beautiful solitude.

Both "Spring Lyric" and "Sleepless on a Bright Moon Night" show how Saikō wrote herself into poetic genres as old as Yuefu and its imitations and reincarnations in late imperial Chinese poetry. Her poems display the lyric affordances of the illness trope, transforming the boudoir plaint through irony: attempts to find a solution to sleepiness and restlessness end in failure, but the lone speaker does not abandon herself to sorrow. Rather, she comes to terms with her longing by finding solitude in the grief of spring and autumn.

POETS LIGHT BUT LAMPS

I conclude this chapter by examining two poems that transform the trope of a *keishū* longing in the inner chamber into Saikō's autobiographical representation of personal grief and philosophical meditation on the passage of time. Saikō composed two heptasyllabic regulated verses that she grouped under the title "Self-Transmission" (Mizukara yaru). These poems encapsulate the concerns of the previous poems examined in this chapter, which represent different aspects of Saikō's sense and sensibility as woman *bunjin*. "Self-Transmission," a title that also means "dispelling grief," mediates her sensual awareness of aging through descriptions of her roles in life as poet, painter, reader, and caregiver, resulting in a representation of self that rang "true" and "new" to her contemporaries. Late Edo scholar and physician Koishi Genzui (1784–1849) compared Saikō's poems to the moving experience of mimesis in *The Tale of Genji*: "The two poems brim with true emotion." Uragami Shunkin (1779–1846) observed how the poems allow for the reader to "sink deeply into new feelings."[80] Such responses by her contemporaries evince how Saikō aspired toward the ideal of "true poetry" (*shinshi*) in *kanshi* poetics. What she attempts to represent in real terms is a poignant awareness of the finitude of human life, concomitant with the inexorable progression of time:

Self-Transmission

One dream fast and fleeting, me half a century old;
Deep thoughts, fine and unending, quietly pain the heart.
The moon wanes, the moon waxes, from full to new;
Blossoms fall, blossoms bloom, in autumn and then in spring.
5   Pictures I once painted seem by a different hand;
Books I once read feel unfamiliar as I read them again.
My only wish is for my life to be without worry;
Yet there in the living room, my father ill and aging.

mizukara yaru   自遣
ichimu sōsō hanbyaku no hito   一夢匆匆半百人
yūkai ruru toshite an ni shin o itamashimu 幽懷縷縷暗愴神

tsuki kake tsuki michite bō to saku to   月虧月滿望兼朔
hana ochi hana hirakite aki mata haru   花落花開秋又春
katsute utsuseru ga wa te no nao betsu naru ka to utagai   曾寫畫疑手猶別
sude ni mishi sho wa me ni kasanete aratanaru to oboyu   已看書覺眼重新
kono mi negau tokoro wa tada tsutsuga naki koto o   此身所願唯無恙
nao kōdō no rōbyō no oya ari   猶有高堂老病親 [81]

The speaker's keen awareness of time is suggested by the way the opening couplet compares the fleetingness of life to the brevity of poetic form. The word "one dream" (*ichimu*) serves as a metaphorical frame for the entire poem, evoking the brevity of its eight lines as well as of life and self-representation in poetic form.[82] The onomatopoeia *sōsō*, "fast and fleeting," is the same phrase as "Yours, in haste" (*sōsō*)—the closing remark to a brief epistolary correspondence. As the speaker figures her life as a fleeting dream, she suggests that her poem, her letter to the reader, is just as fleeting.

While human life and poetic experience are limited by the forms that embody them, the senses and feelings contained therein are limitless. In line 2, Saikō places the onomatopoeia *ruru*, or "fine and unending," in parallel opposition with *sōsō*, or "fast and fleeting." The word *ruru* evokes an image of a fine, endless thread and describes the minuteness of "deep thoughts" (*yūkai*). The opening couplet suggests that to render the totality of everyday life into poetic form involves contending with the economy of words, but once the speaker has done this, poetic form has the potential to represent endless threads of profound feeling, pulling quietly and painfully in the depths of the reader's heart.

Saikō expands the opening couplet into two more couplets that compare the continuity of the natural world with the discontinuity of human life. Lines 3 and 4 echo the feeling of "fine and unending" (*ruru*) in Line 2 by describing the constancy of lunar phases and seasonal change, suggesting nature's continuous progression. The repetition in this couplet expresses the speaker's lyrical excitement, if not envy, for this continuity: "The *moon* wanes, the *moon* waxes, from full to new; / *Blossoms* fall, *blossoms* bloom, in autumn and then in spring." Chinese literature scholar Cecile Sun has examined repetition in the English and Chinese traditions: "For the lyric, unlike any other mode of discourse, is obsessed with repetition, expressed not only through the overtly palpable rhythm and cadence of the emotions and thoughts, but also through a variety of covert and hence artful means of repetition, to deliver its thoughts and emotions in terms of something else."[83] Jonathan Culler has described the something-else-ness of rhythm and repetition in lyric poetry as "an event without representation."[84] Using repetition to evoke the non-representational form of music, Saikō celebrates the way the moon and blossoms return the same month after month, year after year.

The feeling of fleetingness in line 1 returns in the line 5 and 6 couplet, which describes how the speaker's sense and feeling have changed with time. The lines begin with adverbs that mark past completion—*katsute* and *sude ni*—and end with adverbs that promise newness—*nao* and *kasanete*. While the natural world moves inexorably in cyclical motion, repeating itself again and again, the mortal speaker changes in ways beyond return. The senses of touch and vision mediate an awareness that she, in the present, is no longer her self from the past. Through these senses, Saikō suggests that the connection between present and past is as "fast and fleeting" (*sōsō*) as a dream, and yet that history of deep thoughts and feelings embodied in poetic form is as "fine and unending" (*ruru*) as a thread. The adjectives "different" (*betsu*) and "unfamiliar" (*arata*) suggest the speaker's awareness of the experiential knowledge that comes with aging, speaking to theories of evolution and human development in early nineteenth-century science and philosophy.

Following upon the idea that aging brings new experiences, the final lines suggest the speaker's wish to continue living; yet the illness of her father becomes a worrying reminder of her own mortality. Line 7 represents a plaintive cry to be free of sickness and all other worries, while line 8 suggests that this cry goes unheard as the speaker is confronted with the empirical reality that her aging and ill father is still there.[85] Saikō's second poem expands upon this wish to be free of worry, and comes to the realization that there is no escape from the ravages of time:

> Long, long-held wishes, many turned out different;
> When life is a dream, what is right from wrong?
> Reined in by worldly thoughts because my reading is shallow;
> Friendships have grown distant since I rarely leave the gate.
> 5   Carrying grief to my pillow—the weak lantern dims;
> Tending to illness by the window—the thin moon fades.
> Who can know if the idle gull on the river's edge is sleeping,
> When the windblown waves keep stirring her from reverie?

yūyū taru sogan koto ōku tagau　　　　　悠悠素願事多違
ichimu jinsei nan no zehi ka aran　　　　　一夢人生何是非

jinsō tsunagaruru wa sho o yomu koto no asaki ni yori   塵想覊因讀書淺
kōyū utoki wa mon o izuru koto no mare naru ga tame nari   交遊濶爲出門稀
urei o idakite chinjō zantō kuraku   抱愁枕上殘燈暗
yamai ni ji shite sōzen ketsugetsu kasuka nari   侍病窓前缺月微
tare ka shiran kan'ō kōhan ni nemuru mo   誰識閑鷗江畔睡
fūha nao bōki ni furen to hossuru o   風波猶欲觸忘機 [86]

The poem opens with a declaration that the speaker's wishes in life have gone unfulfilled. Line 1 begins with the onomatopoeia *yūyū*, or "long, long-held," which gives her wishes a temporal and spatial dimension as endless longing in boundless space. Line 2 offers some relief to this grief by returning to the word *ichimu*, "a dream," arguing that there is no difference between a "right" life and a "wrong" one. This is a reference to the Daoist idea of nondistinction, from the famous butterfly parable in *Zhuangzi* that questions the distinction between waking life and dream.

But the speaker is not convinced and states the reasons for her life not turning out the way she had wished. In lines 3 and 4 she describes herself as a shallow reader with shallow thoughts as well as a recluse and caregiver who has alienated herself from friends. This self-deprecation is part of her performance as a *keishū* and as a daughter who subscribes to Confucian norms, but it is also an indirect way of describing the speaker's choice to devote herself to poetry and painting in solitude. Even in these pursuits, everyday life gets in the way: lines 5 and 6 describe the grief she feels as a caregiver for her ailing father. While earlier poems figure the pillow and window in the inner chamber as a place for creative and sensual exploration, here they are reminders of mortality. The dimming lantern and the fading moon cast the scene and atmosphere in growing darkness, suggesting that the lights she hopes will shine inexhaustibly eventually go out.

The final couplet concludes the poem with a metaphor for the speaker's awareness of time: a seagull tries to sleep and tune out from the world, but the windblown waves wake her from "reverie" (*bōki*). The term *bōki* literally means "to let go of the impulses of the heart and mind." One meaning of *ki* is "impulse," referring to the human impulse to respond to the world through sense and feeling. Another meaning of *ki* is "trigger," referring to that which sets the world in motion: the workings of nature or the progression of time.[87] Through the metaphor of the seagull unable to tarry in reverie, the speaker attempts to forget her impulse to sense and feel, to ignore the trigger that sets everything in motion. But the waves, like the moon and the blossoms, serve as constant reminders of how time

progresses inexorably, indifferent to her finite existence. Perched precari-
ously at the edge of the river, the seagull's only recourse is to take flight.
As a seagull, the speaker can soar to new heights, even with grief weighing
heavily on her wings.

Reusing and reinventing the tropes of the inner chamber, Saikō wan-
dered within and without poetic convention, crafting a lyric voice that was
personal and ironic. Her poems offer a glimpse into the history of perception and feeling in Late Edo literati culture and into her own sense and
sensibility as a woman *kanshi* poet and *bunjin*. The feelings of anxiety and
longing she represented in her poetry were echoed by modern writers
Masaoka Shiki and Natsume Sōseki in their prose poems, the subject of the
following chapters.

NOTES

1. Three hundred and fifty of Saikō's *kanshi* are anthologized in *Shōmu ikō*
   (1871; Posthumous manuscript of the dreamer of Xiang), a posthumous
   poetry collection compiled by her family. For more poems see Ema Saikō,
   San'yō sensei hiten: Shōmu shisō.
2. Saikō composed a poem (ca. 1828) representing her childhood memories and early nineteenth-century cosmopolitanism:

> Winter Night
> A father leafs through European books,
> A child reads Tang and Song verses.
> Sharing the light of a single lamp,
> Each following their own course.
> The father reads, not knowing when to stop;
> The child tires, and thinks of nuts and potatoes.
> What a shame her mind cannot keep up with his;
> The father is eighty years, but his eyes are not cloudy.

tōya	冬夜
chichi wa himotoku ōran no sho	爺繙歐蘭書
ko wa yomu tōsō no ku	兒讀唐宋句
kono ittō no hikari o wakachite	分此一燈光
genryū onoono mizukara sakanoboru	源流各自泝
chichi wa yomite yamu koto o shirazu	爺讀不知休
ko wa umite ritsuu o omou	兒倦思栗芋

hazuru ni tau seishin chichi ni oyobazu   堪愧精神不及爺
chichi wa toshi hachijū me ni kiri nashi   爺歳八十眼無霧

Ema Saikō, *Ema Saikō shishū Shōmu ikō*, 2: 253-255. From here on *SI*. Translations are mine unless otherwise noted.

3. Maki Fukuoka has examined the emergence of realist representation in the early nineteenth century. She offers a new history of Japanese visuality through an examination of the discourses and practices surrounding the nineteenth-century "transposition of the real" in the decades before photography was introduced. Fukuoka examines texts by the Shohyakusha, a motley crew of scholars comprising doctors, farmers, and government officials. She traces the word *shashin* in medical, botanical, and pictorial texts, and reveals how the term creates new discourses concerning the representation of objects in scientific practice. Fukuoka, *The Premise of Fidelity*.

4. Suzuki, *Edo shiikashi no kōsō*, 6–30.

5. Nagase, "Truly, they are a lady's words," 279–305.

6. *SI*, 2: 274–275. The poem is one of four in the series "Poems on the Four Pleasures of Leisure" (Enkan shitekishi): "The Zither" (Kin), "Chess" (Ki), "Calligraphy" (Sho), and "Painting" (Ga).

7. Imanishi, *The Akita Ranga School*, Chapters 4 and 5.

8. Many of these framing ideas derive from treatises on gardening and landscape by Chinese literatus Li Yu (1611–1680). Li authored the preface to *The Mustard Seed Garden Manual of Painting*, which was published in Japan in 1679 and served as a primer for late Edo *bunjin*. In his essay collection *Leisure Notes* (1671; Xianqing ouji), Li describes living quarters of a Chinese house and outlines his theory of windows, arguing that windows could serve as natural substitutes for a scroll painting. Sarah E. Kile has discussed Li's *Leisure Notes* in the larger context of late imperial Chinese cultural history, arguing that these essays concentrate on the material world with an emphasis on quotidian and individual experience. Kile, "Toward an Extraordinary Everyday." Li's ideas informed the paintings of Odano Naotake and Uragami Gyokudō (1745–1820).

9. The *gui* (J. *kei*) etymologically refers to "the small gate of an inner courtyard, palace, or city." The term is used in combination with other words to denote the space for Chinese women—*guige* (inner chamber), *guikun* (inner quarter), and *guifang* (bedrooms)—and various aspects of the female subject that occupies the *gui: guixiu* (talented woman of the

inner chamber; J. *keishū*), *guiyan* (beauty of the inner chamber), *guiwa* (girl of the inner chamber), and *guiying* (the eminent of the inner chamber). Xiaorong Li has shown how women poets in late imperial China constructed new feminine subjectivities by transforming the *gui* in their poems. Li argues that such writings by women prescribed a feminine subjectivity that conformed to Confucian ideals for women, but they also "provided women with new possibilities for self-understanding and projection." X. Li, *Women's Poetry*, 5, 13, 14.

10. In the Confucian tradition, the *gui* functioned as a physical and social space of separation and was gendered as a woman's space. In Yuefu poetry and in the Six Dynasties collection *New Songs from a Jade Terrace* (Yutai xinyong), the *gui* was often figured as a space of lament, where an abandoned woman longed for a lover. The latter collection established the genre conventions for "palace-style poetry" (*gongti shi*): tropes such as the abandoned woman (*qifu*), themes such as the boudoir plaint (*guiyuan*), topoi such as the boudoir (*gui*), and luxurious objects that depict feminine beauty—bejeweled garments, diaphanous curtains, trousseaus, mirrors, and perfume. While stock imagery, artifice, and cliché define palace-style poetry, the syntagmatic relationship between poetic images reveals how Six Dynasties poets evoked palatial atmospheres in the poetic imagination. The *gui* topos returned in Song dynasty *ci* (song lyric) poetry. *Collection from Among the Flowers* (940 CE; Huajian ji) established the boudoir as a genre that both Chinese men and women poets used to represent feminine subjectivity.

11. In the Chinese tradition, male literati ventriloquized women voices, representing emotion through a female lyric persona. For a study on the subject in early Chinese male-authored writings, see Rouzer, *Articulated Ladies*. In the Song dynasty, male *ci* poets also borrowed the voice of women. Maija Bell Samei has examined the complexities of voice in the *ci* genre, arguing that it ultimately disrupts gender binaries. Samei, *Gendered Persona*. Wai-yee Li has examined how late imperial male poets "hide themselves" by assuming the voice of a woman during times of national and political crisis. W. Li, "Hiding Behind a Woman."

12. The social conditions in early modern Japan also show that the separation of the sexes was an ideal, not a reality. Marcia Yonemoto has argued that women in the Edo period held roles inside and outside the family, and that they were not subject to the same segregated seclusion as their

female contemporaries elsewhere in East Asia. In Japan's case, Yonemoto contends, the separation of the sexes was more the exception than the rule. Yonemoto, *The Problem of Women*, 14.

13. The quote comes from the preface to a collection of Yuan's poems by Jiang Yingke (1553–1605). Ibi, *Edo Shiikaron*, 68.

14. Liu Xie's ideas were reiterated throughout Chinese literary history, and *Wenxin diaolong* (J. *Bunshin chōryō*) had circulated in Japan by the early eighteenth century or earlier.

15. Owen, *An Anthology of Chinese Literature*, 346; *Bunshin chōryō*, 2: 395–396.

16. Cai, *A Chinese Literary Mind*.

17. Burwick, *Romanticism*, 137. William Blake (1757–1827) evoked both kinds of inspiration in his epic poem *Milton* (1810–1814), in which he discusses the poet's relationship to his literary forebears, such as John Milton (1608–1674), whose work weighed heavily on many Romantic poets. Blake opens the poem with the claim that the muses of Beulah mediate his unification with Milton as they travel directly from his brain down his arms, and in the end the spirit of Milton manifests on the page, or in Blake's case, the illustrated plate of the poem: "Come into my hand, /By your mild power descending down the nerves of my right arm / From out the portals of my Brain." Blake, *The Prophetic Books*, 1.

18. Anka Mulhstein has shown that the afflictions of artistic inspiration can be found in Honoré de Balzac's account of fictional seventeenth-century painter Frenhofer: "In Frenhofer, 'the creative principle itself is threatened, sapped, an ultimately destroyed by an overabundance of talent and imagination.' The destructive forces that fell Frenhofer do not come from the outside world, from the ordeals that all artists have to confront, but from within himself." Mulhstein, *The Pen and the Brush*, 61.

19. As Burwick remarked on the works of Swedish scientist, philosopher, and theologian Emanuel Swedenborg (1688–1772): "demonic possession was a phenomenon competing with divine inspiration." English Romantic poet John Keats (1795–1821) also evoked the idea of demonic possession in his poetry. Burwick, *Romanticism*, 139.

20. Shunkin Gakujin [Uragami Shunkin], *Rongashi*, 2: 2–3. Rpt. in Taketani and Uragami, *Bunjin garon*, 137–138. *Rongashi* is remarkable in the genre of treatises on painting (*garon*). Most treatises on painting were written in prose, and if they included poetry, the poems were often hep-

tasyllabic quatrains (*shichigon zekku*). Taketani Chōjirō has highlighted how the treatise itself is composed entirely of pentasyllabic ancient-style poems (*gogon koshi*). *Rongashi* is two volumes, each comprising thirty poems of ten lines; the poems are interspersed with commentary in prose by other *bunjin*. In sixty poems, Shunkin conveys the essence of literati painting, its aesthetic ideals, its formal features, and its history in the Chinese and Japanese traditions. The entire poem:

> Ages and ages of arguments on painting;
> Too many claim authority over the other.
> The men of the Song knew how to expound theory,
> So well, their theories were profuse and pell-mell.
> The Southern and the Northern schools emerged,
> Their differences have been passed down clearly.
> Through them we trace painting to the ancients,
> And can also search for its origins.
> Transformation follows the trend;
> Propensity likewise accords with nature.

yoyo garon o arawasu	世世著畫論
shūshō sukoburu tatan nari	聚訟頗多端
sō hito yoku ri o toku	宋人能説理
sono ri o mata funpun tari	其理亦紛紛
nanboku no setsu hajimete okori	南北説始起
hamyaku ruden o akiraka ni su	派脈晰流傳
kore ni yotte kojin ni sakanobori	依之遡古人
aruiwa sono minamoto o saguru beshi	或可探其源
henka kiun ni shitagai	變化隨氣運
ikioi mo mata shizen ni yoru	勢亦因自然

21. Alexander Pope's (1688–1744) idea of nature is "a principal of natural order or natural law that applied to human behavior and morality and also governed poetic expression." However, William Wordsworth (1770–1850) saw nature as a tutelary presence, believing in an inter-dependency between the individual mind of the poet and his external surroundings in nature. Burwick, *Romanticism*, 185. Wordsworth's Romantic attitude toward nature and literati attitudes toward nature in the nineteenth century are strikingly similar. For example, Satake Shōzan's (1748–1785) landscape paintings resemble the kind of

European Romantic landscapes where nature is depicted as large and overbearing, and man small and vulnerable.

22. This idea was reiterated by fellow painter and scholar Nukina Kaioku (1778–1863), whose commentary can be found throughout *Rongashi*, and whose modern attitude can be found in Saikō's poem. Kaioku remarked that Shunkin's claim "transformation follows the trend" is not limited to painting: "'Transformation follows the trend,' How can this be just about painting? A truthful claim." Taketani and Uragami, *Bunjin garon*, 138. Kaioku's own landscapes also varied in style; most of his brushwork is soft and inconspicuous, but the brushwork in paintings such as "Viewing Plum Flowers in Snow" (Setchū kenbai zu) "ha[s] a bravura quality accentuated by strong tonal contrast, which emphasize a sense of depth between the foreground figure and the distant mountain peaks." Berry, *Literati Modern*, 172.

23. For a partial translation of Hokuzan's treatise, see Shirane, *Early Modern Japanese Literature*, 910–913.

24. *SI*, 2: 276–278.

25. The first of Su Shi's two poems:

Saying that to paint is to resemble	論畫以形似
Is like seeing through the eyes of children.	見與兒童鄰
To say a poem must be a kind of poem	賦詩必此詩
Proves ignorance of the poet's craft.	定非知詩人
Poetry and painting are one in principle:	詩畫本一律
Natural and creative, pure and new.	天工與清新
Bian Luan depicts sparrows true to life;	邊鸞雀寫生
Chao Chang's blossoms communicate soul.	趙昌花傳神
How is it that their paintings evoke	何如此兩幅
Distance and blandness held in perfect balance?	疎澹含精勻
Who says that just one splash of red	誰言一點紅
Can lodge the infinitude of spring?	解寄無邊春

In a discussion of the poetry and paintings of Wang Wei (ca. 699–759 CE), Su Shi famously remarked that the two mediums complement one another. In the first poem, the speaker says they are "one in principle" (*ben yi lü*). The lines all suggest that poetry and painting are supposed to suggest something beyond itself, beyond reality, and along this train of thought, he concludes the poem by indirectly praising Secretary

Wang's awesome craft: "just one splash of red / Can lodge the infinitude of spring." The second poem:

Thin bamboo is like a secluded man;	瘦竹如幽人
A secluded blossom is like a young maiden.	幽花如處女
Above and below, sparrows sit on branches;	低昂枝上雀
In waving sheets, the rain falls on flowers.	搖蕩花間雨
As a pair of wings gets ready to take flight,	雙翎決將起
A mass of leaves just scatters into the air.	眾葉紛自舉
How lovely the bees scour the blossoms,	可憐採花蜂
Transporting fresh pollen on two limbs.	清蜜寄兩股
In the same way men abound in natural talent:	若人富天巧
Spring colors emerge when the brush touches paper.	春色入毫楮
Even from afar I know your potential in poetry:	懸知君能詩
Conveying a voice, seeking wondrous words.	寄聲求妙語

Su Shi, *Su Shi quan ji jiao zhu*, 5: 3170–3176.

26. Such a view resonates with Su Shi's Neo-Confucianist attitude toward aesthetics, which was more interested in the metaphysical aspects of representation, rather than the imitative and derivative.

27. Fister, "Feminine Perceptions," 5.

28. Li Yu: "All rooms with such windows should have considerable depth. If the viewer is looking at a mountain from a place somewhat distant from the window, the exterior of the window becomes the mounting for the picture scroll, what is within the frame becomes a landscape painting, and the landscape and the mounting work together as a continuous whole. Thus the viewer will perceive it without explanation as a 'natural painting.'" Imanishi, *The Akita Ranga School*, 264.

29. Casey, *Representing Place*, 17.

30. Screech, *The Western Scientific Gaze*, 3.

31. *SI*, 1: 226–227.

32. Kado Reikō has discussed this poem in the context of Saikō's feminism, arguing that it writes against the grain of poetic conventions created and enforced by men in the history and practice of Chinese poetry. For a recent study of women poets challenging conventions of self-expression in late imperial China, see Yang, *Women's Poetry*. The questions Yang lays out in her study echo the question posed by Saikō's poem: "While *shi* poetry is often treated as autobiographical, to what extent could a woman

express a 'self' in her poem when the genre has been excluding her for hundreds of years and when the very idea of expressing herself to an audience beyond her immediate family could bring severe criticism, suspicion of her moral qualities, and even denial of her femininity?" Yang, xiv.

33. The claim that such feelings will not "burn to ash" (*kai narazu*) also challenges the traditional idea in Confucian ideology that art and literature need only have moral—not aesthetic—purposes. Such a view resulted in the immeasurable loss of works by women in the Chinese tradition, many of whom burned their manuscripts.

34. Bamboo is one of the "Four Gentlemen" (*shikunshi*): plums (*ume* or *bai*), orchids (*ran*), bamboo (*take* or *chiku*), and chrysanthemums (*kiku*). For a study of Saikō's career as a painter, see Fister, *Japanese Women Artists*, 111–113.

35. *SI*, 1: 93–94

36. Ibi, *Edo Shiikaron*, 93–121.

37. Stewart, *Poetry and the Fate of the Senses*, 145.

38. Kurokawa Momoko has examined the representation of light (*hikari*) in Saikō's ink-wash paintings of bamboo, showing, in one example, how Saikō used white space to represent snowfall on bamboo and the illusion of moonlight illumination. Kurokawa, "Ema Saikō jigasan."

39. Focillon, *The Life of Forms in Art*, 162.

40. Stewart, *Poetry and the Fate of the Senses*, 164–165.

41. Hiroaki Sato's translation: "in light shades, aslant-aslant, emerges through my hand." Sato, *Breeze Through Bamboo*, 68.

42. Xiaorong Li has linked the popularity of the boudoir topos to the resurgence of the *ci* genre in late imperial Chinese literature, arguing that the boudoir was one vehicle that served the *ci* genre's call for true and sincere self-expression. X. Li, *Women's Poetry*, 47–51.

43. Stewart, *Poetry and the Fate of the Senses*, 162.

44. Screech, *The Western Scientific Gaze*, 2.

45. Maurette, *The Forgotten Sense*, 18.

46. *SI*, 2: 461–462. The *kundoku* is a blend of the versions in *SI* and in Fukushima, *Joryū*, 95–96.

47. Saikō wrote herself out of feminine genres, composing poems on a wide range of topics, including nature, history, drinking, family, friendship, and travel. Nagase, "Women Writers of Chinese Poetry," 177–180.

48. Saikō's representation of the sea conjures imagery similar to that of Anglo-European Romanticism. Margaret Cohen has examined the

sublimation of the sea in eighteenth- and nineteenth-century English fiction, arguing that the sea emerged as an aesthetic object in the Romantic period: "dark-heaving, boundless, endless, and sublime." Cohen, *The Novel and the Sea*, 115–118.

49. *SI*, 2: 462. I have modified the *kundoku* by Iritani and Kado in *SI*.
50. In her discussion of other eighteenth-century lenses and viewing devices, Imanishi distinguishes between two types of painting: *uki-e* and *megane-e*. The former refers to a painting that uses linear, one-point perspective (today called *ukiyo-e*). The latter refers to paintings that were produced to be viewed through an optical apparatus that had either the "reflective type" (*hansha-shiki*) or the "direct type" (*chokushi-shiki*) of lens. The former lens uses a mirror to reflect the image; the latter does not: "What is important about both [*megane-e* and *uki-e*] is that people enjoyed them in playful or recreational contexts. Moreover, both the viewing apparatus and the contrivance of using linear perspective were seen as 'tricks' to delight the human eye. Those tricks invited people to feel that they were standing in an actual scene or landscape, a sensation that added to the interest these images generated." Imanishi, *The Akita Ranga School*, 116–129.
51. Fukuoka, *The Premise of Fidelity*, 2.
52. Decades earlier, Rai San'yō composed a heptasyllabic ancient-style poem entitled "Song of a Dutch Ship" (Oranda sen no uta), representing a Dutch ship docking in Nagasaki in 1818. Aboard a skiff, the speaker observes the port patrol boats escort the ship to the quay. The lines below describe the ship's massive size and machinery:

> The barbarian ship in water reaches a hundred feet tall;
> A sea breeze faintly soughs, flags and fishnets billow.
> Three sails on timber yards, set by myriad lines of rope,
> With a pulley to hoist and lower them like a well sweep.

bansen mizu o idete hyakushaku takaku	蛮船出水百尺高
kaifū sekiseki toshite keibō o soyogasu	海風淅淅颼罽旄
sanpan hobashira o tatete bantō o hodokoshi	三帆樹桅施萬條
ki o mōkete shinshuku suru koto kekkō no gotoshi	設機伸縮如桔橰

Rai San'yō, *Rai San'yō shisen*, 88–93. The poem strives toward verisimilitude by describing the ship in detail—down to the block and tackle system used to set the sails—and by comparing the hoisting and lowering motion to a well sweep, a device that draws water from a well using a pulley mechanism. Cohen remarked in the case of European writing: "the real seas were in the vanguard of science, technology, communications, and commerce." Cohen, *The Novel and the Sea*, 117. San'yō's poem shows how this is also the case for early nineteenth-century Japan.

53. Naotake's painting *Shinobazu Pond* (1770; Shinobazu ike) exhibits these modern characteristics: reflection on water, distant perspective, chiaroscuro, fading blues in sky and water, and three-dimensional representation of objects. For images of sea-faring ships, see the images of Naotake's *Seascape from Takanawa* (Takanawa kakei-zu) and *Night Fishing* (Yachō-zu) in Imanishi, *The Akita Ranga School*, 121.

54. The color *sei* can also mean green, gray, and black. In the context of the poem it makes sense to read it as blue to mirror the blue that follows it, *ran*, which is also the word for indigo (*ai*).

55. Screech, *The Western Scientific Gaze*, 215–228. In Chinese poetry "climbing up high" (*deng gao*) has been a common theme, if not genre, since the Tang dynasty—for example, "Climbing High" (Deng gao) by Du Fu (712–770 CE). In the poem, the speaker ascends a tower and gazes upon an autumn landscape, whereupon he becomes overwhelmed by sadness. Saikō's poem incorporates this tradition as well (especially with the use of *bōbō*), but her poem is more about an optical illusion, rather than autumnal sadness.

56. Yonemoto, *Mapping Early Modern Japan*, 45.

57. Yonemoto: "in the case of both *haikai* and early modern tale literature, one can see not only an expansion of literary sensibility, but also a vernacularization of spatial concepts, as spatial and place-based references became the stuff of increasingly popular poetic and prose genres." Yonemoto, *Mapping Early Modern Japan*, 47.

58. The perceptual movement and confusion in Saikō's poem conjure the affective and dissonant wandering in eighteenth- and nineteenth-century English women's poetry. Ingrid Horrocks has shown how mobility in the Romantic tradition is a gendered genre in which literary works authored by women often depict the lyric subject as a poetic wanderer with feelings of anxiety about mobility. Horrocks argues that the poetic wanderer reveals the vulnerability of the modern subject, as people are increasingly subjected to movement throughout the world with the expansion of the British Empire. See Horrocks, *Women Wanderers*.

59. Imanishi, *The Akita Ranga School*, 251–275.
60. Itasaka Noriko, "The Woman Reader as Symbol."
61. Ibid.
62. See H. Li, "Didactic Readings" and Nakamachi, "*Genji* Pictures."
63. Nagase, "Women Writers of Chinese Poetry," 181–182.
64. Fukushima, *Joryū*, 73–79. I have modified the *kundoku* for Line 22.
65. For the reception of *Genji* in the Edo period see Caddeau, *Appraising* Genji.
66. Schaberg, "The Ruling Mind," 46.
67. Harper and Shirane, *Reading* The Tale of Genji, 440–441.
68. Tomiko Yoda highlights one of the contradictions in Norinaga's theory of *mono no aware,* arguing that communication in *Genji* often ends in failure. Yoda shows that the poetic responses delivered by women characters to their male suitor (Genji) and the intrusions by the narrator disrupt the romantic connection and consequently contradict the ideal of "communal harmony" in *mono no aware*. Yoda, "Fractured Dialogues."
69. Annotators Fukushima and Iritani and Kado have replaced the Chinese graph *shō* 鐘 (bell) in Saikō's manuscript with *shō* 鍾 (to gather, hence *atsumuru* in *kundoku*). The correction makes sense, but to address both meanings, I rendered the line "the emotion most resonant" as opposed to "the emotion that gathers the most."
70. Harper and Shirane, *Reading* The Tale of Genji, 471.
71. Woolf, "How Should One Read a Book?" 259.
72. Saikō's *keishū* persona evokes the contrarian persona that Qing poet Gu Zhenli (1623–1699) displayed in her poetry. Xiaorong Li has argued that Gu's alternative representation of the boudoir was a means of "articulating her idiosyncratic sense of self." X. Li, *Women's Poetry*, 88. Saikō likely read Gu, since she was familiar with late imperial Chinese women's poetry.
73. *SI*, 1: 63–65.
74. Fong, "Writing and Illness," 19–47.
75. Saikō represented the water clock, or clepsydra, in the following quatrain on a long summer day:

> Improvisation on a Summer Day
> The long days are like years, the water clock at noon drips slow;
> A steady fall of light rain, it is the season of ripening plums.

I take a long nap by the window, deep in my chamber it is quiet;
I even copy from the perfume box, four bedazzling poems.

kajitsu gūsaku	夏日偶作
eijitsu toshi no gotoku chūrō ososhi	永日如年晝漏遲
hibi taru saiu jukubai no toki	霏微細雨熟梅時
gosō nemuri tarite shinkei shizuka nari	午窓眠足深閨靜
nozomi etari kōren shien no shi	臨得香奩四艷詩

Fukushima, *Joryū*, 3.

76. Poem No. 12 of the "Nineteen Old Poems" from the Han dynasty ends with an abandoned woman longing to be reunited with her husband like a pair of swallows:

Heart racing, I fiddle with my inner belt,	馳情整中帶
Muttering softly, for a while pacing to and fro.	沉吟聊躑躅
Longing for us to become a pair of flying swallows,	思爲雙飛燕
I carry mud in my mouth and nest in the eaves of your house.	銜泥巢君屋

Koshigen, 204.

77. *SI*, 1: 130–132.

78. Saikō's poem evokes Li Bai's "On a Silent Night I Long," in which the speaker is lying in bed, and mistakes the bright moonbeams shining into his bedroom for frost glinting on the ground. He raises his head and gazes longingly at the bright moon, then lowers his head and longs for home:

By the foot of the bed I see moonlight:	牀前看月光
It looks like frost shining on the ground.	疑是地上霜
I raise my head, and gaze at the moon above the mountain;	舉頭望山月
I lower my head, and long for home.	低頭思故鄉

Tōshisen, 167–168.

79. Fong: "Generally constructed within the spatial location of the women's quarters, their poems draw on a limited lexicographical range that emphasizes acute bodily sensations of being cold and thin and a heightened level of sensory perception, particularly the auditory senses, often due to the inability to sleep at night. The persona hears the water clock

dripping and the wind blowing at night, the cock crowing and the orioles singing at dawn." Fong, "Writing and Illness," 33.

80. *SI*, 2: 375.
81. Fukushima, *Joryū*, 80–81.
82. John Hollander writes that both dreaming and poetry question the intentionality of the dreamer and the poet: "There are dreams in and out of poems, poems in and out of dreams. There is the common and interesting challenge that both poems and dreams pose to the idea of intentionality; both the dreamer and the poet could be said to will elements in each of these, but unwittingly." Hollander, *The Work of Poetry*, 78.
83. Sun, *The Poetics of Repetition*, 216.
84. Culler, *Theory of the Lyric*, 138.
85. By writing about her ill father, Saikō evokes a tradition of women's writing on the relationship between daughters and fathers. Esperanza Ramirez-Christensen has explored why the works of women writing at the intersection of the tenth and eleventh centuries in Japan "still touch us, and both comfort and distress us." Copeland and Ramirez-Christensen, *The Father-Daughter Plot*, 49–88.
86. Fukushima, *Joryū*, 82–84.
87. This reading comes from its usages in *Zhuangzi*. The Chinese graph *ki* 機 alone can mean "what gives birth to myriad things" as well as "the workings (of nature)."

REFERENCES

Berry, Paul. *Literati Modern: Bunjinga from Late Edo to Twentieth-Century Japan.* Seattle: University of Washington Press, 2008.

Blake, William. *The Prophetic Books of William Blake: Milton.* Edited by E.R.D. MacLagan and A.G.B. Russell. London: A.H. Bullen, 1907.

Bunshin chōryō. Edited by Toda Kōgyō. Vols. 64 and 65, *Shinshaku kanbun taikei.* 121 vols. Tokyo: Meiji Shoin, 1974.

Burwick, Frederick. *Romanticism: Keywords.* Chichester, England: John Wiley & Sons, Ltd., 2015.

Caddeau, Patrick W. *Appraising Genji: Literary Criticism and Cultural Anxiety in the Age of the Last Samurai.* New York: State University of New York Press, 2006.

Casey, Edward. *Representing Place: Landscape Painting and Maps.* Minneapolis: Minnesota University Press, 2002.

Cai, Zong-qi. *A Chinese Literary Mind: Culture, Creativity, and Rhetoric in Wenxin diaolong.* Stanford, CA: Stanford University Press, 2001.

Cohen, Margaret. *The Novel and the Sea.* Princeton, NJ: Princeton University Press, 2010.

Copeland, Rebecca, and Esperanza Ramirez-Christensen, eds. *The Father-Daughter Plot: Japanese Literary Women and the Law of the Father.* Honolulu: University of Hawaii Press, 2001.

Culler, Jonathan. *Theory of the Lyric.* Cambridge, MA: Harvard University Press, 2015.

Dickinson, Emily. *Dickinson: Selected Poems and Commentaries.* Edited by Helen Vendler. Cambridge, MA: The Belknap Press of Harvard University Press, 2010.

Egan, Ronald. *The Burden of Female Talent: The Poet Li Qingzhao and Her History in China.* Cambridge, MA: Harvard University Asia Center, 2013.

Ema Saikō. *Ema Saikō shishū Shōmu ikō.* 2 vols. Edited by Iritani Sensuke and Kado Reiko. Tokyo: Kyūko Shoin, 1992.

———. *San'yō sensei hiten: Shōmu shisō.* Edited by Kobayashi Tetsuyuki. Tokyo: Kyūko shoin, 1997.

Fister, Patricia. "Feminine Perceptions in Japanese Art of the Kinsei Era." *Japan Review* 8 (1997): 3–21.

———. *Japanese Women Artists 1600–1900.* Lawrence, KS: Spencer Museum of Art, University of Kansas, 1988.

Focillon, Henri. *The Life of Forms in Art.* Translated by George Kubler. New York: Zone Books, 1992.

Fong, Grace S., and Ellen Widmer, eds. *The Inner Quarters and Beyond: Women Writers from Ming through Qing.* Boston: Brill, 2010.

Fukushima Riko, ed. *Joryū: Ema Saikō, Hara Saihin, Yanagawa Kōran.* Vol. 3, *Edo kanshisen.* 4 vols. Tokyo: Iwanami Shoten, 1995.

Fukuoka, Maki. *The Premise of Fidelity: Science, Visuality and Representing the Real in Nineteenth-Century Japan.* Stanford, CA: Stanford University Press, 2012.

Harper, Thomas, and Haruo Shirane, eds. *Reading* The Tale of Genji: *Sources from the First Millennium.* New York: Columbia University Press, 2015.

Horrocks, Ingrid. *Women Wanderers and the Writing of Mobility, 1784–1814.* Cambridge, MA: Cambridge University Press, 2017.

Hollander, John. *The Work of Poetry.* New York: Columbia University Press, 1997.

Ibi Takashi. *Edo Shiikaron.* Tokyo: Kyūko shoin, 1998.

Imanishi, Riko. *The Akita Ranga School and the Cultural Context in Edo Japan.* Translated by Ruth S. McCreery. Tokyo: International House of Japan, 2016.

Itasaka Noriko. "The Woman Reader as Symbol: Changes in Images of the Woman Reader in Ukiyo-e." In *The Female as Subject: Reading and Writing in Early Modern Japan,* edited by P.F. Kornicki, Mara Patessio, and G.G. Rowley, 87–108. Ann Arbor: Center for Japanese Studies, University of Michigan, 2010.

Kile, Sarah E. "Toward an Extraordinary Everyday: Li Yu's (1611–1680) Vision, Writing, Practice." PhD diss., Columbia University, 2013.

Koshigen. Edited by Uchida Sen'nosuke. Vol. 4, *Kanshi taikei*. 24 vols. Tokyo: Shūeisha, 1964.

Kurokawa Momoko. "Ema Saikō jigasan 'bokuchikuzu' kō": sono hikari no hyōgen o megutte." *Wakan hikaku bungaku* 47 (August 2011): 54–76.

Li, Haruki. "Didactic Readings of *The Tale of Genji*: Politics and Women's Education." In *Envisioning* The Tale of Genji: *Media, Gender, and Cultural Production*, edited by Haruo Shirane, 157–170. New York: Columbia University Press, 2008.

Li, Xiaorong. *Women's Poetry of Late Imperial China: Transforming the Inner Chambers*. Seattle: University of Washington Press, 2012.

Li, Wai-yee. "Hiding Behind a Woman: Contexts and Meanings in Early Qing Poetry." In *The Rhetoric of Hiddenness in Traditional Chinese Culture*, edited by Paula M. Varsano, 99–122. New York: State University of New York Press, 2016.

Maurette, Pablo. *The Forgotten Sense: Meditations on Touch*. Chicago: The University of Chicago Press, 2018.

Mulhstein, Anka. *The Pen and the Brush: How Passion for Art Shaped Nineteenth-Century French Novels*. Translated by Adriana Hunter. New York: Other Press, 2017.

Nagase, Mari. "Women Writers of Chinese Poetry in Late-Edo Period Japan." PhD diss., University of British Columbia, 2007.

———. "'Truly, they are a lady's words': Ema Saikō and the Construction of an Authentic Voice in Late Edo Period Kanshi." *Japanese Language and Literature* 48, No. 2 (October 2014): 279–305.

Nakamachi, Keiko. "*Genji* Pictures from Momoyama Painting to Edo *Ukiyo-e*: Cultural Authority and New- Horizons." In *Envisioning* The Tale of Genji: *Media, Gender, and Cultural Production*, edited by Haruo Shirane, 171–210. New York: Columbia University Press, 2008.

Owen, Stephen. *An Anthology of Chinese Literature: Beginnings to 1911*. New York: W.W. Norton, 1996.

Rai San'yō. *Rai San'yō shisen*. Edited by Ibi Takashi. Tokyo: Iwanami Shoten, 2012.

Rouzer, Paul F. *Articulated Ladies: Gender and the Male Community in Early Chinese Texts*. Cambridge, MA: Harvard University Asia Center, 2001.

Samei, Maija Bell. *Gendered Persona and Poetic Voice: The Abandoned Woman in Early Chinese Song Lyrics*. New York: Lexington Books, 2004.

Schaberg, David. "The Ruling Mind: Persuasion and the Origins of Chinese Psychology." In *The Rhetoric of Hiddenness*, edited by Paula M. Varsano, 33–51. New York: State University of New York Press, 2016.

Screech, Timon. *The Western Scientific Gaze and Popular Imagery in Later Edo Japan*. Cambridge, MA: Cambridge University Press, 1996.

Shirane, Haruo, ed. *Early Modern Japanese Literature: An Anthology, 1600–1900*. New York: Columbia University Press, 2002.

Stewart, Susan. *Poetry and the Fate of the Senses*. Chicago: The University of Chicago Press, 2002.

Sun, Cecile Chu-chin. *The Poetics of Repetition in English and Chinese Lyric Poetry*. Chicago: The University of Chicago Press, 2011.

Su Shi. *Su Shi quan ji jiao zhu*. Edited by Zhang Zhilie, Ma Defu, and Zhou Yukai. 20 vols. Shijiazhuang Shi: Hebei ren min chu ban she, 2010.

Suzuki Ken'ichi. *Edo shiikashi no kōsō*. Tokyo: Iwanami Shoten, 2004.

Taketani Chōjirō and Uragami Shunkin. *Bunjin garon: Uragami Shunkin Rongashi hyōshaku*. Tokyo: Meiji shoin, 1988.

Tō shisen. Edited by Saitō Shō. Vol. 7, *Kanshi taikei*. 24 vols. Tokyo: Shūeisha, 1965.

Uragami Shunkin [Shunkin Gakujin]. *Rongashi*. 2 vols. N.P.: Jukeidō, 1842.

Woolf, Virginia. "How Should One Read a Book?" In *The Second Common Reader*, edited by Andrew McNeille, 258–270. New York: Harcourt, Inc., 1932.

Yang, Haihong. *Women's Poetry and Poetics in Late Imperial China: A Dialogic Engagement*. New York: Lexington Books, 2017.

Yoda, Tomiko. "Fractured Dialogues: *Mono no aware* and Poetic Communication in *The Tale of Genji*." *Harvard Journal of Asiatic Studies* 59, no. 2 (December 1999): 523–557.

Yonemoto, Marcia. *Mapping Early Modern Japan: Space, Place, and Culture in the Tokugawa Period, 1603–1868*. Berkeley: University of California Press, 2003.

———. *The Problem of Women in Early Modern Japan*. Berkeley: University of California Press, 2016.

CHAPTER 4

Representing Life in the Prose Poems of Masaoka Shiki

To imagine a language means to imagine a life-form.
—Ludwig Wittgenstein, *Philosophical Investigations* (1953)

Words are things, and a small drop of ink,
Falling like dew, upon a thought, produces
That which makes thousands, perhaps millions, think.
—Lord Byron, *Don Juan*, III: 88 (1821)

The body is the house of the mind;
the mind is the master of the body.
—Masaoka Shiki, *Propensity of the Brush* (1884)

This chapter examines how Masaoka Shiki (1867–1902) carried forth the legacy of *bunjin* culture into the Meiji period (1867–1912) and used literary form as an allegory for the life and death of the literati tradition. His lyricism combined the poetic artifices afforded by the literati repertoire with the realism of modern vernacular prose, creating organic forms—prose poems—that mediated his senses and feelings in symbiosis with literati culture.

Shiki was born into a samurai-class family at the start of Meiji and was one of the last modern writers to receive formal training in *bunjin* poetry

M. Mewhinney, *Form and Feeling in Japanese Literati Culture*,
https://doi.org/10.1007/978-3-031-11922-4_4

and painting. Over the course of his lifetime, he composed nearly 2000 *kanshi* and modernized the traditional poetic genres *haikai* and tanka (or *waka*).[1] The fruits of his labor included the emergence of *hokku* as a modern lyric genre called "haiku." By raising Japanese poetry to the level of the Western lyric Shiki participated in a national effort to forge a modern literary language. In concert with the *genbun'itchi* (unification of speech and writing) movement of the late 1880s and 1890s, Meiji writers aimed to abandon classical poetic tropes, experimenting in a new vernacular language that represented common everyday speech. The literary realism that emerged from this experiment laid the foundation for the modern Japanese novel (*shōsetsu*).

Shiki's experiments in the modern vernacular, however, held on to the poetic tropes and genres of the literati tradition. His brand of realism took form in a literary style called *shasei*, or "sketching from life," wherein the empirical representation of objects was informed by the pictorial realism and naturalism of nineteenth-century European painting and literature. Shiki was the progenitor of this style in Japanese literature; he employed it in haiku, tanka, and *kanshi*, as well as in various genres of "prose poems," including *haibun* (*haikai* prose), *zuihitsu* (essays), and *nikki* (diary).[2]

The term *shasei* has roots in the literati tradition. During the Edo period, *shasei* denoted a practice wherein the artist communed with a natural object and represented its "spirit-resonance" (*kiin*) in poetry and painting.[3] By the late nineteenth century, *shasei* had imported the conventions of Western-style realism, and had gained cultural currency as an ideal for modern artistic and literary composition by Japanese poets and painters.[4] In other words, *shasei* became a metonym for empirical and realist representation, referring to a work that represented an object "as is" (*ari no mama*) with accuracy, precision, and objectivity.[5]

The object of representation in *shasei* is "life," yet despite the style's purported objectivity, Shiki's *shasei* was personal, subjective, and ironic. It was informed by the poetics of Late Edo literati culture as well as by the lyricism and "science of feeling" of Anglo-European Romanticism. Shiki employed *shasei* in prose poems that evoked the Romantic ideal of "organic form"—a morphological metaphor for poetic form that unfolded naturally according to the thoughts, senses, and feelings of the poet. When tuberculosis left him bedridden, Shiki used the prose poem to represent his weak and fragile mind and body. In Japanese literary criticism, this representation has often been read as autobiography that conflates the represented Shiki with the historical Shiki. I, however, contend that for Shiki self-representation was a call made to order for a virtuosic poetic performance that speaks to John Paul Eakin's notion of "the theater of autobiography."[6] Thus when I refer to Shiki in the texts under examination, I mean the poetic Shiki performed by his speaker and/or his narrator.

This chapter tours various prose poems, organic forms in which Shiki represented his inner world: his essay *Propensity of the Brush* (1884–1892; Fudemakase), his travelogues *Journey Within a Journey Within a Journey* (1892; Tabi no tabi no tabi) and *Summer Ten Years Ago* (1898; Jūnen mae no natsu), and his deathbed narratives *A Drop of Ink* (1901; Bokujū itteki) and *A Six-foot Sickbed* (1902; Byōshō rokushaku). Each of these prose poems displayed the vital power of Shiki's poetic imagination and attempted to *sha-sei* in the literal sense—"represent-life" (*sha-sei*). The works simulated a living and dying organism through a discursive style of narrative prose interrupted by poetic references, quotations, and other tropes from Romanticism and the *bunjin* tradition. This chapter demonstrates how this contrapuntal narrative motion creates an organic rhythm through which Shiki both mediated his senses and feelings and represented the decline of literati culture.

LETTING THE BRUSH GO WHERE IT GOES

Shiki employed *shasei* in a series of prose poems or vignettes that display his idiosyncratic attitude as a modern *bunjin* blending elements from the literati tradition with modern ideas about sound and rhythm in poetry to create a new literary form. These vignettes were published in four volumes under the same title, *Propensity of the Brush* (1884–1892; Fudemakase). The tenuous—if not entirely absent—connection between the vignettes is one reason the work has been categorized as a *zuihitsu* (essay; lit. "following the brush"),[7] a prose genre practiced by writers as early as the thirteenth century.[8] By the late eighteenth and nineteenth centuries, *zuihitsu* had become a popular genre that embraced the empiricism of the age and represented daily life.

In *Propensity of the Brush*, Shiki displays his playful attitude toward genre, expressing an ambivalence about categorizing his own work as a *zuihitsu*. In the vignette "The *Zuihitsu* Style" (Zuihitsu no bunshō), Shiki calls the piece a *zuihitsu*, stressing that the work records his "inner thoughts" (*kokoro issun kanjitaru koto*):

We may call this *zuihitsu* my memorandum, we may call it my wild ramblings, but it is a recording of my inner thoughts as they are, so needless to say, there are many imperfections. I began writing the piece a few days ago, dashing off whatever comes to mind, faster than a locomotive, without concern for style or grammar: there's Japanese text, Chinese text, translated text; the grammar is classical, modern, and my own. Once I write something down, I don't review it or make corrections. So, read it with that in mind.[9]

Shiki argues that the representation of inner life requires a form that is free, unpredictable, and idiosyncratic, as well as unconstrained by a particular literary genre.

Shiki's disclaimers about inaccuracy and randomness describe the way his thoughts naturally take form on the page. In the title *Fudemakase*, or "propensity of the brush," "propensity" refers to the "propensity," or the Chinese word *shi* (J. *sei* or *ikioi*), that François Jullien describes as the natural movement of the brush in Chinese calligraphy.[10] By featuring this notion in his title, Shiki calls upon the traditional idea that a literatus becomes one with his brush, allowing it to go where it goes. And where it goes subscribes to the traditional principle of naturalness, which governs all of nature's forms—including the mind of the poet.[11]

During the mid-1880s, Japanese prose still resembled Edo styles of writing: a hodge-podge of classical Japanese and Chinese elements on the levels of rhetoric, diction, and syntax. Although the *genbun'itchi* debates were well in swing by the time Shiki began writing *Propensity of the Brush*, he chose to use the eclectic style of his Edo *bunjin* forebears.[12] The opening vignette "Poem in a Dream" (1884; Muchū no shi) exemplifies this style of language:

February 13, my cold severe, and I have no voice. In the middle of the night, I wake up from a dream, and hear snow falling on the window: in a dream or in a hallucination, I compose a couplet:

Falling on the window, a sound faint, softer than rain;
Spread out on the floor, colors bright, white like frost.

The next morning I wake up, and my heart is still hazy.

二月十三日風邪劇シク聲全ク出デズ　夜半夢驚クノ際雪ノ窓ヲ打ツヲ聞ク　夢カ幻カ一聯ヲ得タリ

mado o utsu koe sasayaka ni shite ame yori mo yawarakaku　　打窓聲小軟於雨
chi ni shiku iro akaruku shite shimo yori mo shiroshi　　　　鋪地色明白似霜

翌曉眠覚メテ後猶模糊心胸ニアリ[13]

The vignette pairs prose with poetry, resembling Edo *haibun*, while also displaying Shiki's fluency in *kanbun* and *kanshi*, or Chinese prose and poetry. The linguistic register is *kundoku* or *kundokutai*, which originated as a gloss for *kanbun* but became its own style of writing.[14] The style is marked by the use of *katakana* and the incorporation of *kanshi*, evident in the middle of the passage.

"Poem in a Dream" exemplifies how Shiki employs illness as a trope to access an alternate temporality through which his speaker can express a heightened awareness of sense and feeling. As Grace Fong has observed, in late imperial Chinese women's poetry, illness played a key role in poetic creation: "For them [late imperial Chinese women poets], the experience of illness—one of temporal duration—often functions as a prelude and even a pretext to writing."[15] In the previous chapter I examined how Ema Saikō used this trope to represent longing and solitude in the boudoir; Shiki, like other male *bunjin*, here borrowed the woman poet's voice to compose poems in the genre of the "boudoir plaint."[16] Although the poetic locus of his vignette is not necessarily the woman's inner chamber, the illness becomes a pretext for the dream or hallucination that follows, which takes form as verse.

Shiki's poems bring together the illness trope in literati culture with the trope of the ill and dying genius in Romanticism. Susan Sontag has described illness as a metaphor for "promoting the self as an image," a characteristic of modern subjectivity in nineteenth-century literature.[17] In this way, Shiki's "Poem in a Dream" also speaks to the "romantic view that illness exacerbates consciousness."[18]

Shiki is sick and cannot speak, so his surroundings speak for him. He hears the sound of falling snow, which is loud enough to stir an ill man with heightened sensitivity. Chinese verse gives his prose a sonic dimension in two lines of verse that form a parallel couplet (or *tsuiku*) in Chinese poetry.

The sound of falling snow and its subsequent figuration in lines of verse display Shiki's facility to use language to mediate different sensory experiences. Susan Stewart argues that "poems compel attention to aspects of rhythm, rhyme, consonance, assonance, onomatopoeia, and other forms and patterns of sound to which attention is not necessarily given in the ongoing flow of prose."[19] The first line opens with the same phrase from the prose—"falling on the window" (*mado o utsu*)—but moves to describe the texture of that sound. The adjective "soft" (*yawarakaku*) describes the audibility of snowfall and its weight and texture. But what does the snow look like? The speaker appears only to hear the sound of snowfall, not to see it. In the second line, sound mediates a transition to a view of moon-light shining on the bedroom floor, which figures the white of the snow. Stewart writes that sound does not intrinsically have a spatial dimension, unlike vision: "We see properly only what is before us, but sound can envelop us; we might, as we move or change, have varying experiences of sound's intensity, but it will not readily 'fit' an epistemology of spatiality, horizon, or location."[20] Stirred by the faint sound of snow falling on the window, Shiki uses line 2 to create a spatial dimension that mediates the sound through the vision of moonlight shining "white like frost."

There are many poems on the plight of the sleepless poet, including Tang poet Li Bai's "On a Silent Night I Long" and Saikō's "Sleepless on a Bright Moon Night," discussed in the previous chapter of this book. In Li Bai's poem, the speaker is lying in bed and mistakes the bright moon-beams shining into his bedroom for frost glinting on the ground. He raises his head and gazes longingly at the moon, then lowers his head and longs for home. As we have seen, Saikō echoes Li Bai's nostalgia in her poem, but Shiki's verse instead breaks off at the image of frost and returns to prose, whereupon we discover that the speaker returns to sleep, but awakes with the same feeling he had before going to bed: "my heart is still hazy" (*moko shinkyō ni ari*). The word *shinkyō* also includes his heart and state of mind, both of which are *moko*, which means "hazy," "indistinct," and "dreamy." Here, Shiki alludes to the opening lines of a poem by Bai Juyi (772–846 CE), anthologized in *Complete Poems of the Tang* (1705; Quan Tang Shi):

Night after night the river and clouds are dark and brooding; 連夜江雲黃慘澹
At daybreak the mountain snow is white and indistinct.   平明山雪白模糊[21]

The allusion to Bai Juyi reveals that the sensation of snow remains with Shiki, almost hauntingly, even after he wakes up: snow transforms into a visual image of his inner feelings, the state of being hazy and indistinct. In other words, while the sound of snow is no longer audible at dawn, its lasting impression can be found in the heart and mind of the speaker as a blankness, an opacity, and an ineffable feeling, soft and fragile as a snowflake.

Shiki's concentration on the sound of falling snow throughout the opening vignette of *Propensity of the Brush* suggests that the work as a whole is interested in the possibilities of language to represent sensory experience. By entitling the vignette "Poem in a Dream," Shiki comments on the experience of lyric as something overheard: poetry is like hearing a sound that makes you want to visualize it, to touch it, and to grant it some palpability so that you can know it. Listening in this way functions as a critical medium for other sensory experiences. In her discussion of German poet Johann Gottfried Herder (1744–1803), Stewart observes that hearing is a "middle" sense that mediates the subject's connection to vision and touch:

> ...it [hearing] mediates the vagueness of touch and the cold brightness of vision; it negotiates the partiality of the immediacy of touch and the objectified 'all at onceness' of vision; and it stands between those objects of touch that are as mute as the fell of dark and those objects of vision that are endlessly describable. Whereas vision and touch refer to stationary objects, hearing indicates movement and change and so hearing is especially conducive to the transformation and unfolding of language.[22]

This same transformation and unfolding of language is evident in how Shiki moves from prose to poetry and back to prose again, an effect that reproduces the experience of hearing a poem being read aloud. In this way, "Poem in a Dream" is a prose poem about poetry, showing how the speaker makes sensory connections with objects using the shifts and changes of language.

The vignettes that follow "Poem in a Dream" reveal Shiki's thoughts on topics of all kinds, among them language, orthography, friendship, happiness, art, literature, music, poetry, letter writing. This overwhelming degree of diversity is his way of exploring the transformative possibilities of language that Stewart raises: this work, as well as his later writings, performs this dynamic relationship in language by mediating different senses, thoughts, and feelings.

This movement in language was informed by Shiki's reading of English philosopher and scientist Herbert Spencer (1820–1903). Shiki wrote a vignette about Spencer's *Philosophy of Style* (1852), in which he argued with Spencer about his claims regarding the economy of mental energy. By mental energy, Spencer meant the mental faculties that we use in the process of reading; he argued that, the more difficult the text, the more reading it depletes our mental energy. This is why in his opening section, "The Principle of Economy Applied to Words," Spencer wrote, on the conveyance of thought, that "the more simple and the better arranged its parts, the greater will be the effect produced."[23] Shiki's concern was what constituted that "effect," and what happens in the heart and mind of the reader through the process of reading. While Spencer argued that the more time we spend over a sentence, the less we gain from it, Shiki contended that sentences that require longer contemplation are the most fascinating.

Spencer cited lines from the Romantic poets, arguing that poetry is superior to prose because of its precision and economy of words. Inspired by this idea, Shiki exclaimed, at the end of the vignette: "the most concise style is the best style" (*sai kantan no bunshō wa sairyō no bunshō nari*), a notion that resonates with his later campaign to reform haiku and let it stand autonomously, cut off from the linked-verse tradition. He quoted English rhetorician Richard Whately (1787–1863)—"Men find pleasure in attaining meaning beyond language"—and replied: "I find pleasure when the writer has mastered the technique of suggestiveness in short sentences."[24] The ideas of "meaning beyond language" (*gengo igai no imi*) and "suggestiveness" (*yoi*) can be found in Shiki's experiments in prose and poetry.

Shiki's discursive meditations on the constitution of literature and the possibilities of language (evident in the range of topics and registers of language that constitute *Propensity of the Brush*) were informed by Spencer's views on the "rhythmical structure" of poetry, namely how such movement makes feelings communicable between poet and reader:

> There is one peculiarity of poetry conducing much to its effect—the peculiarity which is indeed usually thought its characteristic one—still remaining to be considered: we mean its rhythmical structure. This, improbable though it seems, will be found to come under the same generalization with the others. Like each of them, it is an idealization of the natural language of strong emotion, which is known to be more or less metrical if the emotion be not too violent; and like each of them it is an economy of the reader's or hearer's attention. In the peculiar tone and manner we adopt in uttering versified language, may be discerned its relationship to the feelings; and the pleasure which its measured movement gives us, is ascribable to the comparative ease with which words metrically arranged can be recognized.[25]

Spencer argued that poetry is pleasurable because of meter. When a reader or listener becomes aware of this structure, exemplified by rhyme and rhythm, he can discern the poet's feelings. Speaking to this point, Shiki ended his vignette on Spencer's essay with poetry:

I am truly wandering inside the boundless indistinctness of cloud and fog.
余は實ニ雲霧茫々の中に彷徨しつつあるもの也。[26]

Shiki employed the four-character phrase *unmu bōbō*, or "boundless indistinctness of cloud and fog," as a metaphor for the recondite thoughts and feelings of the human mind and heart. He wrote that the speaker is "wandering" (*hō'ō*), a rhyme with *bōbō*—the dense, vast, and indistinct space that cloud and fog occupy. The line is in prose, but Shiki's usage of figurative language points to "meaning beyond language" with all its "suggestiveness." Most striking is how the line presents the speaker moving in a space pregnant with anxious feeling. The sections to follow will continue to explore this space in his other prose poems.

Mind and Landscape

Shiki blended the traditional idea of *shasei* as the merging of mind and landscape with the Romantic idea of returning to nature after having been alienated from it. As a poet who liked to roam in "boundless indistinctness," he recorded his feelings of wonder and anxiety while traveling, including a short piece called *A Journey Within a Journey Within a Journey* (1892; Tabi no tabi no tabi), in which he recounts his trip to Hakone.[27] (From here forward, I refer to this piece as simply *Journey*.) The language of the travelogue resembles *haibun* (*haikai* prose) works from the Edo period. In *haibun* pieces about travel, the writer describes a place and inserts haiku to distill his or her thoughts and feelings about a particular observation of the natural environment.

Shiki's descriptions of the natural landscape in *Journey* have continuity with *haibun* and the travelogue tradition in how the lyric subject abandons himself to spiritual communion with the natural object under empirical observation. They also evoke Romantic fascination with the sublime and the beautiful, as discussed by William Wordsworth in his essay "The Sublime and the Beautiful" (1811–1812).[28] The following examination shows how Shiki's mind reconciles these two aesthetic categories when his first-person narrator reaches the summit of a mountain in Hakone and gazes at Mt Fuji towering in the distance.

The travelogue begins with the sound of a steam engine whistle, marking the narrator's departure from Tokyo:

> The steam whistle blew [*kiteki issei*], I left the capital behind, and in one day watched fifty-three stations go by. The exquisite views of the riverside towns and mountain hamlets were more fugitive than cloud and smoke passing before the eye [*un'en kagan*], ever more fleeting than the sight of famous ruins on the signboards of photography shops, that after one glance, they were gone without a trace. Someone would call this a journey. This journey is no different from a dream.[29]

The narrative opens with *kiteki issei*, a four-character Chinese compound that means "the steam whistle blew." Its sound carries over to the following sequence of words, and like vanishing plumes of smoke, the capital recedes from view, and along with it fifty-three train stations. The rhetoric of the opening description is Romantic, painting an image of the traveler stepping out of the city and making a foray into the enchanting space of the countryside. The narrator pairs the image of the fleeting capital with the image of the fugitive towns, using a Chinese metaphor to do so: *un'en kagan* (Ch. *yun yan guo yan*), or "cloud and smoke passing before the eye." The locus classicus of the phrase is "Record of the Hall of Treasured Paintings" (Baohui tang ji), an essay by Song dynasty literatus Su Shi (1037–1101).[30] As I discussed in the previous chapters of the present volume, the writings of Su Shi had a profound influence on Japanese literati culture. Here, Shiki used figurative language from the literati tradition to describe the fleeting beauty of a modern rural landscape.

To reinforce the feeling of fleetingness, the narrator compares the exquisite bucolic landscape to the advertisements of ruins posted outside a photography shop. By the late Edo period, travel had become more convenient because of new roads and infrastructure. As Kate McDonald has observed, by the Meiji period in the late nineteenth century, with the emergence of Japan as an imperial power, tourism and travel had become a critical tool for broadening the social imagination alongside the expansion of the empire.[31] During this period, Japan created an image of itself as a nation state with a national language and cultural heritage, and photography became important for visualizing and disseminating ideas associated with that cultural past and identity. The narrator's comment on the photography shop signboards betrays a subtle lamentation about the speed by which the modern subject encounters an image in a single glance (*ichibetsu*), only to forget it, as it leaves no trace (*ato kata o todomezu*). In order to categorize the fleetingness of such images, especially those associated with the historical past, the narrator assumes a third-person perspective, calling his experience a *tabi*, or "journey." Rehearsing the cliché of fugitive experience in premodern literature, he compares the journey to a dream interwoven with mournful feelings for the fleeting beauty of the countryside at the expense of modernization.

The repetition of words in the prose creates a rhythm similar to that of premodern oral performance, when the performer would utter a word, and qualify it in the next sentence by repeating the phrase. This rhythm continues as the narrator describes his journey into the countryside, conjuring the space of the rural demimonde:

> When I tap on my hand a cup of wine suddenly appears; when I tap on my wallet, a beautiful woman with a nice smile shows up later. Someone would call this a hotel. This hotel is very noisy like a communal villa. I felt an affinity to a previous life where the straps on my sandals would wear away after climbing a hill for a few miles, my reward for pilgrimaging into the unknown, where I would be scolded by the road-horse man and ridiculed by the palanquin bearer for setting out aimlessly on the road, treading on white clouds and picking herbs and blossoms. Only in these moments can one truly understand *mono no aware*.[32]

The narrator seems to enjoy romping in rustic places with fine wine and fine women at the snap of his finger. In homage to itinerant poets from the past, he describes this feeling as akin to a former life (*tashō*) in which he would be pilgrimaging with horses and carriage, traveling without a destination and merely "treading on white clouds and picking herbs and blossoms." As he dreams about walking on sunshine, he writes that these are the moments when a person can truly understand *mono no aware* (lit. "the pathos of things"). When a poet feels *mono no aware*, an emotion wells up from within, and he usually composes a poem to distill and encapsulate it.

The narrator writes that he has been traveling in the "floating world" (*ukiyo*) for twenty-five years, has been away from his hometown in the south for ten years, and has been away from Tokyo for ten days. Struck by the repetition of his peripatetic movements he composes the following haiku, from which the title of the piece derives:

> A journey within a journey
> Within another journey
> In the autumn wind.

tabi no tabi / sono mata tabi no / aki no kaze
旅の旅その又旅の秋の風 [33]

The repetition of *tabi* on the one hand illustrates Shiki's playful lyricism, which also evokes the cyclical nature of Buddhist thought; on the other, it bespeaks a modern fascination with numbers and enumeration in modern poetry.

Evident in *Propensity of the Brush* and many other prose works that fit under the umbrella of *zuihitsu* is Shiki's passion for counting, listing, and cataloguing. Seth Jacobowitz has viewed this as the poet's fascination with creating archives of information—an obsession symptomatic of a modern media overload. [34] I would also argue that the excessiveness of enumeration and repetition in Shiki's oeuvre gives form to feelings of infinitude, as well as to Romantic anxiety about the unhappiness of recollection, echoing ideas discussed by Danish philosopher Søren Kierkegaard (1813–1855). In the haiku above, one journey follows another in an almost endless cycle of repetition, only to find company in the autumn wind. In *haikai* poetry, the autumn wind functions as a *kigo* (seasonal referent); here it also works as an ironic figure for autumnal sadness. While the repetition of *tabi* initially produces a comic effect, the elation of humor is soon deflated by the biting cold of the autumn wind.

The rest of *Journey* represents Shiki's feelings about the enchanting landscape of Hakone. The narrator's descriptions in prose are regularly distilled by poems. When he reaches the summit of a mountain in Hakone, he is struck by his view of Lake Ashi and begins to express fear and wonder as he describes the landscape unfolding before his eyes:

> After climbing the peaks of mountains stretching for a thousand leagues, and breaking off fragments of the hanging white clouds, I reached the summit. How vast my heart felt the first time I set eyes on the polished mirror of Lake Ashi! Enraptured by the superbly exquisite view, and unable to stand, I sat on a tree stump and just stared continuously: the mountains grew all the more quiet when the wind was still, and the cold felt like winter, creeping up from my feet and spreading through every corner of my body through the crown of my head. [35]

The opening of the passage immediately evokes the "Climbing High" (Ch. *deng gao*) trope in classical Chinese poetry, in which the poet would ascend a tower or mountain and look out at the vast landscape before him.[36] White clouds (*hakuun*) evoke the dreamy and ethereal space of the immortal realm, where Daoists transcend the vulgar world and indulge in drink and merriment.

Whereas many classical Chinese poems about climbing high often end in poignant reflections about the distant past, the narrator's description tarries in the ecstasy of the present and displays a Romantic fascination with the unfamiliar landscape. The image he paints in words conjures the painting in oil of the peripatetic poet staring into a vast expanse of rolling clouds and smoke depicted in *Wanderer Above the Sea of Fog* (1818) by German Romantic painter Caspar David Friedrich (1774–1840). Philip Fisher has called wonder the sudden recognition of a visual presence: "Wonder and learning are tied by three things: by suddenness, by the moment of first seeing, and by the visual presence of the whole state or object."[37] Shiki's narrator sees Lake Ashi for the first time; the vastness of the unfolding landscape maps onto his heart and mind; and his body feels paralyzed by ecstasy (*kōkotsu*).

His rapture continues as he gazes into the landscape and describes in detail what he sees and feels. What he perceives seems to be a combination of the sublime and the beautiful. The more he stares the more he finds quietude: the farther his gaze passes into the dark density of the valley, the quieter it grows; the wind is still, and yet a wintry cold penetrates his entire body. The way the cold envelopes his body, indicated by the verb *shimiwataru* (to penetrate and spread throughout), suggests that the feeling is overwhelming. Wordsworth writes: "Where the beautiful and the sublime co-exist in the same object, if that object be new to us, the sublime always precedes the beautiful in making us conscious of its presence."[38] After or mid-trance, Shiki's narrator describes rare and placid views of the local wildlife:

> Wagtails were flying past each other over the waves, swiftly coming, swiftly going. Struggling in the autumn wind, the butterflies fluttered about powerlessly, hovering over and grazing the water surface—who knew that a mountain peak in Hakone could be so comforting![39]

He seems to be most struck by these creatures' movement in flight. Wagtails weave in and out of each other's path; butterflies brave the autumn wind, struggling to stay above the water, but just barely. The solace and comfort (*kokoro-zuyoshi*) he feels comes not only from the crisp clarity of the view but also from his identification with these creatures, which reify the feeling of rapture and ecstasy in concrete images. The adverbs used to describe the flight of the wagtails—*tachimachi* (suddenly)—and the butterflies—*hirahira* (flutteringly)—echo the abstract and indistinct feeling of the rapture: in a perpetual state of flux moving at a pace beyond one's control.

The narrator then gazes into the distance, where he discovers the stately, symbolic, and sublime image of Mt Fuji, a powerful presence that stirs yet more feelings of awe:

> Far away in the sky I found only white clouds, but above them there was Mt. Fuji towering still, reaching what even from here looks like three thousand fathoms. Its shadow sunk down so far and deep that on the water surface its image wrinkled with the ripples. Nothing could be more impressive.[40]

He notices that the same white clouds that he found at the summit in Hakone stretch far away into the sky, where Mt Fuji towers in all its magnificence. Wordsworth writes that when we encounter the sublime, the sensation we feel resolves itself in three parts: "a sense of individual form; a sense of duration; a sense of power." Shiki's description of Mt Fuji strikes all three. The adverbial phrase "towering still" (*kotsuzen toshite*) suggests the solid and singular presence of the mountain. The narrator even estimates how much taller it stands from his perspective on the summit of a mountain in Hakone. But what strikes him the most, giving us a sense of duration and of the concomitant presence of august power, is Fuji's shadow: as it falls onto the surface and into the depths of Lake Ashi, its image ripples. Wordsworth again: when the form of the object meets with duration, then we feel a sense of the sublime. The narrator ends the description with a statement that comes close: "Nothing could be more impressive" (*mata naku okashi*). The adjective *okashi* has multiple meanings, but in literary contexts it often describes an object (or person) that is extraordinary, fascinating, charming, or magnificent.

Once the narrator descends the mountain, he discovers a ruin that inspires him to compose a tanka. This composition evokes the Japanese poetic tradition and reifies the modern romanticism about ruins displayed in the photography shop advertisements. The scene encapsulates the meaning behind *utamakura* (lit. "poem-pillow"), the poetic toponyms

for famous places that are represented in *waka*. The Hakone Barrier
(Hakone no seki) is not a traditional poetic toponym since it was constructed in the early Edo period, but Shiki makes it an *utamakura* in
his poem:

> From there, I descended the mountain, and as far as I could see, everything
> was pampas grass. I wondered where Hakone Barrier was, but there was no
> one to ask, and no traces to seek. Thinking it could be an *utamakura*, I
> compose a *waka*:

> The barrier keepers
> Beckon me—
> I come and take a look:
> The ends of pampas grass ears,
> And the wind passing through.

> *sekimori no / maneku ya sore to / kite mireba / obana ga sue ni / kaze*
>   *wataru nari*
> 関守のまねくやそれと来て見れば尾花が末に風わたるなり [41]

Shiki did not begin promoting *shasei* in his campaign to reform Japanese
poetry until the mid-1890s, making this tanka an early example of his realism. While making the Hakone Barrier an *utamakura* would seem to contradict *shasei* ideals by linking the poem to convention and the entire
poetic tradition, Shiki composed a poem that fits the bill for a classical
waka and also represents a scene a poet beholds outside the poetic tradition. The barrier keepers (*sekimori*) are a metaphor for the panicles of
blooming pampas grass flowers that wave to the poet as the wind passes
through them.

The blandness and banality of the scene also exemplify Shiki's ideas
about *shasei*—including the inseparability of life from death. Pampas grass
(*obana*; also *susuki*) is one of the Seven Herbs (*nanakusa*) of autumn,
appearing in poems as early as *Collection of Ten Thousand Leaves* (ca. 759
CE; Man'yōshū); it is often used as a trope for a former lover beckoning
the poet. As a seasonal referent for autumn, the tone of poems on pampas
grass is often mournful and bittersweet, like in Shiki's poem. The "ends"
(*sue*) indicate the part of the pampas grass flowers that wave in the wind,
but also suggest that their life is reaching an end.

Late in his life, Yosa Buson left a *hokku* on pampas grass that evokes the
sadness and morbidity associated with the autumn plant:

> The mountain darkens,
> On the moor at twilight:
> Ears of pampas grass.

yama wa karete / no wa tasogare no / susuki kana
山は暮れて野は黄昏の薄かな [42]

As scholars Ogata Tsutomu and Morita Ran have observed, Buson's *hokku* paints a twilight scene in which the sunset leaves the mountain falling into darkness (*kurete*) while meanwhile, on the moor, the ears of pampas grass glimmer faintly in the remaining light. Buson, ever the painter, here places light and dark in opposition, creating a scene in which darkness increasingly envelops the landscape. In Buson's poetry, darkness inspires wonder just as much as light does. Shiki held Buson in high esteem and used his elder's poetry to promote his own modern views on *shasei* and to reform modern haiku.[43] Shiki viewed Buson as a *shasei* poet par excellence because of his "objective beauty" (*kyakkanteki bi*), a characteristic that became one of the tenets of modern *shasei*.

Like Buson's poem, Shiki's tanka depicts an autumn landscape. While the former is entirely visual, the latter refigures what the poet hears with what he sees. When describing experiences of wonder, Fisher writes that the visual comes front and center, especially in poetry: "Lyric poetry has always, among the arts of time, had uniquely potent means to reach out for the effects of wonder that are more at home in the visual. In language it is the work of familiar syntactic structures and the work of grammar that builds in a strong component of expectation at every moment."[44] Buson's and Shiki's poems fall under the umbrella of *shasei* poetry in that they both describe what the poet immediately sees "as is," yet both poems rely on the traditional trope of the pampas grass in order to express a farewell and a feeling of sadness.

A Buson-like painterly aesthetic can be found in many of Shiki's poems, as well as in the descriptions of natural landscapes in his prose pieces. Years later, he wrote another travelogue entitled *Summer Ten Years Ago* (1898; Jūnen mae no natsu; from here on, shortened to *Summer*), a retrospective piece on a journey he made to Nikkō in Tochigi Prefecture.[45] Like his earlier travelogue, *Summer* juxtaposes prose with poetry to describe the natural landscape. But the lapse in time from when Shiki made the journey to when he sat down to recount it changes the tone of his remembrance. The tone of *Summer* is more philosophical, and he exhausts the possibilities of language in order to communicate to the reader the experience of beholding beauty via a recollection.[46] Shiki's recollection also tries to restore a past experience by recounting the sights and sounds of a personal encounter with the sublime and the beautiful.

The opening to *Summer* sounds Wordsworthian: "When I look back, twelve years have passed."[47] Like Wordsworth in "Lines Composed a Few Miles above Tintern Abbey" (1798), Shiki begins his piece with a temporal rupture, and uses the remainder of the narrative to fill in what has been lost over time. The narrator romanticizes his youth, writing that then he was young and healthy, with unlimited hope and ambition. We learn that he ends up traveling with four other friends from Tokyo to Nikkō, on a quest to "traverse mountains and waters and exhaust the patterns of nature" (*sansui o basshō shite shizen no aya o kiwamen*).[48] As a retrospective piece, *Summer* transports the past into the present through visual description informed by modes of representation in painting. When he visits Tōshōgū Shrine, the resting place of Edo period founder Tokugawa Ieyasu (1543–1616), the narrator describes what he sees as "painted landscapes" (*gakei*) and "strange views" (*kikan*):

> The next day, we went to Tōshōgū. On heaven and earth a painted landscape of a single red bridge surrounded by nothing but green, and a strange view of myriad stocks of cryptomeria and moss of three hundred years covering the withered bones of a hero—these sensations stirred my mind and heart in material [*yūkei*] and immaterial [*mukei*] ways.[49]

His visual observations of the area surrounding Tokugawa's grave stir feelings and sensations (*kanji*) that "have form" (*yūkei*), denoting a visible or corporeal manifestation, and that "lack form" (*mukei*), denoting an invisible or spiritual manifestation. The way he describes his sensations echoes earlier claims in the piece where he talks about his "heart's intent" (*kokorozashi*) as being formless and in constant flux, but also certain that future opportunities await him on the journey. Some of this hope for what he and his fellow travelers will encounter comes from his discernment: he writes that knowing the philosophy of art allows one to judge the beautiful (*bi*) from the ugly (*shū*).[50] The tone of *Summer* thus differs from *Journey*: whereas the latter reads more in line with the travelogue genre, *Summer* becomes an aesthetic treatise as well as a paean to the sublime and the beautiful.

When he arrives at Kegon Falls, the narrator describes the sublime and beautiful mountain landscape. The companions visit waterfalls and a lodge by Lake Chūzenji, located at the foot of Mt Nantai: "When we were finally deep in the mountain, the thicket of trees was different from anything on earth."[51] Before the nineteenth century, Lake Chūzenji was regarded as a sacred place; from the Meiji period onward it became a popular tourist site for Japanese and foreigners alike.[52] Writing a retrospective piece in 1898, Shiki emphasized the lake's unfamiliarity—a Romantic way of rediscovering beauty that had been lost. Such recompense can be found in the narrator's description of what he sees and feels:

> When I first set eyes on Lake Chūzenji, I knew it was a place I could never forget. Mountain verdure as dense as darkness, the appearance of the water a tranquility that pierces bone, the air sunk into stillness, the lonely rays of the setting sun glimmered, coldness like the forehead of a dead man, tree leaves quiet like a mouth in a portrait, moss from eons ago without human traces, mysterious plants unknown to a botanist—struck by all these strange and wondrous sensations, I could do nothing but join the silence around me.[53]

This description evokes the description of Lake Ashi in *Journey*, but moves in a different direction by emphasizing the landscape's alienness. The metaphors in the passage evoke life as much as death. Shiki represents a sensitivity to his body interwoven with a dark and deadly atmosphere as still as a portrait or a landscape painting. As the narrator describes objects that are unknown to man and unknown to science, he paints a scene of unfamiliarity that stirs sensations "strange and wondrous" (*kii*), rendering him nonplussed and silent.

As he finds himself unable to do anything but join the silence of his natural surroundings, he begins to lose his footing in time and space, and ultimately his sense of self:

> After coming here, the feeling of summer was first to disappear from my mind, followed by the feeling of being in the world, and then when I had finally lost all sense of self amid the awesomeness, I sensed a single beam of life moving through the myriad forms silent around me. It was as if this was the first time here that I could feel mystical beauty.[54]

Shiki's description anticipates William James's (1842–1910) discussion of mystical experiences in "The Varieties of Religious Experience" (1902), in which he argued that the subject loses a sense of self when he feels overcome by the Other—in the case of *Summer*, nature itself.[55] As the narrator is overcome by its "awesomeness" (*bōzen toshite*), he senses a "single beam of life" (*ichidō kakki*) moving through every living thing around him, and comes to the realization that he has felt "mystical beauty" (*shinpiteki bi*).

In a state of ecstasy, his mind enters a trance that abandons him to thought, feeling, and desire, leaving him seeking to experience the moment forever, whereupon he composes a haiku to capture the moment in seventeen syllables:

> From then on, thoughts of staying here at Lake Chūzenji went back and forth ceaselessly in my mind, as mystery constantly awaited me. Indistinct [*kō tari* 恍たり], profound [*kotsu tari* 惚たり], alluring [*kei tari* 盼たり], beautiful [*sen tari* 倩たり].

> The moon on the water,
> The chill of the night—
> There are spirits.

> *tsuki ni mizu / suzushiki yūbe / kami aran*
> 月に水涼しき夕神あらん [56]

Like the near paralysis the narrator in *Journey* experiences on the Hakone summit, gazing at Lake Ashi and Mt Fuji, the narrator in *Summer* is stunned by Lake Chūzenji. As his thoughts ceaselessly move back and forth, entering a state of limbo, language starts to break down: the stative verb *kōkotsu* (entranced; enraptured) splits into its constituent elements *kō* (indistinct) and *kotsu* (profound), and *senben* (attractive eyes and mouth) splits into *ben* (alluring) and *sen* (beautiful). In the classical Chinese tradition, these words are used to describe a poet's encounter with beauty, often personified by a goddess.[57]

As the narrator's thoughts break down into lone adjectives without a clear object, he composes a haiku to distill a scene of light and dark: moonlight shines on the water and a chill fills the night air, whereupon the speaker senses the presence of the divine.[58] The final measure of the verse—*kami aran*—indicates the presence of either one or multiple spirits, but considering the Shinto belief that deities exist in all living things, the divine presence is likely more than one. Among unfamiliar sights painterly and strange, Shiki has a mystical experience in which he encounters the sublime and the beautiful. These encounters inspired him to compose lyric poems and also to shape his prose into poetry. Shiki displayed this poetry with representations of his thoughts, feelings, and sensations that occur when he perceives a natural object or landscape that forces him to suggest meaning beyond words.

In his travelogues and retrospective prose poems about the beauty of Hakone and Nikkō, Shiki engaged with the poetic tradition and represented his encounters with nature. Where nature was the object of representation in *shasei*, Shiki represented the sensual experience of encountering landscape, a realism that is informed by the poetics of late imperial *kanshi*, literati painting, Spencer's philosophy, and Romantic ideas of the sublime.

A Small Drop of Ink

Shiki continued his *shasei* experiments to the very end of his life in death-bed narratives where he made his own ill body the object of representation. By the start of the twentieth century, Shiki was writing in the new vernacular language of *genbun'itchi*, but he did not entirely abandon tropes and genres from Late Edo literati culture. Instead, he integrated them with modern prose in lyrical, discursive, fragmentary, biographical, and encyclopedic prose poems that were published in daily installments in the newspaper *Nippon*. In a prose poem entitled *A Drop of Ink* (1901; Bokujū itteki), Shiki created a poetics of irony, representing life as illness and impending death. Illness influences the form of the work, manifesting in shifts across registers, genres, and languages. In his final poems, Shiki represented his ailing body as a polygonal picture comprising a multitude of dissonant fragments held together tenuously by rhythm and repetition.

The Japanese title *Bokujū itteki* has been interpreted as a metaphor for writing about life. As Janine Beichman writes, "the title of *A Drop of Ink* shows how closely he [Shiki] identified his words with life, for the ink of the title was a metaphor for his life's blood."[59] The association between words and blood is evident in the prose poem, which reads like a diary in that every installment ends with a date of composition, and the register of language is personal and vernacular. *A Drop of Ink* also opens with keen observations of objects around the poet's body, and ends with a humorous discussion on how to compose haiku on sushi. In one installment, the speaker lists ten tanka that he composes extemporaneously, and declares that "there is no order" (*junjo nashi*).[60] This declaration serves as meta-commentary on the rambling and organic quality of the entire piece.

Jean-Jacques Origas has observed in his reading of Shiki's deathbed narratives that there is a sensuous logic that organizes Shiki's thoughts.[61] His thoughts about the senses are mediated by poetry. Considering the number of poems that punctuate prose throughout the work's installments, the title *A Drop of Ink* also seems to suggest that everything—words, objects, discourses about poetry and painting, people, history itself—becomes an object of observation and contemplation. In this way, the prose poem transcends autobiography, as its words stir the imagination of readers, transporting them toward myriad possibilities of meaning.

The title and the function of its words allude to the opening lines of a stanza in canto III of the long satiric poem *Don Juan* by English Romantic poet Lord Byron (1788–1824): "Words are things, and a small drop of ink, / Falling like dew, upon a thought, produces / That which makes thousands, perhaps millions, think."[62] Shiki owned a collection of Byron's works, so it is possible that he had the Englishman in mind. Like *Propensity of the Brush*, from over a decade earlier, *A Drop of Ink* falls under the umbrella of *zuihitsu*, but its language is more diverse, and its content dwells on the public as much as the personal in its discursive and polemical discussions on painting and poetry. Shiki's sensual tour of different languages, registers, and genres in the latter work speaks to how words, to echo Byron, "make[s] thousands, perhaps millions, think."

How words function in *A Drop of Ink* also transports the reader to the genre of ekphrasis, but here the painting described is a constantly changing representation of Shiki's life, feelings, and thoughts. The first installment, from January 16, 1901, opens with a description of the objects around Shiki's pillow. As Origas has observed, the poet evokes a picture for readers by naming objects one by one, as if he were describing a painting:[63]

Ill by my pillow, where there is a box containing scrolls, letters, and envelopes. Above it rests a thermometer. Decorating the thermometer is a straw wreath to remind me that in my sickness I can somewhat celebrate the new year; the way fern leaves reach out left and right makes me all the more joyful. Below it is an orange, and next to the orange is a globe of nearly the same size. The globe is my twentieth century new year's gift, given to me by Sokotsu.[64]

The narrative begins in medias res with the word *yameru* (being ill). Readers of *A Drop of Ink* have often conflated the author Shiki with the

Shiki represented in the literary work. Like the historical Shiki, the speaker—the poetic Shiki—is bedridden until his death a year later. I argued above that this distinction applies to all of Shiki's autobiographical works, but I stress it here because Shiki the author is conscious of his public audience and assumes the persona of an ill Romantic genius, offering the readers of *Nippon* many entertaining feats of lyric performance.

The speaker's focus on the boxes with scrolls, letters, and envelopes is in part a *shasei* description of his immediate observations. Makoto Ueda has argued that selection is essential in *shasei*, making it subjective.[65] The speaker's choice to mention the contents of the boxes thereby invites the reader's critical attention. Because he is immobile, the only way for him to communicate with the outside world is through post—his connection to anything beyond the confines of his bedroom is mediated through written language. Each installment in *A Drop of Ink* reads like a letter, a diary entry, or a fragment of a paper scroll on which a literatus might record his poetic musings.

As he continues his *shasei* description, the speaker describes a *wakazari*, the straw wreath decoration that celebrates the New Year. But his attention is especially drawn to a globe that his friend, the haiku poet Samukawa Sokotsu (1875–1954), gave him as a New Year's present:

> I scrutinize the planet earth, three inches in diameter, and find the country of Japan, ever so small, colored especially red. Below Taiwan is written "New Japan." Korea, Manchuria, Jilin, and Heilongjiang all fall into the purple-colored region, but it makes me uneasy to find no mention of Peking or Tianjin. At the end of the twentieth century I wonder how the globe will look different from these red and purple colors; one cannot know just by looking at a globe from the start of the twentieth century.[66]

As he scrutinizes the globe, the world and all its possibilities come to mind. Geographical boundaries are represented by color, but unlike in painting, where everything is depicted in completed form, the globe he beholds represents a world in a state of transformation. He wonders whether the globe will look different 100 years later, no doubt a curiosity stirred by Japan's imperial expansion and colonization of Taiwan upon its victory in the Sino-Japanese War (1894–1895). These opening images set the tone for the entire work, suggesting that in *A Drop of Ink* the world is his oyster: he can freely write at length about every topic, using all kinds of words as well as diverse forms, genres, and styles of language.[67]

Just as he distills prosaic observations of beauty with a poem in the works examined thus far in this chapter, Shiki ends the first installment of *A Drop of Ink* with a tanka that condenses his earlier, prose observations, and also ironizes them in lyric form:

> At any rate, the box filled with letters and envelopes, and the thermometer, orange, and globe that rest above it make up the *hōrai* in my bedroom.

> By the pillow
> On the thermometer
> Hangs a straw wreath
> To celebrate the new year,
> And it may unravel.

> *makura be no / samusa hakari ni / shinnen no / toshi hogi nawa o / kakete hogu kamo*
> 枕べの寒さ計りに新年の年ほぎ縄を掛けてほぐかも [68]

The speaker restates the objects that he describes earlier in the passage, writing that they make up his *hōrai*, a term that the reader may interpret in a number of ways: as the Japanese transliteration of "Penglai," the legendary island of eternal youth from Chinese myth; as another name for Taiwan; or, in the context of the New Year decorations, as another term for the stand upon which food offerings were placed. In all of these interpretations, the tone is ironic. The tanka repeats the same images but puns on the word *hogu*, which in the context of the new year means "to celebrate," but on its own is synonymous with the verb "to fall apart." The very object that gives the speaker a sense of joy at the start of a new year is the same object that points to the year's—and the poet's—end.

This pun demonstrates Shiki's interest in the stuff of poetry as well as in the balance of oppositional elements, like chiaroscuro in painting. Beichman observes: "Shiki employed his special ability to speak of two opposing ideas in one breath. When the one was the surface meaning of a statement and the other its true meaning, the result could be biting sarcasm."[69] The playfulness of Shiki's language can create a mood of lighthearted irony, evoking the humor in the *haikai* tradition. But when the punchline of the joke is death, Shiki's humor takes on a much darker tone. Beichman claims that Shiki's best writing is "imbued with a consciousness of the coexistence of life and death."[70] This dialectic of life and death appears throughout *A Drop of Ink*, especially in passages where the speaker mediates feelings and sensations through poetic forms that suggest his own impending death. In this way Shiki's writing mirrored how Romantic poets represented life as a paradox—or as Ross Wilson puts it, "what is often taken to be life does not live."[71]

Shiki mediates thoughts and feelings about his own mortality through metaphor, for example in the installment from March 26. He writes that his pupil, tanka poet Itō Sachio (1864–1913), stopped by with a bucket of spring water and three koi fish, and placed it next to his bed so that he could enjoy the season. The immobile speaker envies the mobile fish, alive and moving, but also sympathizes with them because they both occupy confined spaces. As Shiki does with the wisteria flowers in his garden, and the potted plants in his bedroom, he uses the koi as material for extemporaneous haiku.[72] He comes up with ten verses, but claims that he is expressing "one thought" (*ichii*) in "ten ways" (*jūyō*):

> After several revisions, I finally came up with ten verses. They amount to ten verses, but they are not ten verses: I only tried to express one thought in ten ways:

The koi in the bucket
In the spring water
Gulping for air.

haru mizu no / tarai ni koi no / agito kana
春水の盥に鯉の喰喝かな

The bucket shallow,
The backs of the koi are visible
In the spring water.

tarai asaku / koi no se miyuru / haru no mizu
盥浅く鯉の背見ゆる春の水

Koi tails
Moving in the bucket—
Spring water.

koi no o no / ugoku tarai ya / haru no mizu
鯉の尾の動く盥や春の水

The koi in the bucket,
Their heads lined up—
Spring water.

tō narabu / tarai no koi ya / haru no mizu
頭並ぶ盥の鯉や春の水

| In the spring water
Full in the bucket,
Koi fins. | *haru mizu no / tarai ni michite / koi no kata*
春水の盥に満ちて鯉の肩 |
| In the bucket.
Spring water—
The koi are alive | *haru no mizu / koi no ikitaru / tarai kana*
春の水鯉の活きたる盥かな |

Spring water—
The koi are alive
In the bucket.

haru no mizu / koi no ikitaru / tarai kana
春の水鯉の活きたる盥かな

Many koi
In the small bucket—
Spring water.

koi ōku / semaki tarai ya / haru no mizu
鯉多く狭き盥や春の水

The koi blow
Bubbles—in the bucket
Of spring water.

koi no haku / awa ya tarai no / haru no mizu
鯉の吐く泡や盥の春の水

In the bucket
Spring water washes
The backs of koi.

koi no se ni / shunsui sosogu / tarai kana
鯉の背に春水そゝぐ盥かな

The koi jump
In the shallow bucket—
Spring water.

koi hanete / asaki tarai ya / haru no mizu
鯉はねて浅き盥や春の水 [73]

Each haiku represents the same objects: the koi, the bucket, and the spring water. But each poem says something slightly different about them. The ten poems may be read together as a single poetic form, analogous to a prism or polyhedron where a poem represents one of ten sides. Shiki's contemporary Marcel Proust (1871–1922) has been described as a novelist who perceived "polygonally" and who imagined "all twenty sides of a question, and added a twenty-first."[74] These visual metaphors reveal how representation in the late nineteenth century merged painting with novelistic and, in Shiki's case, poetic expression. For Shiki, though, the additional side of the prism is the new form: the whole that is greater than the sum of its parts.

The visual metaphor illuminates how the speaker's statement "one thought in ten ways" manifests in literary form with varying dimensions of space in temporal suspension. For example, the first haiku conjures a purely visual image of the koi gulping for air in the bucket; in the second haiku the subject changes to the speaker, who sees the backs of the koi in the water; the third haiku moves from the back of the koi to their tails; by the fourth haiku, the speaker has turned his focus to the heads of the koi. The poems' emphasis on various actions of the koi—gulping, moving, filling, living, blowing, washing, and jumping—exemplifies the empirical observation in *shasei*. This focus on the movement of the fish also serves as a foil for the speaker's own immobility and lack—at least physical lack—of vigor and vitality.

The repetition of koi, bucket, and spring water creates a sense of rhythm in the installment, a rhythm that changes beat throughout *A Drop of Ink*, continuing as permutations of repetition in prose and poetry. Here the repetition of key words that constitute the haiku sequence becomes the poet's way of moving as the koi do in the bucket. Jonathan Culler writes that rhythm has a somatic quality that draws the reader into another world:

> Rhythm gives lyric a somatic quality that novels and other extended forms lack—the experience of rhythm linking it to the body and, perhaps, to the rhythms of various natural processes—and thus contributes both to a different sort of pleasure from those promoted by novels and to a sense of a special otherness: lyrics are language, but language shaped in other ways, as if from elsewhere.[75]

Shiki's "one thought" is the source of the rhythm that runs through the body of the haiku sequence. His preface to the sequence suggests that the reader consider the ten haiku as one whole. As a whole, the sequence creates a rhythm, presenting "a different sort of pleasure."

The haiku sequence shows how Shiki created a poetic form using the very tropes of literati culture but represented them in new idiom. The sequence furnishes a discursive space to make statements about koi, a bucket, and spring water; as lyric, the materiality of language allows the poems to say something beyond mere description of the three objects. As Mutlu Blasing writes, "Lyric poetry is not mimesis,…it offers an experience of another kind of order, a system that operates independently of the production of meaningful discourse that it enables."[76]

Rhythm is the system that allows the ill poet to simulate movement using only words.

Shiki creates another kind of movement via rhythm and repetition of thought in prose that seems to go nowhere, or rather ends where it starts. In the installment for March 15, the speaker describes his dislike of the Fifth Month:

> May is a horrible month. Over the past few days it has finally begun to feel like May, and the displeasure is unbearable. My head is foggy, and my thoughts do not in the least cohere.
>
> In a dream, I would be walking carefree even now. But whenever I have to jump over something, I always think twice. I am also surprised that the recent weather forecasts have been wrong.
>
> When I feel the pain pressing upon my body, I want nothing else but to float in the sky, where nothing can touch me, where the weight of a human being is the same as the weight of air.
>
> Around this time last year, I was able to move into the other room by crawling on my knees, but this year, at present, just turning over in bed has grown difficult. I suspect that by next year, I will be unable to move at all.[77]

The writing is terse, as one might expect from a diary entry, and the connection between thoughts in each paragraph is tenuous. The speaker begins with a statement about how much he dislikes May, then talks about his inability to think clearly, and then moves on to talking about dreaming. Only after the non sequitur about the weather forecast does the reader discover that the overarching theme of the installment is the movement (or obstruction) of thought and the mobility (or immobility) of the body. The speaker's desire to float in the sky and to be untouchable and weightless is a response to his state of intense pain, in which he feels the pressure of everything, even the air itself.

Shiki then abandons the themes of the body and of mobility to introduce new images that sound like more non sequiturs:

> I went to the trouble of informing Sokotsu that I discarded the 'bad luck' fortune card I drew the other day at Anamori Shrine.
>
> I want to forage for bamboo shoots.
>
> At Nikkō a rain squall quickly passes through the new green leaves—how delightful. Out of the dripping wet verdure a single crow takes off, almost touching the leaves.
>
> Postscript: Upon review, the form is not unified. Evidence of my vacuity.[78]

The speaker sounds delirious. And yet, he returns to the concerns of the opening paragraph by concluding with a poetic description of a spring scene. He writes in the present tense, so the reader assumes that he is imagining the scene in Nikkō from his Tokyo bedroom. The reverie evokes the dream and his sensitivity to touch from earlier passages. He notes that the crow flies away, "almost touching the leaves" (*ha ni furesō ni*), a somatic sensation that falls between his desire to not touch anything and his present predicament of feeling the pressure of everything. He also leaves a postscript, as if he is writing a letter to the reader, that reiterates his earlier claim that his thoughts are incoherent. By the end, therefore, the installment comes full circle, much like how in a lyric poem the start points to the end, and vice versa. In seemingly incoherent prose, Shiki created a poetic form of detour through non sequiturs and subtle repetitions of images and thoughts.

A Drop of Ink thus evinces how Shiki used incoherence to create rhythm in literary form. The postscript about the lack of unified form points to the work's awareness of its own performativity, revealing poetic irony. As a *shasei* work, *A Drop of Ink* also questioned what it means to "represent life" as the permutations of thought in the form of poetic prose. In this way, the work can be read as a representation of the life of the mind and of poetic contemplation.[79]

The installment for June 9 in *A Drop of Ink* offers another telling example of how Shiki represents thought through different genres of poetry. But, due to his illness, here his speaker's thoughts move in and out of coherence:

> My fever high, my body in pain. It began with moaning, then turned into shouting, and by the end I was reciting poems and singing loudly: my tone of voice shifted in and out of tune, catching bits and pieces of Dodoitsu, Hauta, and Noh plays, changing so quickly that even I could not keep track. One night, as usual I develop a fever, and one or two lines from a poem or from a gatha pile and fold on one another as I rave in delirium: the first line that comes out, I do not record; but when I reach the middle, I take a moment to record one or two lines, ending up with four. How strange and wondrous that there are parts coherent and incoherent.[80]

As in the opening of the earlier installment, the speaker prefaces the descriptions to come with a statement of his illness and pain. These prefatory remarks about being ill or mentally vacuous serve as a frame for introspection and sensual observation. In late imperial Chinese poetry illness often served as the pretext for writing. Shiki was aware of this practice, but here his speaker uses illness, fever, and pain to represent spontaneity, genius, creativity, and the craft of poetry. He outlines another sequence of progression, inviting the reader to consider the stages of delirium as a metaphor for the creative process: it starts off with moaning, then moves to shouting, and by the end of it the creator is singing anything and everything that comes to mind.

Illness, delirium, and mental vacuity are ways a literatus attains *xian* (J. *kan*), or "a state of tranquility" that stimulates creativity. François Jullien defines *xian* as a kind of vacuity: "The vacuity to which a spirit liberated from all preoccupations gains access (*xian*) allows for such a concentration of intentionality that will guide the drawing."[81] Shiki's writing diverges from the "concentration of intentionality" enabled by *xian* by straddling oppositional ideas and allowing coherence to clash with incoherence. The language of the passage is heavily informed by *kanbun*, which lacks particles to mark grammatical subjects and objects. A trained reader can parse the prose without gloss, but at first glance the language is dense. As the speaker describes how word fragments from traditional genres of Japanese song and performance—Dodoitsu, Hauta, and Noh plays—come to him without rhyme or reason, the language of the passage visually reproduces the polyphony of tunes with the proliferation of Chinese graphs. In other words, the incoherence of form here mirrors the incoherence of content.

Although what he is thinking, hearing, or saying is opaque to the reader, Shiki establishes a semblance of order by thinking in sequence: as he is uttering verses, he does not record first lines but waits until he gets to the middle of the poem and then jots down one or two lines. By the end, he has composed a pentasyllabic quatrain (*gogon zekku*):

A star falls down into a white lotus pond;
By the pond embankment, green colors are even.
Walking and walking, never going to find Buddha;
On one road, and I cannot tell east from west.

hoshi wa otsu hakuren no ike	星落白蓮池
chitō sōshoku hitoshi	池塘草色齊
iki-ikedomo butsu ni awazu	行行不逢佛
ichiro tōzai o oshinau	一路失東西 [82]

The images of white lotus, the pond, and Buddha suggest that the poem is describing the Pure Land or a place of Buddhist enlightenment, and yet, ironically, the poet cannot find Buddha, nor does he have any sense of direction. The installment ends with just the poem, no comment. If the reader takes Shiki at his word, the poem is supposed to be "coherent and incoherent" (*kai subeku kai subekarazaru*), which he finds to be "strange and wondrous" (*kimyō*). His use of the adjective *kimyō* suggests that the poem should be taken as wild ramblings and as a work of marvel. While he claims there is continuity in content, the form suggests otherwise: the order of the regulated nature of *kanshi* opposes the discursive rambling in the preceding prose.

The poem's content can be interpreted as a metaphor for contemplation itself, representing the contradictions of Buddhist thought. Zen Buddhism blends together Daoist ideas that figure the world in oppositions such as presence and absence. Buddhist statements about truth are phrased in contradictory and oppositional language, much like riddles or paradoxes. A secular reading of the poem reveals that the speaker has somehow found himself in a place of perfection, and yet his movements in any direction lead him nowhere. In this sense, the poem becomes a metaphor for Shiki's representation of thought and feeling in *A Drop of Ink*: "Walking and walking" (*iki-ikedomo*) refers to their organic unfolding in the narrative, without directionality or teleological closure. In other words, the poem suggests that the larger prose poem represents thought and feeling in a state of perpetual motion.

WANDERING IN THE ENIGMA OF FORM

Shiki composed another prose poem entitled *A Six-foot Sickbed*, which was serialized in *Nippon* in 1902, the year of his death. In this work, Shiki represented his life through the rhythm and repetition in poetry, while also questioning the limits of *shasei* by obtruding different poetic genres from the literati tradition upon the reader. The work presents a contrapuntal narrative motion from the disequilibrium between the genres of past and present.

A Six-foot Sickbed is structured almost exactly like *A Drop of Ink*: each installment begins with a number and ends with a date of composition. Amounting to a total of 127 installments, *A Six-foot Sickbed* returns to many of the themes in *A Drop of Ink*, but departs slightly in its increasing emphasis on philology, *haikai* poetics, and literati painting.[83] Shiki's speaker continues to discuss the matters of daily life from the confines of his bedroom, but mostly in the vernacular—the one exception is the classical Japanese poetry. The latter text also engages more with discourse on aesthetics and literary criticism.

A Six-foot Sickbed opens by reframing the narrative setting from the confined space to boundless possibilities: "A six-foot sick bed—this is my world. And this sickbed six feet long is too big for me."[84] These lines recall the opening installment of *A Drop of Ink*, in which Shiki scrutinized the globe he had received from Sokotsu. Here, his bed becomes his world, but he writes that he reads newspapers and magazines on a daily basis to stay up-to-date with the world outside. When he learns of new information and decides to write about it, his feelings about the topic register in the form of the prose, and begin to reach out beyond the confines of his bed through rhythm, repetition, and quotation.

In installment 25, he receives continual news reports that educator Nishimatsu Jirō (1855–1909; penname Hōhi sanjin) has asked educated men across the land about the call of owls. Intrigued by this inquiry, he describes the call he remembers hearing in his hometown of Matsuyama, and then discusses his past experiences listening to owls in Ueno, Tokyo. As it turns out, his illness makes him a light sleeper, and the owl's call often wakes him in the middle of the night:

> Ill, and after falling asleep, even all the way in Negishi I hear that call, so even these days sick in bed I am up listening every night. After sundown it starts calling, and at times calls through the night; sometimes I can even hear two of them calling without stopping. Other times, I hear one calling by the tree in my garden, but when I hear one calling even closer, it feels dreadful indeed. But when the nights finally get cold in mid-autumn, they stop calling entirely. I would like an informed person to tell me whether they just roost until mid-autumn in Ueno and move elsewhere, or do they remain in Ueno, and just stop calling.[85]

The speaker describes the proximity and frequency of the owl's call, which is loud enough to reach him kilometers away in Negishi, from Ueno, as well as frequent enough to keep him awake. The way the call is described makes it sound haunting, especially with Shiki's repetition of *naku* (to call; to cry), along with its various verbal inflections (*naki*; *naka*) and homonym *naku*, a negation suffix (see underlined text). The haunting repetition of the word "call" mirrors Shiki's emphatic repetition of "k" sounds in the original Japanese prose (see boldface):

yamai ni nete nochi mo yahari rei no __nakigoe__ wa negishi made kikoeru node, kono goro demo byōshō de maiban kiite iru. hi no kure kara __nakidashite__ yofuke ni mo __naku__ koto ga aru ga, toki toshite wa niwa no tsure__naki__ ni __naku nakigoe__ ga kikoeru koto ga aru. mata aru toki wa waga niwa no ki chikaku e kite __naku__ koto mo aru ga, amari ni chikaku __nakareru__ to sasuga ni monosugoku kanjiru. sōshite aki no __nakaba__ shōshō yosamu no koro ni naru to itsumo __nakanaku__ natte shimau. shite miru to ueno niwa aki no __nakaba__ made sunde ite, sorekara yoso e tenkyo suru no dearōka, mata wa ueno ni iru keredo mo __nakanaku__ naru no dearōka, monoshiri ni oshiete moraitai no dearu.

This subtle, but clearly audible, repetition of the "k" in the passage performs the repetitive nature of the owl's call for the reader, as if the repetition of *naku* was not enough. Keith Vincent has argued that bedridden Shiki relied on poetic devices like the repetition and accentuation of syllables in order to make the representation of sensory experience palpable to and pleasurable for the reader.[86] In Japanese and Chinese poetry, "k" sounds and other glottal stops are emphatic, and hence associated with deep emotion. In this passage the feeling is a mixture of fear and wonderment. Repetition that registers in the process of reading enlists us, as the readers, into the process of lyric experience. Clive Scott has argued that "rhythm is the mediating force between text and reader, reader and self, the place where these conflicting impulses of will play out in their drama."[87] The drama here is a haunting spectacle that also evokes the sublime. Culler argues that rhythm and other forms of repetition bring forth "miniature versions of the sublime."[88] No doubt this has to do with the fact that rhythm evokes a place that is elsewhere; here it is the affective space created by the dreadful call of owls.

The haunting feelings stirred by the rhythm and repetition in the prose make the speaker think of Samuel Taylor Coleridge's long and unfinished narrative poem "Christabel" (1798). He quotes an excerpt from the opening stanza:

Whenever I start talking about this matter concerning the bird's call, I always think of Coleridge's 'Christabel':
    And the owls have awakened the crowing cock!
    Tu-whit!—Tu—whoo! [89]

Of Coleridge's poems, it is not surprising that Shiki thought of this one, as "Christabel" was associated with Gothic literature of the eighteenth and nineteenth centuries, and has been described by English scholars as "a poem of supernatural and psychological terror."[90] The poem tells the story of an innocent young woman named Christabel who encounters, in her bed, a being named Geraldine, whom she discovers is either a ghost, demon, witch, or Gothic temptress.

Karen Swann has argued that "Christabel" dramatizes and provokes the hysteria of the time, and that the protean nature of Geraldine is a metaphor for the unstable and changing "bodies of literary convention" in late eighteenth-century England.[91] In *A Six-foot Sickbed*, the speaker's obsession with a particular topic—painting, haiku, philology, owls, his illness—oftentimes sounds like hysteria, and his proclivity or compulsion to safeguard his words with the voices of others in the form of poetic quotation may be symptomatic of an anxiety about Japanese literary form at the turn of the twentieth century. By the late Meiji period, many Japanese writers had abandoned premodern modes of expression to write in the plain style closest to modern speech.[92] Evident in his choice to cleave to traditional modes of expression (e.g., *haikai, kanshi, sōrōbun*), Shiki was far from an exemplar of *genbun'itchi*, but he did smooth out his prose in *A Six-foot Sickbed* by writing almost entirely in the vernacular. Moments where the speaker slips into English, or others where he composes poems or quotes the verse of others, are ruptures in the text that resonate with Swann's observations about the instability of genre during Coleridge's time.

The important thing to consider in Shiki's quotation of Coleridge's poem is the reification of sound and its attendant feelings of dread. The entire installment is about the call of the owl, and Shiki concludes it with "Tu-whit!—Tu—whoo!"—onomatopoeia for an owl's call evoking its locus classicus in the winter scene from Shakespeare's comedy *Love's Labour's Lost*. By ending the installment about sound with sound, the language enters multiple visual and sonic dimensions. The quotation from "Christabel" only heightens the eeriness and subtle sublimity of the scene, transporting Shiki's empirical observations beyond his bedroom, and into the world of Romantic poetry and the English tradition.

Shiki's deployment of various literary genres and forms may be symptomatic of the instability and imbalance that plagues his mind and body. In installment 39, his symptoms of illness feed into his persona as a madman and the Romantic genius who seeks sympathy from his readers, a persona that allows his mind to wander freely because his body cannot:

During the intervals when I could move my body, lying on my sick bed, there was no need to think that illness is tough, and I just lay there in peace. But recently being unable to move my body has made my mind anxious, and almost every day I feel like I am suffering from madness. Hoping that I would not succumb to such suffering, I thought of different ways to force my immobile body to move. This only stirred more anxiety. My head is a mess. When I can no longer endure it, the bag that I have borne loses its last thread, and before long rips itself apart.[93]

Once again, Shiki writes eloquently here about mobility and immobility. With his body no longer able to move, he feels frustration and anxiety, yet something is released in the process. He puns on the idiom "the patience bag loses its thread" (*kannin bukuro no o ga kireru*), representing the moment when all the stitching comes loose and everything falls out:

When it comes to this, I am hopeless. Screaming. Wailing. More and more screaming. More and more wailing. I do not know how to describe this suffering and this pain.[94]

The image of the bag ripping itself open represents the mental state of a person unhinged. The speaker dramatizes the characteristics of madness through a staccato rhythm and repetition of words evoking terrifying sounds. The verbs "screaming" (*zekkyō*) and "wailing" (*gōkyū*) only intensify by their repetition with "more and more" (*masu masu*), and the passage devolves into a pain and suffering beyond what words can describe.

When language fails to capture feeling, Shiki uses the form of prose to communicate the pain pounding his mind and body. The installment closes with the same kind of repetition, but instead of words and phrases, whole sentences recur, ringing in a crescendo of pain:

I thought I would be happier if I became a real madman, but I could not even do that. If I could die, that would be more desirable than anything, but when a person cannot even die, there is nothing that can kill him. When one day's suffering would finally diminish by night, and when that day's anguish would finally be over, then I would rise the next morning feeling anguish all over again. There is no time more painful than waking up. Is there no one who can save me from this suffering? Is there no one who can save me from this suffering?[95]

For Shiki, there is no escape from pain, probably because he finds it productive.[96] He writes that he wants to be a "madman" (*kyōjin*), but he cannot; he writes that he would rather die, but he cannot—nothing can put an end to his misery. These statements preface his claim that waking up is the most painful. Part of this may have to do with the reality that his pain diminishes at night and returns in the morning, but the recursive rhetoric of the passage suggests that this is all a performance of cyclicality and endless repetition, much like the screaming and wailing. He is unable to save himself by turning into a madman or embracing death, the reasons for which he chooses to omit. The passage ends with him repeating the same question, a pitiful plea or pathetic prayer to a sympathetic reader.

The progression of pain finds its echo in the form of the text: as the pounding gets louder and longer, so does the text. Whereas other installments have no connection to each other, the following installment returns to the same question; the speaker comments that a religious figure would argue that he was seeking spiritual salvation. But he rejects the association with religion, explaining that he has fallen into a state where everything causes him pain and suffering: "In the end, finding harmony with my surroundings has grown extremely difficult."[97] Morphine no longer eases his pain, so he has resigned himself to constant suffering.

If the dissonance he feels with his surroundings is the catalyst for setting something in motion, then what would that something be? This setting in motion references Spencer's idea of rhythm in *First Principles* (1880), where he argued that rhythm "is a necessary characteristic of all motion."[98] In his chapter "The Rhythm of Motion," Spencer uses empirical observations of a sailboat on water and trees on shore to illustrate that when one object encounters another, there is conflict that results in what he calls "rhythmical action." When the wind blows, the sails ruffle, and the boat swings from side to side, generating undulations in the water; meanwhile, on shore, trees sway to and fro, and blades of grass rise and fall. The ideas about rhythm in *First Principles* are evoked by Shiki's language in his prose poems. He represents himself as a bedridden poet—an inert object—whose senses are stimulated by surrounding objects, from his bed to the call of owls. This stimulation from sensory perception has a residual effect—or a wake, to echo Spencer's boat metaphor—that makes ripples in language, taking form as linguistic leaps through different genres and registers in the work.

The multi-sensory experience afforded by *shasei* evokes the sensual plenitude that Shiki argues is characteristic of modern *shasei*, and not of works from the tradition. During the mid-1890s, Shiki publicly promoted *shasei* in his writings published in the newspaper *Nippon*. *A Six-foot Sickbed* was one such work, and in installment 45, he argues for the importance of *shasei* in artistic production:

> The practice known as *shasei* is extremely essential for painting pictures and writing descriptions. Without it, paintings and descriptions would be impossible. This is a method that has been used in the West from early on, but the *shasei* of the past was an imperfect *shasei*; since then there have been more improvements, and by now it has become a method of precision on a whole new level. In Japan, *shasei* since long ago has been terribly neglected, which consequently obstructed the development of painting, and impeded the progress of writing and poetry.[99]

Shiki enjoyed polemics, and he made his critical voice heard in his writings. Here, his speaker promotes the modern advancements of Western realism, while denigrating the tradition of *shasei* in Japan. He suggests that this approach, as a polemical stance, was nothing more than embracing a *risō*, or "ideal," that trapped artists in the worlds of convention and cliché:

> Whether in painting or in poetry, there are many people who advocate for what is called an 'ideal,' but they are the people who do not know the flavor of *shasei*, and who dismiss *shasei* as highly superficial. But actually, an ideal is much more superficial: it cannot compare to the many variations of charm in *shasei*. I do not mean that works that display an ideal are necessarily bad, but when the ideal commonly manifests in a work of art, many in fact turn out bad. An ideal reveals a human being's intention, so unless the human being is a rare genius, his work inevitably cannot avoid being entirely imitation or cliché.[100]

He explains why modern *shasei* works are good and why *risō* works are bad. By *risō*, or "ideal," he is referring to the centuries of artistic practice when a painter would render an object according to traditional modes of representation. As a direct heir to the literati tradition, Shiki learned these modes, and yet his speaker rejects them.

As he sets up his argument in praise of modern *shasei* as a means of expression with the promise of newness and variation in contrast to traditional ideals, he contradicts himself by creating and promoting an ideal of his own at the end of the installment:

When you view a work of *shasei*, it may look slightly superficial, but the more you savor it deeply, you will find its variations many, and its charms profound.... An ideal work is often like trying to jump onto a roof in a single breath, but then falling into the center of a puddle. While it may be bland, *shasei* avoids such failures. Thus when we find something lodging the finest flavor at the heart of blandness, that wondrous beauty is truly ineffable.[101]

He views *shasei* as a form of perfection, an ideal he claims is not an ideal. He concedes that *shasei* is "bland" (*heitan*), and it does not fail at being bland. Blandness (Ch. *pingdan*) is an aesthetic ideal that derives from traditional Chinese painting, and it evokes plenitude in the beauty of the ineffable. He believes that such beauty can be found in modern *shasei* as well.

The speaker's denigration of idealistic modes of representation comes at the expense of his own idealization of *shasei*. Such contradiction abounds in Shiki's writing, evincing a process of contemplation constituted by oppositional movement that mediates thought and feeling. Throughout the installment, and in his other poetic writings, Shiki uses the word *henka*, which means "change," "transformation," or "variation."[102] He argues that each viewing of a *shasei* painting will show something different, and that this difference is what makes *shasei* so compelling and beautiful.[103]

Shiki gives an example of the beauty afforded by *shasei* in a series of haiku. In installment 70, his speaker wonders about image pairs in literati poetry and painting, and composes a haiku sequence like that discussed above in *A Drop of Ink*. He claims that he can easily compose poems about willows (*yanagi*) and kingfishers (*kawasemi*), the reasons for which are left unstated. In this final example in which he intersperses prose with poetry, he ends up embracing the conventions and clichés that his *shasei* ideal had originally set out to avoid, and yet he succeeds in creating another variation of the tradition by rendering one thought in ten ways. By the end of the sequence, the speaker mediates his duel with death through a celebration of life in a polygonal painting of kingfishers and willows:

Like they say for plums and warblers, and bamboo and sparrows, the coupling of willows and kingfishers has been treated in sketches for so long that it is cliché. Whenever I pick up a picture book these days, I often see these cliché couplings. And yet, I am strongly moved by their beauty, and I get more and more intrigued by them. So, I decided to compose ten haiku for fun on the topic of willows and kingfishers. I recall that I did the same last spring with koi in spring water, and composed ten verses too.[104]

The pairs that he mentions—plums and warblers, bamboo and sparrows, willows and kingfishers—have been conventional in literati painting for centuries. He mentions *ryakuga* (sketches), a term that refers to the crude illustrations of natural objects found in painting manuals and picture books (*ehon*), a genre of illustrated material that disseminated widely among literati and artists alike throughout the early modern period. The term *ryakuga* seems to originate, with Shiki, in installment 6, where he describes an illustration of a single blade of grass and a lone tree.[105] Although he states that such illustrations are cliché, the speaker cannot help but be moved by their beauty. This contradicts his earlier claim that *shasei* is superior to representational modes of the past because it avoids convention and cliché.

Shiki's speaker often changes his mind, so it is not surprising that here he decides to find praise for convention and cliché. This thought sets in motion another haiku sequence, but this time with images that accord with one another in harmony:

A kingfisher
Eyes the fish   *kawasemi no / uo o ukagau / yanagi kana*
By the willows.   翡翠の魚を覗ふ柳かな

Concealing
The kingfisher,   *kawasemi o / kakusu yanagi no / shigeri kana*
Willows overgrown.   翡翠をかくす柳の茂りかな

The willows
Where the kingfisher comes, *kawasemi no / kitaru yanagi o / ai su kana*
I adore.   翡翠の来る柳を愛すかな

The kingfisher—
Circling the pond,   *kawasemi ya / ike o megurite / mina yanagi*
Around all willows.   翡翠や池をめぐりて皆柳

The kingfisher
Does not come on the day   *kawasemi no / konu hi yanagi no / arashi kana*
Storm strikes the willows.   翡翠の来ぬ日柳の嵐かな

A kingfisher
And a heron   *kawasemi mo / sagi mo kite iru / yanagi kana*
By the willows.   翡翠も鷺も来て居る柳かな

The willows cut down,
And the kingfisher
Never came back.

yanagi kitte / kawasemi tsui ni / kozu narinu
柳伐つて翡翠終に来ずなりぬ

The kingfisher
Finds some footing
By the willows.

kawasemi no / ashiba o erabu / yanagi kana
翡翠の足場を選ぶ柳かな

The kingfisher
Gone—the willows
In the evening sun.

kawasemi no / satte yanagi no / yūhi kana
翡翠の去って柳の夕日かな

The kingfisher
Has flown far away
From the willows.

kawasemi no / tonde shimaishi / yanagi kana
翡翠の飛んでしまひし柳かな[106]

Like the ten poems on koi in the bucket of spring water, the haiku sequence here paints a multifaceted picture of the kingfisher and willows. While the koi sequence served more as a metaphor for Shiki's immobility, the kingfisher poems are more about the presence and absence of natural objects and traditional tropes that are meant to be together. Each poem exists in a dialectical relationship with the poem that precedes and/or follows it: in the first poem, the kingfisher and willows are both present, but the gaze is directed at fish; in the second, the kingfisher is there, but concealed; in the third, the kingfisher and willows are together; in the fourth, the kingfisher outlines the space of the pond; in the fifth, a storm strikes and the kingfisher is absent; in the sixth, the kingfisher shares the willows with a friend; in the seventh, the kingfisher and the willows are gone; in the eighth, the kingfisher tarries in the willows; in the ninth, the kingfisher is gone, and the willows recede from view; and in the tenth, the kingfisher is gone and the willows remain. Each poem could stand as an autonomous scene in a literati painting, and each also displays the empiricism of modern *shasei*.

By the end of the sequence, the repetition of *kawasemi* conjures a beautiful painting that is constantly changing, as the bird appears and disappears. The kingfisher's plumage is green and blue; in *kanshi*, the Chinese graphs for the kingfisher are read as *hisui*, which also means "jade green." The bird's associations with this most cherished precious stone in the Chinese tradition imbue the image with exquisiteness, elegance, timelessness, and ineffable beauty.

The speaker states that the conventional nature of the pairing made composition easier, but it also revealed the truth about the limits of what a poet can do with genre:

> When I wrote on the koi in spring water, I kept getting stuck on the words, but this time with the willows and kingfishers there was more room to play. This let me vary some of the ideas and imagery. But as for how they turned out, there were more bad ones among the kingfisher poems. When composing these kinds of verses, it may seem like nothing more than a brief diversion, but I discovered the best way to learn haiku conventions is when you actually try and compose poems. In other words, I find it interesting to realize that when composing haiku, knowing what goes with what is one thing, but knowing what makes a good verse from a bad one, is something you can only learn by doing it.[107]

This comment on how a poet uses convention evokes the idea in traditional Chinese literature that forms and genres can have infinite variations dependent only on the writer's ability to use language.[108] The speaker claims that poetic inspiration came more easily when writing within a genre, but even with variation of ideas and imagery (*shukō no henka*), more bad poems resulted.

Shiki ends the installment with the idea that composing within a genre is a heuristic for learning how to discern a good poem from a bad one. Because genre already delimits what a poet can or cannot say, a writer must be creative within those generic constraints. And yet, Shiki is also championing a *shasei* approach to poetic composition through empirical practice and his trial-and-error method. At the core of his concluding remarks on what makes a good poem is the conflict within this artist who advocates that the poet must free haiku from the conventions of the past in order to make it anew. Relying on traditional tropes for content, Shiki makes his transformative leaps in form, composing ten poems as one.

But this new poetic form mediates only feelings of longing. The kingfisher's disappearance in the final haiku leaves the reader with the image of willows, a trope for farewell. A reader might interpret such an ending as a metaphor for Shiki's impending death and his valediction to literati culture, as the tropes—even in new form—have reached their twilight.

The next chapter turns to Shiki's contemporary, novelist Natsume Sōseki, and examines how he forges new poetic forms, allegorizing the death of literati culture in Meiji.

Notes

1. As early as twelve years old, Shiki composed poems in Chinese, a sensibility first nurtured by his grandfather, Confucian scholar Ōhara Kanzan (1818–1875). Shiki produced nearly 2000 *kanshi*, 600 of which are anthologized in a self-compiled collection called *Kanshikō* (1878–1896; Chinese poetry manuscript). As Watanabe Katsumi has observed, for Shiki literature begins with *kanshi*. Masaoka Shiki, *Shiki zenshū*, 8: 683. From here on *SZ*.

2. *Shasei* transformed the topical range of haiku to include any object from everyday life, which Shiki demonstrates in two of his most famous poems:

   > Surely there were
   > Fourteen or fifteen
   > Cockscomb blossoms.
   > 鶏頭の十四五本もありぬべし

   > I bite into a persimmon,
   > And a temple bell booms—
   > Hōryūji.
   > 柿くへば鐘が鳴るなり法隆寺

   Masaoka Shiki, *Shiki jinsei ronshū*, 143–144. Translations are mine unless otherwise noted.

3. The term *shasei* appears as one of the three principles of composition in writings on eighteenth-century painting: *shai* (painting the idea), *shasei* (painting life), and *ikkaku* (the artist's untrammeled personality). As Melinda Takeuchi has discussed in the works of Ike no Taiga (1723–1776), to paint the "life" of an object means to "apprehend the spirit-resonance of nature's forms in order to probe the essential truth of nature." Takeuchi, *Taiga's True View*, 144. When composing a *shasei* in the Edo period, the artist must embrace the ideal of representing the underlying reality of nature, its "spirit-resonance."

4. Karatani, *The Origins of Modern Japanese Literature*, 26.

5. Although "detached objectivity" was the goal, in actual poetic practice Shiki and other modern poets invariably communicated their own individuated subjectivity. In his collection of essays *Views on Poetry* (1924; Kadō shōken), tanka poet Shimagi Akahiko (1876–1926) observes that the meaning of *shasei* was misunderstood by painters in the Meiji period, arguing that the term has always meant an "immediate expression of the workings of feeling" (*kanjō katsudō no chokusetsu hyōgen*). Shimagi Akahiko, *Kadō shōken*, 35–37.

6. Eakin: "When we settle into the theater of autobiography, what we are ready to believe—and what most autobiographers encourage us to expect—is that the play we witness is a historical one, a largely faithful and unmediated reconstruction of events that took place long ago, whereas in reality the play is that of the autobiographical act itself, in which the materials of the past are shaped by memory and imagination to serve the needs of present consciousness. The mediation of the past by the present governs the autobiographical enterprise." Eakin, *Fictions in Autobiography*, 56.

7. The *zuihitsu* (Ch. *suibi*) is a genre of writing with Chinese provenance in the Song dynasty that is known for its randomness. Donald Keene writes: "Most are short and they are seldom linked. One gets the impression that, whenever anything attracted his attention, whether great or small, Shiki felt compelled to set down his reactions immediately." Keene, *The Winter Sun Shines In*, 155.

8. As Linda Chance has observed in her study on the medieval writer Yoshida Kenkō's *Essays in Idleness* (fourteenth century; Tsurezuregusa), the *zuihitsu* is a genre that lacks generic boundaries, making it an "anti-genre." Chance, *Formless in Form*, 46–76.

9. *SZ*, 10: 87.

10. François Jullien writes: "*shi* can be defined overall as the *force* that runs through the *form* of the written character and animates it aesthetically." Jullien, *The Propensity of Things*, 76.

11. These traditional principles are governed by the Chinese ideas of *yi* (appropriateness) and *li* (the principle of nature). Whenever a literatus picks up his brush, he produces something that is "appropriate" to the theme, topic, or situation about which he is writing, and that accords with "the principle of nature."

12. Shiki explains his frustration with *genbun'itchi* in the vignette "The Pros and Cons of *Genbun'itchi*" (Genbun'itchi no rigai) in the first volume of *Fudemakase*. While Shiki believes writing in a way that is comprehensible to everyone is important in the case of certain genres of writing (speeches, lectures, etc.), he does not believe this should be the case for literature, especially poetry. *SZ*, 10: 143–4.

13. *SZ*, 10: 13. The *kundoku* is from *Masaoka Shiki shū*, 10.

14. A. Ueda, "Sounds, scripts, and styles."

15. Fong, "Writing and Illness," 19.

16. Shiki composed a *kanshi* in 1882, borrowing the voice of an abandoned woman:

Boudoir Plaint
The dying lamp, the shadows cold—in a dream I long for you;
In the golden duck the incense burned out, the jade clepsydra grieves.
Endless threads hanging wistfully—the willows on the river shore;
Thinner than I was that day long ago, when I bid farewell to my beau.

keien	閨怨
zantō kage hiyayaka ni shite yume ni aiomou	殘燈影冷夢相思
kin'ō ka kiete gyokurō kanashi	金鴨香消玉漏悲
banru ii tari kōjō no yanagi	萬縷依依江上柳
sekijitsu kimi o okurishi toki yori mo yasetari	瘦於昔日送郎時

SZ, 8: 42, 242.

17. Sontag, *Illness as Metaphor*, 29.
18. Ibid., 36.
19. Stewart, *Poetry and the Fate of the Senses*, 68.
20. Ibid., 100.
21. Shiki did not appear to own a copy of the late imperial Chinese poetry collection *Complete Tang Poems* (Quan Tang shi), but Bai Juyi was one of the most popular Tang poets in Japan since the Heian period. The word *moko* (Ch. *mohu*) also appears in Su Shi's (1037–1101) "Snow at the Hall of Constellations" (Juxingtang xue). Bai Juyi's "Improvisation in the Snow, A Reply to Wei Zhi" (Xue zhong ji shi da Wei Zhi) is cited as the locus classicus for Su Shi's usage of the word. Shiki owned collections of Su Shi's poetry.
22. Stewart, *Poetry and the Fate of the Senses*, 101.
23. Spencer, *The Philosophy of Style*, 11.
24. *SZ*, 10: 378.
25. Spencer, *The Philosophy of Style*, 39.
26. *SZ*, 10: 378.
27. *Journey* was first published in four installments in the newspaper *Nippon* from October 31 to November 6, 1892.
28. Shiki owned a collection of Wordsworth's poetry and likely read him alongside Coleridge and other Romantic poets.
29. *SZ*, 13: 493.
30. For an English translation of the essay, see Egan, *The Problem of Beauty*, 165–167.
31. See McDonald, *Placing Empire*.
32. *SZ*, 13: 493.
33. Ibid., 494.
34. Jacobowitz, *Writing Technology*.

35. *SZ*, 13: 495–6.
36. Paula Varsano traces the earliest example of the trope to a *fu* (poetic exposition) by Wang Can (177–217 CE) titled "Climbing the Tower" (Deng lou fu): "In poems treating this theme, the poet ascends the tower or a mountain and looks out at the vast landscape unfurled before his eyes. Confronted with the evidence of nature's cycles, he reflects upon his own impermanence and the intransigence of the ills of the world. By virtue of the nature of the sentiment being express, treatment of the theme could hardly help but grow more poignant as the theme itself receded into the past and poems on the subject proliferated." Varsano, *Tracking the Banished Immortal,* 175.
37. Fisher, *Wonder,* 21.
38. Wordsworth, *Selected Prose,* 264.
39. *SZ*, 13: 496.
40. Ibid.
41. Ibid.
42. Yosa Buson, *Buson zenshū,* 1: 239.
43. Mark Morris observes that Shiki takes interest in Buson as early as 1893. For more on the relationship between Shiki and Buson, see Morris, "Buson and Shiki: Part Two."
44. Fisher, *Wonder,* 22.
45. *Summer* was published in *Hansei zasshi* (Reflection magazine) on August 1, 1898.
46. The piece also evokes Wordsworth's "Lines Composed a Few Miles above Tintern Abbey" (1798), which Paul Fry has argued is a recompense for loss, that what was beautiful then can still be beautiful now. Fry writes that the crisis of loss in Wordsworth's poetry is "not so much a loss as a failure to understand that what seems to have been lost is always within reach. In itself unaltered, that which was lost in a form that makes it seem different, more consistent with the ethical humanism of mature reflection in response to suffering, yet still harboring Wordsworth's original insight as a poet." Fry, *Wordsworth,* 177–178.
47. Wordsworth's opening to "Tintern Abbey": "Five years have passed. Five summers, with the length / Of five long winters!"
48. *SZ*, 12: 224. Shiki's use of the word "pattern" (*aya*; also *bun*) to describe nature references the centuries of literature on *wen* in traditional Chinese thought. In the opening chapter of *The Literary Mind Carves Dragons,* Liu Xie writes: "As an inner power of things, pattern (*wen*) is very great indeed, and it was born together with Heaven and Earth. How is this?" Owen, *An Anthology of Chinese Literature,* 344.
49. *SZ*, 12: 226.
50. Ibid.

51. *SZ*, 12: 228.
52. In 1896, British diplomat and Japanologist Ernest Satow (1843–1929) built a summer resort near the lake, and since then the area has gained international recognition.
53. *SZ*, 12: 228.
54. Ibid.
55. James: "In mystic states we both become one with the Absolute and we become aware of our oneness"; "Mystical states, when well developed, usually are, and have the right to be, absolutely authoritative over the individuals to whom they come." James, *The Varieties of Religious Experience*, 419, 422.
56. *SZ*, 12: 228. The graph *kei* 盻 is variant for *hen* 盼, which forms a compound word with *sen* 倩: *senben*, which describes the eyes and mouth of a divine beauty.
57. The scene here conjures images from Qu Yuan's (340–278 BCE) "Encountering Sorrow" (Li sao) in *Lyrics of Chu* (Chu ci), and later Cao Zhi's (192–232 CE) *Rhapsody on Goddess of the Luo* (Luo shen fu).
58. Shiki's language breakdown can be read alongside lines from "Two Voices" by Alfred Lord Tennyson (1809–1892):

> Moreover, something is or seems,
> That touches me with mystic gleams,
> Like glimpses of forgotten dreams—
> Of something felt, like something here;
> Of something done, I know not where;
> Such as no language may declare.

Qtd. in James, *The Varieties of Religious Experience*, 383.
59. Beichman, *Masaoka Shiki*, 124.
60. *SZ*, 11: 186.
61. Jean-Jacques Origas is speaking specifically about *A Six-foot Sickbed*: "Since *Byōshō rokushaku* is a *zuihitsu* one may think that it lacks an organized structure, but the reader can viscerally sense several structures manifesting in the text. To speak from my own sense, I can see sequence and order manifesting there." Origas, *Mono to me*, 131.
62. The quote appears in canto III of *Don Juan*. The rest of the stanza:

> 'Tis strange, the shortest letter which man uses
> Instead of speech, may form a lasting link
> Of ages; to what straits old Time reduces
> Frail man, when paper—even a rag like this,
> Survives himself, his tomb, and all that's his.

The sentiments expressed here in Byron's poem are echoed in *A Drop of Ink* as a single word "may form a lasting link / Of ages," and for a writer approaching death these words will be what survives him.

63. Origas, *Mono to me*, 138–139.

64. *SZ*, 11: 93.

65. M. Ueda, *Modern Japanese Poets*.

66. *SZ*, 11: 93.

67. Underlying Shiki's omniscient worldview may be the same imperialist gaze that he finds so unsettling, and yet his conscious choice to employ a variety of literary forms, genres, and styles may also be an attempt to resist the imperial language and modern systems of expression, including teleological narrative (i.e., the novel).

68. *SZ*, 11: 93.

69. Beichman, *Masaoka Shiki*, 142.

70. Ibid., 115.

71. Wilson, *The Meaning of "Life,"* 9.

72. *A Drop of Ink* is most famous for the sequence of tanka Shiki composed on wisteria. For a beautiful translation and reading of the poems, see Beichman, *Masaoka Shiki*, 117.

73. *SZ*, 11: 93.

74. The quote is by French poet Fernand Gregh (1873–1960): "At twenty, Marcel looked on life the same way a fly does, with a multifaceted eye. He saw polygonally. He saw all twenty sides of a question, and added a twenty-first which was prodigiously inventive and ingenious." Muhlstein, *The Pen and the Brush*, 200.

75. Culler, *Theory of the Lyric*, 138.

76. Blasing, *Lyric Poetry*, 2.

77. *SZ*, 11: 189.

78. Ibid.

79. It is tempting to read Shiki's *A Drop of Ink* alongside Coleridge's *Biographia Literaria* (1817), as they are both encyclopedic compendiums of essays that bridge and blend biography, literary criticism, and philosophy. Recent scholarship on Coleridge has mined *Biographia Literaria* for clues about Coleridge's ideas concerning poetic contemplation. See "Special Issue: Coleridge, Contemplation, and Cultural Practice," *Poetica* 85 (2016).

80. *SZ*, 11: 206.

81. Jullien, *The Great Image Has No Form*, 169.

82. *SZ*, 11: 206, 360.

83. Shiki's third and last deathbed narrative *Supine Notes* (1902; Gyōga man-roku) takes the concern for Japanese art even further by placing sketches and abstract illustrations of natural objects alongside the text.

84. Trans. Donald Keene. Keene, *The Winter Sun Shines In*, 171. *SZ*, 11: 231.
85. *SZ*, 11: 266–7.
86. Vincent, "Better than Sex?" 220–241.
87. Culler, *Theory of the Lyric*, 138.
88. Ibid., 185.
89. *SZ*, 11: 266–7.
90. Coleridge, *Coleridge's Poetry and Prose*, 160.
91. Swann: "In 'Christabel,' Coleridge both capitalizes on and exposes culture's tactical gendering of formal questions. The poem invites us to link displacing movement of cultural forms through subjects to the 'feminine' malady of hysteria and the 'feminine' genres of the circulating library; at the same time, it mockingly and dreamily informs us that hysteria is the condition of all subjects in discourse, and that the attribution of this condition to feminine bodies is a conventional, hysterical response." Swann, "*From 'Christabel,'*" 710–722.
92. Kunikida Doppo's *Musashino* (1901), Tayama Katai's *No no hana* (1901), and Shimazaki Tōson's *Kyūshujin* (1902) were written in the modern vernacular language of *genbun'itchi*.
93. *SZ*, 11: 266–7.
94. Ibid.
95. Ibid.
96. My reading considers the fact that Shiki was writing for a public audience and performing until his death.
97. *SZ*, 11: 284.
98. Spencer, *First Principles*, 235.
99. *SZ*, 11: 289–290.
100. Ibid.
101. Ibid.
102. Tabe Tomoki has argued that Shiki introduced *henka* (variation) from linked verse (*renku*) into his haiku and new-style poetry (*shintaishi*), affording them new possibilities of expression. Tabe, "Masaoka Shiki ni okeru renku no ichi," 16–28.
103. The emphasis on transformation evokes essential ideas about organic form in traditional Chinese aesthetics. In "Poetic Exposition on Literature" (Wen fu), Lu Ji (261–303 CE) describes shifts and changes in language as the places where the reader can discern the thoughts and feelings of the writer.
104. *SZ*, 11: 322.
105. *SZ*, 11: 239.
106. *SZ*, 11: 322.
107. Ibid.

108. In chapter 29, "Continuity and Variation" (Tong bian), of *The Literary Mind Carves Dragons*, Liu Xie highlights how genres of writing have been constant throughout literary history, but the vital voice of the writer behind the words achieves longevity through a limitless process of continuity and variation. In other words, a form or genre of writing has infinite variations depending on the writer's ability to use language. Owen, *An Anthology of Chinese Literature*, 351.

References

Beichman, Janine. *Masaoka Shiki*. New York: Kodansha International, 1986.

Blasing, Mutlu Konuk. *Lyric Poetry: The Pain the Pleasure of Words*. Princeton, NJ: Princeton University Press, 2007.

Byron. *Don Juan*. Edited by T.G. Steffan, E. Steffan, and W.W. Pratt. New York: Penguin, 2004.

Chance, Linda H. *Formless in Form: Kenkō, Tsurezuregusa, and the Rhetoric of Japanese Fragmentary Prose*. Stanford, CA: Stanford University Press, 1997.

Coleridge, Samuel Taylor. *Coleridge's Poetry and Prose*. Edited by Nicholas Halmi, Paul Magnuson, and Raimonda Modiano, Norton Critical Edition. New York: W. W. Norton, 2004.

Culler, Jonathan. *Theory of the Lyric*. Cambridge, MA: Harvard University Press, 2015.

Eakin, John Paul. *Fictions in Autobiography: Studies in the Art of Self-Invention*. Princeton, NJ: Princeton University Press, 1985.

Egan, Ronald. *The Problem of Beauty: Aesthetic Thought and Pursuits in Northern Song Dynasty China*. Cambridge, MA: Harvard East Asia Center, 2006.

Fisher, Philip. *Wonder, The Rainbow, and the Aesthetics of Rare Experiences*. Cambridge, MA: Harvard University Press, 1998.

Fong, Grace S., and Ellen Widmer, eds. *The Inner Quarters and Beyond: Women Writers from Ming through Qing*. Boston: Brill, 2010.

Fry, Paul H. *Wordsworth and the Poetry of What We Are*. New Haven: Yale University Press, 2008.

Jacobowitz, Seth. *Writing Technology in Meiji Japan: A Media History of Modern Japanese Literature and Visual Culture*. Cambridge, MA: Harvard East Asia Center, 2015.

James, William. *The Varieties of Religious Experience: A Study in Human Nature*. New York: Longmans, Green, 1920.

Jullien, François. *The Propensity of Things: Toward a History of Efficacy in China*. Translated by Janet Lloyd. New York: Zone Books, 1995.

———. *The Great Image Has No Form, or On the Nonobject through Painting*. Translated by Jane Marie Todd. Chicago: The University of Chicago Press, 2009.

Karatani Kōjin. *The Origins of Modern Japanese Literature*. Translated by Brett de Bary. Durham, NC: Duke University Press, 1993.

Keene, Donald. *The Winter Sun Shines In: A Life of Masaoka Shiki*. New York: Columbia University Press, 2013.

Masaoka Shiki. *Shiki zenshū*. 25 vols. Tokyo: Kōdansha, 1976.

———. *Shiki jinsei ronshū*. Tokyo: Kōdansha, 2001.

Masaoka Shiki shū. Vol. 27, *Shin Nihon koten bungaku taikei: Meiji hen*. 30 vols. Edited by Kanai Keiko, Munakata Kazushige, and Katsuhara Haruki. Tokyo: Iwanami Shoten, 2016.

McDonald, Kate. *Placing Empire: Travel and Social Imagination in Imperial Japan*. Berkeley: University of California Press, 2017.

Morris, Mark. "Buson and Shiki: Part One." *Harvard Journal of Asiatic Studies* 44, no. 2 (December 1984): 381–425.

———. "Buson and Shiki: Part Two." *Harvard Journal of Asiatic Studies* 45, no. 1 (June 1985): 255–321.

Mulhstein, Anka. *The Pen and the Brush: How Passion for Art Shaped Nineteenth-Century French Novels*. Translated by Adriana Hunter. New York: Other Press, 2017.

Origas, Jean-Jacques. *Mono to me: Meiji bungaku ronshū*. Tokyo: Iwanami Shoten, 2003.

Owen, Stephen, ed. and trans. *An Anthology of Chinese Literature: Beginnings to 1911*. New York: W.W. Norton, 1996.

Poetica 85. "Special Issue: Coleridge, Contemplation, and Cultural Practice." Tokyo: Maruzen-Yushodo, 2016.

Shimagi Akahiko. *Kadō shōken*. Tokyo: Kōdansha, 1978.

Sontag, Susan. *Illness as Metaphor and AIDS and Its Metaphors*. New York: Picador, 1989.

Spencer, Herbert. *The Philosophy of Style: An Essay*. New York: D. Appleton and Company, 1876.

———. *First Principles*. New York: A. L. Burt, 1880.

Stewart, Susan. *Poetry and the Fate of the Senses*. Chicago: The University of Chicago Press, 2002.

Swann, Karen. "*From 'Christabel'*: The Wandering Mother and the Enigma of Form." In *Coleridge's Poetry and Prose*, edited by Nicholas Halmi, Paul Magnuson, and Raimonda Modiano, Norton Critical Edition, 710–722. New York: W.W. Norton, 2004.

Tabe Tomoki. "Masaoka Shiki ni okeru renku no ichi: 'henka' ni taisuru hyōka wo jiku ni." *Renga haikai kenkyū* 130, (March, 2016): 16–28.

Takeuchi, Melinda. *Taiga's True Views: The Language of Landscape Painting in Eighteenth-Century Japan*. Stanford, CA: Stanford University Press, 1992.

Ueda, Atsuko. "Sounds, scripts, and styles: *kanbun kundokutai* and the national language reforms of 1880s Japan." In *Translation in Modern Japan*, edited by Indra Levy, 141–164. New York: Routledge, 2010.

Ueda, Makoto. *Modern Japanese Poets and the Nature of Literature*. Stanford, CA: Stanford University Press, 1983.

Varsano, Paula M. *Tracking the Banished Immortal: The Poetry of Li Bo and Its Critical Reception*. Honolulu: University of Hawaii Press, 2003.

Vincent, J. Keith. "Better than Sex? Masaoka Shiki's Poems on Food." In *Devouring Japan: Global Perspectives on Japanese Culinary Identity*, edited by Nancy K. Stalker, 220–241. New York: Oxford University Press, 2018.

Wilson, Ross, ed. *The Meaning of "Life" in Romantic Poetry and Poetics*. New York: Routledge, 2009.

Wittgenstein, Ludwig. *Philosophical Investigations*. Translated by G.E.M. Anscombe. Malden, MA: Blackwell, 1953.

Wordsworth, William. *Selected Prose*. Edited by John O. Hayden. New York: Penguin, 1988.

Yosa Buson. *Buson zenshū*. Edited by Ogata Tsutomu, et al. 9 vols. Tokyo: Kōdansha, 1992.

CHAPTER 5

Anxiety and Grief in the Prose Poems of Natsume Sōseki

How beautiful, if sorrow had not made
Sorrow more beautiful than Beauty's self.
—John Keats, *Hyperion*, Book I (1856)

In this hither and back of mutual and manifold influence,
the interior of the picture vibrates, rises and falls back into itself,
and does not have a single unmoving part.
—Rainer Maria Rilke, *Letters on Cézanne* (1907)

The end is immanent, rather than imminent.
—Frank Kermode, *The Sense of an Ending* (1967)

This chapter examines how modern novelist Natsume Sōseki (1867–1916) carried forth the legacy of the literati tradition into the modern period and simultaneously mourned its death. Of the four writers treated in this book it is Sōseki's relationship to literati culture that was the most ironic. As shown in the previous chapter, Masaoka Shiki (1867–1902) saturated his modern prose poems with an array of traditional tropes, representing the literati tradition in a diffuse and dissonant form on the brink of collapse—just like his own body. In Sōseki's works, the end of the literati tradition is

---

The original version of the chapter has been revised. A correction to this chapter can be found at https://doi.org/10.1007/978-3-031-11922-4_7

© The Author(s), under exclusive license to Springer Nature Switzerland AG 2022, corrected publication 2023
M. Mewhinney, *Form and Feeling in Japanese Literati Culture*,
https://doi.org/10.1007/978-3-031-11922-4_5

represented as having already arrived, or, to echo Frank Kermode, as immanent.[1]

In literary history, Sōseki is mostly known as a novelist who produced thirteen major works, many of which were serialized in the *Asahi* newspaper. In his personal life, he displayed another talent as a prolific poet who composed thousands of poems across genres, including English verse, new-style poetry (*shintaishi*), tanka, haiku, and *kanshi*. Sōseki is perhaps most known for the latter two poetic genres, which afforded him a claim to Late Edo literati culture. In his novel *Pillow of Grass* (1906; Kusamakura) and his memoir *Recollecting and Such* (1910; Omoidasu koto nado), he combined haiku and *kanshi* with modern vernacular prose, forging new poetic forms through which he mediated feelings of grief, anxiety, and longing for literati culture.

Contrary to their genre categorizations in literary history, I read *Pillow of Grass* and *Recollecting and Such* as modern prose poems because their narratives unfold according to the thoughts, senses, and feelings of their first-person narrators (Sōseki's lyric "I").[2] As these narrators express their feelings of grief (as nostalgia and melancholy) in a combination of modern vernacular prose, haiku, and *kanshi*, the narratives' oscillation between prose and poetry creates an organic rhythm between stasis and movement that evokes the alternation between loss and restoration in the process of grieving and simulates the beating pulse of a living organism. This contrapuntal motion represents what psychologists call "the paradox of grief."[3]

The narrator in *Pillow of Grass* is a poet-painter who embarks on a journey to capture beauty. Seeking inspiration for a painting, he travels to an idyllic and pastoral landscape, far away from the concerns of modern urban life and the threat of war. His grief takes form in images that evoke languid motion in mythic time and space, eternal slowness, and an aesthetic of indistinctness drawn from Chinese poetry and painting. This slowness stalls the linear progression of the narrative, which concludes with a pat ending that ironizes the journey as well as the artist's goal to complete his painting: his epiphany that he can paint after seeing the sadness on the woman innkeeper Nami's face becomes ironic in the context of the novel's unresolved representation of grief and longing.

In *Recollecting and Such*, the narrator convalesces from a near-death experience. The narrative is retrospective and non-chronological. As the narrator recounts past events, alternating between prose and poetry, this stasis and movement in his recollections creates a narrative pulse that simulates an ill body in a state of recovery. Although the narrator regains his memory of past events through sensory embodiment in lyric poems, *Recollecting and Such* concludes by ironizing the efficacy of that recuperative process, representing the narrator's grief and loss as unending.

As modern poetic experiments, *Pillow of Grass* and *Recollecting and Such* show how Sōseki participated in the literati tradition by embracing it ironically. Sōseki concludes both works with Romantic irony, I argue, to cope with the immanent death of literati culture in modern times, holding on to the idea that "only the fragmentary, finite, and incomplete…can give us a sense of infinity that lies behind any closed form."[4] As feelings of grief take form in each work, irony—the permanent interruption of meaning that makes the reader question the narrative presented before him— allows that grief to continue, unresolved, beyond the containment of form and the finality of literary closure. Both works thereby evince that the process of grieving can only be represented through the organic open-endedness afforded by the prose poem.

A "Haiku-Style Novel"

In the same year of its publication in 1906, Sōseki described *Pillow of Grass* as a "haiku-style novel" (*haikuteki shōsetsu*), while acknowledging that such a term was unusual.[5] The writer did not elaborate further on what he meant by the term, only that it pointed to how the work was doing something new in Japanese literature. As shown in the previous chapters of this book, haiku (formerly known as *hokku*) played an integral part in Late Edo literati culture. Yosa Buson (1716–1783) transformed the genre by infusing his poems with the diction of Chinese poetry and painting, creating ekphrastic forms that represented Chinese landscapes. Although Ema Saikō (1787–1861) composed only *kanshi*, the wit and humor of *haikai* poetics likely informed the way she ironized genre conventions.[6] By the late nineteenth century, Shiki was using haiku to promote his modern ideal of *shasei*, representing personal and subjective observations of life, which transformed haiku into a modern lyric genre.

Robert Backus described haiku as a form of contrast and incongruity, stating that its brevity is an "effort to sharpen our consciousness of what we live in confusion by reordering the shreds of experience into new, quickly apprehensible, totalities."[7] *Pillow of Grass* is neither quick nor brief, as its narrative plods along slowly, following the rambles of the first-person narrator. Moreover, the work contains *kanshi*, tanka, and English verse in addition to haiku. For Sōseki to call it a "haiku-style novel," then, seems to suggest that haiku is a metonym for all the lyric poetry in the narrative and that his neologism attempts to capture the work's organizational principle as a lyrical prose poem.

In the spirit of haiku, the sensuous and affective language in *Pillow of Grass* creates poetic oppositions that give the narrative its movement, which Masao Miyoshi described as "determined by the juxtaposition and reversal of short scenes or thought sequences."[8] This narrative structure also speaks to what Ralph Freedman has described as the nineteenth-century "lyrical novel," which he claims is distinct for its "internal conflict, a precarious balance of different, sometimes antithetical, techniques which creates a poetic effect."[9]

The poetic oppositions in the narrative occasion irony, or what could be called Romantic irony. As D.C. Muecke has put it, "Romantic Irony is the expression of an ironical attitude adopted as a means of recognizing and transcending, but still preserving those contradictions. The theory of Romantic irony is the theory that this is the only course open to the modern artist."[10] The narrator in *Pillow of Grass* is a modern artist who recognizes and transcends the boundaries between Eastern and Western aesthetics, while preserving their contradictions by quoting from, referencing, and composing in different genres of language and registers of speech.

The narrative opens with poetic opposition, setting the tone for the rest of the work. The narrator, a poet-painter, contemplates the Romantic discord between humanity and nature. In Romanticism, modern man has lost his connection with nature, and longs to make recompense by communing with the natural landscape. Thinking about this conflict between man and nature, the narrator embarks on a quest in the countryside to find inspiration for a painting:

> As I ascended the mountain path, I pondered:
> Work by reason, and you will encounter rough patches; Dip your oar into the tide of sentiment, and you will be swept away; Always having your way only constrains you. Suffice it to say, the human world is a hard place to live.
> When this difficulty intensifies, you long to move to an easier place. At the moment you have realized that life is hard no matter where you are, a poem is born, and a painting takes form.
> If the human world is not the work of a god, it is not the work of a demon either. It is the work of ordinary people just living their lives in the row of houses next door. You may think it is hard to live in a world created

by ordinary people, but surely there is nowhere else to go. If there were, that would only mean going to the nonhuman realm. But I imagine that life in the nonhuman realm would be even harder than life in the human world.[11]

Like the title *kusamakura*—a poetic epithet for travel meaning "pillow of grass"—the opening line frames the entire novel as a tour of the narrator's mind: while his body is in a state of motion (*noborinaga*), his mind is deep in thought (*kangaeta*).[12] Over the course of the narrative, his journey becomes a process of thinking about the relationship between humanity and nature.

The narrative unfolds into a long aesthetic journey through the deployment of images and tropes from the English, Japanese, and Chinese poetic traditions. The opening ascent of a mountain alludes to the "Climbing High" (Ch. *deng gao*) trope in classical Chinese poetry as well as to the Romantic quest into the mystery of nature. Poetic traditions blend as the narrator ascends, a journey that stirs contradictory thoughts about life in nature vis-à-vis life among people. He finds life in the modern "human world" (*hito no yo*) difficult because it lends itself to extreme ways of being that result in conflict and discord. This difficulty sets up an argument for living elsewhere, a place that seems not to exist. If it were to exist, he continues, then it would be the "nonhuman realm" (*hito de nashi no kuni*)—the prelapsarian world of nature, untainted by the problems of man. But just as he praises life in the nonhuman realm, he contradicts the thought by saying that life there would be more difficult than life among people. This back and forth between ideas anticipates other poetic oppositions that occur later in the narrative.

The binary created by the "human world" and the "nonhuman realm" is echoed by other antipodes, most notably *ninjō* (human feelings; attachment) and *hininjō* (nonhuman feelings; detachment).[13] Pairs such as *ninjō* and *hininjō* are among many antipodes that constitute the dialectical system through which the narrative unfolds, occasioning irony: going back and forth between antipodes; stating that the novel is in search of one thing, then evoking its opposite.[14] The meaning of each term is redefined in its evocation, only to be undermined later by a lyric poem or lines of figurative prose.

This back and forth creates slippages in meaning that reveal the lyric impulses of *Pillow of Grass* as a whole. The work purports to be in search of *hininjō*, which Karatani Kōjin has described as a time and space outside of realism and inside the imaginative world of poetry and painting.[15] While purporting to be a work unconcerned with real life in modern times, *Pillow of Grass* shifts into the world of *ninjō* by commenting on war, by featuring cliché interactions between the narrator and a mysterious woman innkeeper named Nami, and by evoking the comic and frivolous exchanges of nineteenth-century melodrama.[16]

In *Pillow of Grass*, the psychology of the lyric subject is projected onto the landscape that he describes. In other words, the narrator's thoughts and feelings take form in his natural surroundings. These scenes allude to tranquil "mountains and streams" (*sansui*) and related topoi from classical Chinese and Japanese poetry, as well as to natural scenes from Romantic poetry of the eighteenth and nineteenth centuries.[17] In late imperial Chinese poetics, this approach is known as the "blending of feeling and scene" (Ch. *qing jing jiao rong*), theorized by Qing dynasty poet Wang Fuzhi (1619–1692). The narrative is written almost entirely in the present tense, which performs the immediacy of the narrator's thinking about the journey, enabling him to form a Romantic communion with the landscape in the lyric present, like the subjects in the poems of William Wordsworth and other Romantic poets whom Sōseki had read.

When the narrator remarks that in times of difficulty "a poem is born, and a painting takes form," he describes how the work's form responds to the thoughts and feelings of the lyric subject. Poetry and painting both manifest in prose descriptions of sight and sound. He offers an example when he hears birdsong:

> Suddenly I hear the voice of a lark below my feet. I gaze down into the vale, but I can see no form or shadow showing where it is singing. All I hear is its song, pellucid and piercing—notes pouring forth hurriedly without pause. It feels unbearable as if the entire boundless blanket of air had been punctured by the bites of fleas. Not for an instant do the notes in the bird's song lull. Seemingly unable to rest until it sings the tranquil spring day to its end, singing it to light, and again singing it to dark. Soaring up and up, and flying on and on, the lark will surely find its death deep in the clouds. Rising to where it can rise no more, it may find itself swept away into the clouds, floating in suspension before its form disappears, leaving behind only its song in the sky.[18]

As the narrator makes his way up the mountain path, he pauses his philosophical discussion on poetry and painting to notice the natural landscape around him. He suddenly hears the song of a lark. The prose then flows into figurative language, evoking Percy Bysshe Shelley's (1792–1822) ode "To a Skylark" (1820). The adverbs "just" (*tada*) and "only" (*dake*) emphasize that it is sound that marks the lark's presence, indicating the song as synecdoche for the singer. The sound of the lark's song takes form in the prose with the repetition of *n* consonants (e.g., a*n*o tori *n*o *n*aku *n*e *n*iwa shu*n*ji *n*o yoyū mo *n*ai). As the image of the bird—which the reader imagines only by way of synecdoche—climbs higher and higher into the void, the song becomes all the more resonant. The passage ends with hyperbole, describing an ascent into the clouds, where the lark disappears in death and leaves only its song as a disembodied and ghostly voice reverberating in the boundless firmament. Like the body of the lark suspended in the sky before it disappears forever, the narrator's feelings tarry in musical splendor, tinged with mournful sentiment.

While the idea of the disembodied song speaks to the conceit behind the "nonhuman world" because it conceals or effaces the existence of a human lyric subject, its ceaselessness even after the lark's disappearance suggests that this world of sonorous pleasure begins to feel more like throbbing pain in the mind of the poet. The possibility of relief adumbrated by the bird's flight toward death makes this point evident, but the narrator's overall description of the lark's song—including the metaphor of air having been punctured by flea bites—suggests that music in this natural landscape is not so pleasurable. Lines later, how apropos then that the narrator quotes the eighteenth stanza from "To a Skylark," and distills the earlier prose description of the lark's song into lines of English Romantic verse:

> *We look before and after*
> *And pine for what is not:*
> *Our sincerest laughter*
> *With some pain is fraught;*
> *Our sweetest songs are those that tell of saddest thought.*

"Looking before, looking after,
We pine for what we want;
Even belly laughter
Can be fraught with pain;
One knows that the sweetest songs contain the saddest thought."

> Indeed, no matter how joyful the poet may be, he cannot hope to sing his joy as the lark does, with such passionate wholeheartedness, oblivious to all thought before and after.[19]

After quoting Shelley, the narrator translates the English lines into modern Japanese poetry.[20] While the narrator's translation explicates Shelley's lines for the Japanese reader, it also repeats the feelings that they convey, echoing the contradictory idea encapsulated in the last line and in the earlier prose passage describing the lark's song. These echoes perform the lark's recursive song in literary form.

After the poem, the narrator discusses how a poet cannot be like a lark that sings its heart out, seizing the present moment and completely ignoring what comes before and after. This is because the speaker's mind is constituted by contradiction, he "pines for what is not," his "laughter, / with some pain is fraught," and his "sweetest songs are those that tell of saddest thought." In the full version of Shelley's ode, the poet addresses the skylark and praises its beautiful song. By ventriloquizing Shelley, Sōseki's narrator is making a general claim about poetry and the Romanticism of *Pillow of Grass* as a whole. The ode is a paean to the skylark's song and a reminder of the poet's inability to sing like the bird. This part of the narrative conjures Shelley's elegiac voice, in which, as Mark Sandy writes, "potential moments of poetic vision and transformation are haunted by an awareness of loss and grief that return us from the possibilities of transcendence and revelation to a confrontation with the limitations of poetry and our own contingent existences."[21] As a prose poem, *Pillow of Grass* features moments of poetic vision and transformation, but the contradictions of thought as well as the mournful and elegiac feelings that take form in the narrative, like Shelley's poetry, ironize the possibility of actual transcendence.

PATHOLOGIES OF MOTION

Pillow of Grass tarries in poetic tropes, stalling the narrative in a time and space outside of teleological closure and producing a languid motion that contradicts the pace of post-industrial life in an age of rising imperialism. This is how the narrative performs the conceit of "nonhuman detachment"—except that human attachment invariably gets in the way, propelling the lyric subject into the heart of human feeling.

Stasis and movement are both evoked in the first chapter, where the narrator discusses another binary: the sleeping world and the waking world. He argues that the imagination of poetic worlds from antiquity—such as the classic Peach Blossom Spring made famous by Six Dynasties poet Tao Yuanming (365?–427 CE)—is an antidote that has palliative effects on the heart and mind. Although the narrator does not state the source of the ailment, the reader may assume that it comes from the modern world of human attachments, the very world the narrator is trying to escape:

> Should sleep be necessary in the twentieth century, the taste of poetry that transcends the vulgar world in the twentieth century becomes all the more essential. It is a pity that composers and readers of poetry are all under the influence of Western writers, so they no longer take the trouble to set off on a skiff free and easy and ride upstream all the way to ancient utopias like the Peach Blossom Spring. Since I have never been a poet by profession, I have no intention to preach to modern society about the poetic worlds of Wang Wei and Yuanming. But for me and only me, the excitement their poetry stirs is more medicinal than theater performances or dance parties, and more moving than Faust or Hamlet. This is the whole reason I plod along slowly on a mountain path in spring, carrying a box of paints and a stool, all by myself. I long to absorb directly from nature the poetic worlds of Yuanming and Wang Wei, and to roam, even for just a while, in the world of nonhuman detachment. Call it a whim.[22]

The narrator places East and West in opposition, as if they are absolute categories. He says that he does not intend to sing the praises of classical Chinese poets but then ironically expresses his wish to immerse himself in their poetic worlds. He writes that the "pleasure" (*kankyō*, lit. "sense pleasure") he feels when roaming in poetic antiquity is more "medicinal" (*kusuri ni naru yō*) than when consuming Western art forms. Considering the binaries at play, the reader imagines that this medicine induces sleep, much like an opiate, numbing the lyric subject from the pain of reality. Dream states induced by opium were made famous by Romantic poets including Samuel Taylor Coleridge (1772–1834) and Thomas De Quincey (1785–1859), both of whom Sōseki had read. The narrator associates dream with intoxication, which is reified in the word "whim" (*suikyō*, lit. "intoxicating pleasure").

Nakajima Kunihiko has argued that "pleasure" (*kankyō*) is a crucial term in Japanese literature written after the Russo-Japanese War (1904–1905). He describes *kankyō* as "an artistic stance and practice to overcome a critical situation," writing: "By the late Meiji period, many writers had met with crisis. Simply put, it was the encounter with the unknown, the fugitive, and the self-threatening."[23] As a postwar work, *Pillow of Grass* is just what the doctor ordered, aiming to provide an antidote to the malaise of modern life and catastrophe in 1906; its palliative effects reside in its language. Just as the narrator "plods along slowly" (*noso noso aruku*), his narrative also moves at a plodding pace through sensual prose and poetry.

An example of plodding prose appears at the end of the first chapter, where the narrator pictures himself as a figure in a painting or a poem. He imagines a painterly scene where raindrops fall like silver arrows across the overcast sky, grey and hazy like faded ink:

> Drenched and moving in the vast and indistinct pale-ink-wash world with silver arrows falling aslant around me, I think of a human form not as myself, but as a poem, as a recitation of verse. When I abandon my material self and observe through a gaze of pure objectivity, for the first time as a figure in a painting I preserve the views of nature and their beautiful harmony.[24]

After he has immersed himself in this painterly landscape, the narrator becomes one with the medium that he evokes: a poem or a line of verse. This self-figuration as a poem or as a line to be recited by the reader speaks to the lyric impulse of this passage and elsewhere in the narrative, where the motion of the lyric subject and other figured objects is mediated through the process of reading.

The narrator then abandons his material self and assumes a "gaze of pure objectivity" that allows him to observe and preserve nature's beautiful harmony. But his reverie does not last:

> The very moment I become concerned by the pain that afflicts my mind in the falling rain and the fatigue that strikes my feet with each step, I am no longer a figure in a poem, nor am I a figure in a painting. I am as before, nothing more than an ordinary townsman. My eyes become blind to the charm of rolling clouds and swirling smoke, my heart unmoved by the pity of fallen blossoms and crying birds.[25]

Once the reality of walking around in the countryside begins to wear on his mind and body, the narrator wakes up from his reverie and loses his ability to feel the empathy stirred by poetry and painting. The repetitive rhetoric in these sentences—"I am...nor am I," "My eyes...my heart"—makes them parallel, much like couplets in classical Chinese poetry and lines of parallel prose in literary Chinese. Although the content of the narrator's speech claims the loss of sensibility, the rhetoric of his language suggests otherwise: the denial of poetry is contradicted by the poetic rhythm in the passage.

The narrator's description of the transition in and out of dream is a fanciful exaggeration that speaks to the conceit of *Pillow of Grass* and why poetry functions as a palliative with opiate-like effects that are temporary. The numbing, dreamlike effects wear off when the natural landscape is not so idyllic. The first chapter concludes with a description that adumbrates how the narrative unfolds, as well as how stasis and movement in language stir disorienting feelings:

> Walking alone in dank desolateness through the mountain in spring, I am able to comprehend the beauty of myself even less. In the beginning, I tilt my hat and stride out. Later I simply walk with eyes fixed on my feet. In the end, I walk with trepidation, with my shoulders hunched. As far as the eyes could see, rain rattles the treetops, and from all directions encroaches upon the lone traveler. This is a little too much nonhuman detachment.[26]

The comic irony with which the narrator concludes the first chapter balances the effusiveness and seriousness with which he discusses aesthetics, philosophy, and his desire to escape the concerns of the mundane world. Such irony falls under the larger umbrella of Romantic irony in *Pillow of Grass* as a self-conscious prose poem representing, to quote Muecke, "the mind's turning in upon itself."[27] In this way, the narrative speaks to what Michael O'Neill has identified as the "self-conscious poem" in Romanticism.[28]

In this passage, the repetition of the verb "to walk" (*aruku*) encapsulates the plodding plot of *Pillow of Grass*; the adverbs that modify the walking narrate the drama of feelings over the course of the narrative. By the end, the narrator finds himself walking unsteadily and with trepidation (*osoru osoru*). He started off ascending the mountain path with wavering thoughts, digressing about springtime tranquility and resplendence. But once the landscape "encroaches" (*semaru*) upon the solitary traveler, dream feels like nightmare.

This opening chapter lays the groundwork for the rest of the narrative, displaying what kind of language the reader can expect and suggesting the feelings and affect that that language generates. What kind of feelings are these, and how are they mediated? They are feelings of grief and anxiety mediated through poetry in the form of poetic prose and poems.

In the third chapter, the narrator records six haiku as they come to him, suspending the narrative and creating a montage of images in haiku form. Below are the two poems that end the sequence, followed by a line of prose:

> Poem upon poem,
> Pacing to and fro   *uta ori ori / gekka no haru o / ochikochi su*
> In the spring moonlight.   うた折々月下の春ををちこちす
>
> Resigned,
> Spring draws to a close,   *omoikitte / fuke yuku haru no / hitori kana*
> And I am all alone.   思ひ切つて更け行く春の独りかな

While composing these verses, at some point I begin to doze off.[29]

The first haiku speaks to the formal movements of *Pillow of Grass* as a narrative that places poem upon poem and wanders back and forth in the narrator's imagination of a spring landscape. The second haiku comments on the entangled relationship between the lyric subject and the landscape in which he is situated. The use of the adverb *omoikitte* (resolutely; determinedly; resignedly) to describe how spring approaches its end is in part a Romantic personification of spring, imbuing the season with the agency to determine its own temporality. But the adverb also speaks to the resignation of the speaker, who laments his solitude as the vagaries of time are beyond his control. And yet, his connection to spring—*haru no / hitori kana*—makes him also part of that season, which has resigned itself to drawing to a close. In other words, the speaker and the spring are one—an idea to which the narrator returns later in the narrative.

The drowsiness induced by composing poetry evokes a liminal space between sleep and waking. The narrator describes this space via the metaphor of a fine silk thread that demarcates the two worlds like an event horizon leading to a black hole full of unknown possibilities:

I think the adjective 'entranced' would be most apt here. In deep sleep, everyone loses recognition of self. When the mind is conscious and clear, no one can be oblivious of the external world. But between these two worlds stretches the horizon to an illusory realm as tenuous as silk thread, too vague to be called waking, too alert to be termed sleep. Such a state is like placing the sleep and waking worlds into the same bottle and thoroughly blending them with the brush of poetry: blur the colors of nature to the threshold of dream, and draw the whole universe, as it is, deeper into the misty realm.[30]

In his state of drowsiness, the narrator falls into deep thought about the word *kōkotsu*, which as an adjective means "entranced; ecstatic; enraptured." The Chinese compound is originally a stative verb that describes entrancement. The prose deploys figurative language to describe this liminal space between sleep and waking. The metaphor of mixture in a form of containment offers a meta-comment on the narrative, knocking on the door of dream and the imagination—where everything is as indistinct as mist and haze—but not entering. The metaphor also undermines the narrative's attempt to maintain a clear distinction between antipodes, as the text is self-consciously aware that such polarities are reconciled by blending.

The figure of the "fine silk thread" (*ru*) for the horizon that lies between the two worlds complements the figure of the "jar" (*bin*) in which they are blended by the "brush of poetry." These figures of containment allude to the containment of the earlier haiku: the silk thread figures that containment as an image of infinity, suggesting the idea of lyric eternity or the eternal present in lyric poetry; at the same time, the jar delimits that containment with an image of finite space. As passages in *Pillow of Grass* hover in figuration and metaphor, the narrative slows down, allowing the narrator's imagination to roam in realms beyond the boundaries of the pastoral and into the infinite space of the cosmos.

The narrator returns to the feeling of entrancement and ecstasy in the sixth chapter, where slowness and languid motion take shape in the form and content of language. The earlier evocations of motion in the haiku and in the figuration of consciousness and unconsciousness meet with a fuller and more figurative description of ecstasy and entrancement, but one that evokes motion without a specific destination:

I am not thinking about anything clearly, nor am I seeing anything with certainty. Nothing of striking color stirs on the stage in my consciousness, so

I cannot say I have become one with anything. Yet I am in motion: motion neither within the world nor without it—just simply in motion. Neither motion as a flower, nor as a bird, nor motion in relation to another human being, just ecstatic [*kōkotsu*] motion.³¹

The narrator describes himself suspended in a liminal state in between antipodes. The negation of motion (*ugoku ni mo arazu*) repeats throughout the passage, reifying his awareness. Language also mediates his movement, which is qualified by the adverb *kōkotsu*, referencing the earlier passage in which the narrator feels drowsy after composing haiku.

When he explicates "ecstatic motion," the narrator conjures the images from the earlier haiku in which he has merged with spring. He explains this fusion through the figure of a "spirit" or "essence" (*seiki*) that has compounded all the elements of spring and saturated his mind:

If I were pressed to explain, I would want to say that my mind is simply moving with spring. I would want to say a spirit [*seiki*]—compounded of every spring color, spring breeze, spring creature, spring song, then condensed and refined into an immortal potion and then dissolved into a numinous elixir from Penglai, and then evaporated in the sun at Peach Blossom Spring—has unbeknownst to me seeped into my pores and saturated my mind unconsciously.³²

As the narrator describes the sublime experience of becoming one with the season, he evokes images from Chinese myth: an "immortal potion" made from cinnabar (*sendan*), a "numinous elixir" (*reieki*), and Penglai, the imaginary realm of the immortals. The predicates of these statements indicate that they are mere approximations, as the ineffable can only be expressed through metaphor, evocations of the imaginary, and suppositional language.

Lines later, the narrator declares more definitively that there is no "stimulant" (*shigeki*) that has initiated his merging with nature: "Normally some stimulant provokes a sense of oneness. One imagines that precisely because there is a stimulant that the experience is enjoyable. But in my oneness, I cannot discern with what I have merged, so there is no stimulant at all":³³

The absence of a stimulant produces a profound and indescribable pleasure [*yōzen toshite meijō shigatai tanoshimi*]. I do not mean some fugitive and wild elation, like waves that heave up toward the sky, by the whip of the wind. I can describe it as like a boundless blue sea that moves between one continent and another above invisible depths of ocean floor.[34]

When the narrator tries to explain what he means by this pleasure, he returns to metaphor. He wants to clarify that the pleasure is not fleeting, like waves heaving at the will of the wind. Rather, he describes this pleasure as immeasurable in time and space, a "boundless blue sea" (*kōyō taru sōkai*) moving between two continents—alluding to his earlier claim that the feeling is "profound" and "indescribable."[35]

The metaphors that constitute the landscape of imagery in *Pillow of Grass* rely primarily on sight, but they also reference sound and touch. The work thus transcends the visual limits of painting, embracing a poetry that calls for full sensory embodiment. Such an experience alludes to the sensual worlds of classical Chinese poetry, including *Lyrics of Chu* (third century BCE; Chu ci) and Qu Yuan's "Encountering Sorrow" (Li sao).[36] The aesthetics from these ancient poems are reproduced in the long tradition of literati poetry and painting; among them is "blandness" (Ch. *pingdan*), the aesthetic from literati painting and poetry that evokes ineffable plenitude.

In his concluding remarks about merging with spring and feeling profound and indescribable pleasure, the narrator writes that his mind is "bland" (*awaki*):

> By 'bland,' I simply mean a taste that is hard to grasp, but without the risk of being too weak. Poetic expressions such as 'teeming tranquility' or 'languid calm' perhaps most fully express this state.[37]

In order to clarify what he means by "bland" (*awashi*), he cites expressions used by Chinese poets: "teeming tranquility" (*chūyū*) and "languid calm" (*tantō*). Both words are composed of Chinese graphs that express the fluidity of water. The word *chūyū* (Ch. *chongrong*) describes a state of harmony and tranquility that is overflowing and also profound; the word *tantō* (Ch. *dandang*) describes a state of boundless calm with faint and languid motion, like a placidly flowing stream.[38] In addition to echoing the many descriptions of the vicissitudes of water's form in *Pillow of Grass*, these expressions distill the tapestry of images that the narrator weaves together through figurative descriptions of the intoxication induced by composing poetry and the attendant feelings of profound and indescribable pleasure that emerge when he finds himself moving under the sway of a force beyond his control.

The states of "teeming tranquility" and "languid calm" also speak to the conceit of nonhuman detachment in the narrative, though treating them as such only touches upon the surface of their meaning. The narrator's effusions of joy and pleasure are ironized by grief evoked in poetry as well as in dialogue, where the historical contingencies of 1906 and the wartime feelings of loss loom large. The feeling of pleasure, like the word *hininjō* that is used time and again to figure it, is external and artificial— just like the surface of a painting. This idea speaks to the way eighteenth-century philosopher Edmund Burke (1730–1797) described "joy and grief" in *A Philosophical Enquiry* (1757): "in grief, the *pleasure* is still uppermost."[39] The irony in Burke's claim evokes Shelley's line "our sweetest songs tell those of the saddest thought." The stasis and movement in *Pillow of Grass* is the contrapuntal narrative motion that represents the process of grieving. The symmetrical and reciprocal relationship between grief and joy speaks to how this process of mourning depends upon the figuration of fantasy as reality, poetry as mimesis.[40]

The following section explores how jouissance in *Pillow of Grass* is ironized by feelings of loss that surface in poetry, and that thereby refigure enchanting spells of numbing ecstasy as ceaseless moments of paralyzing grief.

NOSTALGIA AND MELANCHOLY

Above I have discussed how the alternation between prose and poetry generates a contrapuntal motion in narrative that gives form to grief. This grief may be described as nostalgia and melancholy, which are both feelings of longing;[41] what distinguishes the two is whether the longing takes an object or not.

Nostalgia can be understood as longing for an object. In her book on nostalgia in the Slavic cultural context, Svetlana Boym writes that "the rapid pace of industrialization and modernization increased the intensity of people's longing for the slower rhythms of the past, for continuity, social cohesion and tradition."[42] *Pillow of Grass* is a case in point: it exhibits nostalgia for a retrospectively sanitized past, crystallized in the idyllic world of *hininjō*. The narrator's desire to embrace *hininjō* inspires him to converse with poems written centuries earlier: in addition to quoting Shelley, the narrator cites poems by Tang poet Wang Wei, whose work evokes the tranquility of Buddhist aesthetics and the contradictions of Buddhist thought.

The narrator's own compositions of haiku and *kanshi* also bespeak nostalgia. Near the end of the novel, he composes a pentasyllabic ancient-style poem (*gogon koshi*). Matsuoka Yuzuru (1891–1969) has described the poem as the "keynote" (*kichō*) of the entire novel.[43] The poem, in part, speaks to the conceit of *hininjō* and the aesthetics of detachment, but it also ironizes that detachment through its evocation of grief:

> As I leave the gate, much on the mind,
> A spring breeze brushes my coat.
> Fragrant grass grows in the wheel ruts
> Of a deserted road receding in the haze.
> 5   I rest my cane and take a moment to look
> At myriad shapes tricked out in sunlight.
> I listen to a warbler tuning its song,
> Watch falling petals fluttering in the air.
> Where my walk ends, a grassy field stretches far;
> 10 I write a poem on an ancient temple door.
> Lonely sorrow high atop the clouds,
> Across the sky a stray goose flies home.
> The human heart, a thing so recondite,
> In formlessness it forgets right and wrong.
> 15 At thirty years I am growing old,
> Still wistful of happier days.
> I wander with the changes of things,
> And calmly encounter their sweet perfume.

mon o idete omou tokoro ōshi	出門多所思
shunpū waga koromo o fuku	春風吹吾衣
hōsō shōtetsu ni shōji	芳草生車轍
haidō kasumi ni irite kasuka nari	廢道入霞微
tsue o todomete me o sosogeba	停筇而矚目
banshō seiki o obu	萬象帶晴暉
kōchō no enten taru o kiki	聽黃鳥宛轉
rakuei no funpi taru o miru	睹落英粉霏
yukitsukushite heibu tōku	行盡平蕪遠
shi o daisu koji no tobira	題詩古寺扉
koshū unsai takaku	孤愁高雲際
taikū dankō kaeru	大空斷鴻歸
sunshin nanzo yōchō taru	寸心何窈窕

hyōbyō toshite zehi o wasuru　　　縹緲忘是非
sanjū ware oin to hosshi　　　　　三十我欲老
shōkō nao ii tari　　　　　　　　韶光猶依依
shōyō shite bukka ni shitagai　　　逍遙隨物化
yūzen toshite funpi ni taisu　　　　悠然對芬菲 [44]

The poem evokes nostalgia in its form and its content. It is a *kanshi*, a genre of classical Japanese poetry that had come to be considered as out-moded in the Meiji period. Like haiku, *kanshi* contradicts the vernacular language of modern Japanese prose. The poem echoes the narrator's digressions about classical poetry by deploying images and tropes that allude to poetry from the Six Dynasties (220–589 CE) in China. A con-temporary of Sōseki, calligrapher Nagao Uzan (1864–1942) made similar observations in his commentary on the poem in *kanbun* (literary Chinese):

> Lofty, ancient, and remote; calm and distant, the mind wanders far into a style as old as the Six Dynasties.
> 高古超迴, 悠然而神遠, 風格敻乎入晉宋 [45]

Nagao's poetic commentary highlights how Sōseki's poem transports the mind of the speaker and his reader to a distant place in antiquity. The var-ied genres of traditional poetry in *Pillow of Grass* take the reader on jour-neys to older, imaginary, and illusory realms, while also keeping the work situated in the modern present through narration in the vernacular. As argued earlier in this chapter, what is "calm and distant" in *Pillow of Grass* is far from detachment and pure tranquility.

A closer examination of the poem reveals how stasis gives rise to motion outside of the linear containment of narrative, motion that gives form to nostalgia and melancholy. As we have seen, the narrator uses metaphor and figuration to evoke states of ecstasy; here the *kanshi* distills that sus-pension of motion in its concatenation of imagery, through which the lyric subject tarries in longing.

Line 1 evokes the opening of *Pillow of Grass*, where the narrator ascends the mountain path with wavering thoughts in his mind, but here, "much on the mind" (*omou tokoro ōshi*) also includes thoughts of longing, as reflected by the different meanings of the verb *omou* in classical poetry.[46] Nostalgia is already suggested in the first line, as the narrator's departure from home is immediately met with conflicting thoughts and feelings.

This first line comments on how travel is depicted in the work as a whole as well as on how departure from home induces anxiety. *Pillow of Grass* evokes the trope of travel in premodern Japanese literature in addition to new anxieties around travel in the Meiji period. As Stephen Dodd has shown, by the late nineteenth and early twentieth centuries, many Japanese writers were using the idea of home to create an alternative sense of belonging and collectivity.[47] Boym makes similar observations in her discussion of the modern meaning of "nostalgia," which "acquired international recognition as a disability of wartime and colonial mobility, a somatic and psychological protest against forced travel, depopulation, emigration, and other kinds of compulsory movement."[48]

With Romanticism floating in the ether of the text, the nostalgia in the *kanshi* evokes the nostalgia in Romantic poetry: Shelley, Meredith, Wordsworth. As Kevis Goodman and Thomas Dodman have shown, before 1900 "nostalgia" was a medical term designating illness; the symptoms that we have come to describe as "nostalgia" were not viewed as such until much later.[49] Swiss physician Johannes Hofer (1669–1752) coined the term "nostalgia," which comes from the Greek words *nostos* (home) and *algia* (pain, suffering). Goodman discusses one of Hofer's studies in which he found an extreme case of nostalgia wherein patients experience "quasi-ecstasy": "They are thus ex-static in a precise sense: they have been 'put out of place'…and seem to occupy another place, preoccupied by absent things as if they were present."[50] The feeling of being "put out of place" is precisely what the narrator feels when he is "just simply in motion…just ecstatic motion."

When the speaker describes what he sees and hears in lines 5–8, he evokes earlier moments in *Pillow of Grass* when he stops his place in the narrative to observe and preserve the spring landscape. The images of "myriad shapes tricked out in sunlight" and the "warbler tuning its song" are emblematic of the other images of beauty that the narrator animates through sensual and effusive language—and of the variation with which poems and poetic prose passages address those feelings of spring resplendence.[51]

By line 8, the poem has revealed the aspect of nostalgia that suspends time and space, as evident in the image of "falling petals fluttering in the air." This image alludes to lines from Tao Yuanming's *Record of the Peach Blossom Spring* (Taohuayuan ji), the conventional figure for the realm of nonhuman detachment for which the narrator longs. But once the walk ends in line 9, the narrative in the poem ceases, echoing the suspension of motion in the fluttering petals. Standing still, the speaker scrawls a poem on the door of an ancient temple. In the following lines this door mediates the speaker's philosophical meditation, concluding the poem with ambiguous thoughts and feelings, just as in the poem's opening.

The act of composing a poem within a poem speaks to the self-consciousness of the narrator's *kanshi* and the narrative it interrupts. The mise en abyme highlights the recursive cycles of self-referentiality and self-reflexivity in *Pillow of Grass*, drawing attention to its irony. The speaker does not reveal the content of his poem, but the couplet that follows it— "Lonely sorrow high atop the clouds, / Across the sky a stray goose flies home"—suggests that it is about longing, in solitude, at a place beyond reach. "Lonely sorrow" (*koshū*) refers to the stray goose on its way home and the speaker who is displaced far from home. The object of longing— home—is implicit in the image of the goose, which thereby evokes nostalgia, and yet lines 13 to 18 refigure that nostalgia as a longing without a clear object.

We might understand this kind of longing as melancholy.[52] Like nostalgia, melancholy (also melancholia) has been associated with illness in the history of Western medical science. Hungarian writer László F. Földényi has traced the history of melancholia in Anglo-European literature and philosophy, and argues that this "illness," in contrast to depression, has always eluded definition because of the impossibility of describing it: "Depression is *describable* by its symptoms, while melancholia is at best only *interpretable*....Only depression has symptomatology, whereas melancholia is a peculiar state of being that is not apprehensible as a certain cluster of symptoms—just as no interpretation of being can be entirely set down, spelled out, or treated as an object."[53] In addition to having an illness that eludes description, "the melancholic...is possibly unaware of his own melancholia," Földényi writes.[54] This characterization of melancholia speaks to the kind of ecstasy—or feeling of out-of-place-ness—that the narrator in *Pillow of Grass* tries to describe in the passages discussed above where he feels a profound and indescribable pleasure. Finding it difficult to diagnose his pleasure, he interprets these feelings and sensations through approximation, by way of metaphor and figurative language.

Within the irony and contradictions in *Pillow of Grass* lies the Romantic idea that grief gives rise to pleasure—or rather the need for the mind to tarry in thoughts of beauty and sadness. I read the work, therefore, as a long prose poem that gives form to the boundless longing of melancholy. As Földényi writes: "Nothing seems more natural than the interweaving of irony and melancholia: it is a kinship that has been unbroken from antiquity to our day."[55] The narrative casts this kinship in the very object-lessness, elusiveness, and indistinctness of the narrator's grief and melan-choly, demonstrating how they inevitably invite contradiction and irony.

As the narrator embarks upon a philosophical digression, he forms a cou-plet that figures the indescribable and open-ended nature of melancholy, alluding to Daoist thought in Chinese philosophy: "The human heart, a thing so recondite, / In formlessness it forgets right and wrong." To "for-get right and wrong" references discussions in *Zhuangzi* about the ability to make distinctions and judgments.[56] For Zhuangzi (the attributed author of *Zhuangzi*), being able to free the self from distinctions is an achievement; "right" and "wrong" are determined categories of knowledge and aban-doning them enables the self to leave matters undetermined and open ended.

The allusion to Zhuangzi addresses the form and representation of longing in *Pillow of Grass*. By couching the claim in the profundity of the heart and mind, the state of "formlessness" (*hyōbyō*; also "boundlessness," and "indistinctness") allows the lyric subject to express feelings without the need to find closure in literary form. *Pillow of Grass* thus speaks to what Anne-Lise François has called "recessive action" in nineteenth-century Anglo-European fiction and poetry that "locate fulfillment not in narrative fruition but in grace, understood both as a simplicity or slight-ness of formal means and as a freedom from work, including both the work of self-concealment and self-presentation."[57] In *Pillow of Grass*, Sōseki may be aiming for a kind of "recessive action" by representing the narrator's longing as an open secret that goes nowhere.

Hyōbyō's centrality in the poem speaks to Földényi's discussion of mel-ancholy as a "boundlessness that disturbs science" because of its very nature as a feeling ever mired in the ambiguity and possibility of meaning, thereby eluding diagnosis. As a word that also describes infinite temporal and spatial boundaries, *hyōbyō* elucidates how *Pillow of Grass* is a prose poem containing emotional or affective eddies that obstruct the linear flow of narrative.

The rest of the poem addresses the contradictory movements of melan-choly. The couplet formed by lines 15 and 16 conveys the speaker's nos-talgia for halcyon days, his mind gazing wistfully into the past while his aging body moves with the linear flow of time in the present. In the pen-ultimate line, the speaker occupies all junctures of time as he wanders with the changes of nature's creatures, but his "free and easy wandering" through time and space is checked in the final line where he "calmly encounters" the appealing fragrances of each moment. The verb *taisu* means "to face," "to oppose," "to meet," and "to encounter"—all of these meanings suggest the speaker's external position to the reverie, to the experience of the past, or to whatever time he has traveled. In his attempt to relive the past, he ironically finds himself at a dead end, seeing earlier times there before him, but unable to relive them. He is ever "ecstatic," "put out of place."

The feelings of pause, dissonance, and unfulfillment at the end of the poem ironize the ending of the novel, where the narrator realizes that he can finally complete his painting. He joins the other characters in sending off a young man as he departs for the war in Manchuria, looks at the beautiful innkeeper Nami, and sees the "pathos" (*aware*) written on her face. Then the narrator has an epiphany, realizing that he can finally paint his painting:

> The painting [*gamen*] within my inner heart and mind [*kyōchū*] is now complete.[58]

In some sense, the narrative has an "ending" because the artist has finally accomplished what he set out to do. However, the feelings in the narrative ironize this closure, making the ending pat. Irony is also occasioned by the word *gamen* (or *emen*; "painting"), a word that during the Meiji period referred to the entire surface of a painting or a picture. The metaphor of his "inner heart and mind" (*kyōchū*) as a "painting" speaks to the aesthetic conceit of *Pillow of Grass* as a representation of thought and feeling, but, as the narrative reveals, what lies beneath the surface of the picture is in constant motion and thus far from resolution.

Pillow of Grass, a sweet song that tells the saddest thought, shows how grief and longing—as nostalgia and melancholy—resist closure. But as the narrator's closing remark suggests, such feelings cannot be without resolution, as the painting is "now complete"—like a wish come true.

As discussed in Chap. 2 of the present volume, György Lukács's (1885–1971) argues that dissonance cannot happen in painting since it is a form outside of temporality; so dissonance must come to resolution, otherwise it is incomplete. Poetry, on the other hand, is a process of "becoming." Lukács asks: "Is not the form-concept of poetry in itself a symbol of longing?" The back and forth between stasis and movement along with the evocations of nostalgia and melancholy in *Pillow of Grass* all suggest that painting as a concrete surface inevitably determines longing, placing it in a particular and reified form. Poetry, however, leaves such representation undecided, undetermined, and open ended. While *Pillow of Grass* and the poetry contained within it will always have a form, the word *hyōbyō* points to the anxiety and indeterminacy of that formal containment.

POETRY AND MEMORY

Next I turn to the representation of grief and longing in Sōseki's prose poem *Recollecting and Such*, in which an ill and immobile lyric subject uses poetry as a means to convalesce from a near-death experience.[59] Irony manifests in the process of sensory healing and memory restoration, again through an alternation between prose and poetry: these shifts in language produce a pulse in the narrative, akin to the pulse of a convalescing human body. *Recollecting and Such* echoes the stasis and movement in *Pillow of Grass*, an oscillation that once more renders the subject out of place and gives form to feelings of grief and melancholy.

As a retrospective piece, *Recollecting and Such* is often read as a memoir that combines premodern literary genres of autobiography, including *haibun* (*haikai* prose), the *zuihitsu* (essay), the travelogue (*kikōbun*), and the diary (*nikki*). However, unlike these premodern genres, the work's narrative lacks chronological order. Blending multiple genres, as Maria Flutsch has argued, the work is a genre unto itself.[60] *Recollecting and Such* goes beyond mere recollection, which is suggested by the adverb *nado* (lit. "and the like") in the original title, *Omoidasu koto nado*. The adverb furtively points to the poetry in the narrative, associating memory with lyric. The work was originally serialized as thirty-two installments in the *Asahi* newspaper; nearly every installment features either a haiku or a *kanshi*. Marvin Marcus observes that these poems provide a "lyrical synopsis of the respective episode while pointing to the author's deep and abiding poetic sensibilities."[61] I read the poems as not so much synopses of the prose that precedes them, but representations of sense and feeling that cannot be captured in prose. *Recollecting and Such* thus mediates recollection through poetry, allowing the lyric subject access to planes of consciousness beyond the realm of the real and strictly mimetic representation.

This prose poem features many self-reflexive and self-referential comments about the function of poetry in the narrative. In installment 5, the narrator argues that the haiku and *kanshi* are to be read as quick communications of mood:

> I insert *kanshi* and haiku into *Omoidasu koto nado* not with the mere intention of presenting myself as a haiku or *kanshi* poet. To tell the truth, whether the poems are good or bad is of no concern to me. I would be content should I be able to impart to the hearts of my readers, at the speed of a glance, the message that I was living under the sway of such moods while ill.[62]

By commenting on the purpose of including his own poetry in *Recollecting and Such*, the narrator is suggesting that he is practicing a genre of writing that may appear to readers as doing something that it is not intending to do.

Such self-consciousness also appears in the poems themselves. Installment 14 concludes with a haiku that recounts a past moment when the convalescing narrator wakes up and finds a spittoon containing a pool of his own coughed-up blood. His physicians fear that he will fall into a coma and use camphor to return him to the world of the living. The installment ends with a scene of the two physicians and a friend preparing for the worst, holding onto the narrator's hands and watching him through the night. At sunup, he composes a haiku:

> Checked my pulse
> Numb
> Early dawn.
>
> *hiyayaka na / myaku o mamorinu / yoakegata*
> 冷やかな脈を護りぬ夜明方 [63]

The preceding prose suggests that the subject of the poem is the physician who holds onto the narrator's hands and monitors his "pulse" (*myaku*) all night long. But by composing a haiku, the narrator places himself in the position of diagnosing his own condition. The adjective *hiyayaka na* literally means "cold," but considering the speaker's awareness of his frail condition—weak and approaching comatose—and the frigidity of an early autumn morning, I suggest that the poem is representing the speaker's feeling of suspension: the cold palsies his body, rendering his pulse "numb."[64]

The haiku provides a coda to a critical moment in *Recollecting and Such*—when the narrator realizes the precariousness of his situation—while also commenting on the work as a whole: checking his pulse is emblematic of how poetry functions as an indicator of sense and feeling. The time of the poem is "early dawn" (*yoakegata*): morning twilight, the brief interval between night and day. Framing the taking of his pulse at this liminal hour alludes to the complexities of time and space in the work: as the narrator alternates between the present and the past, he interrupts his retrospective narrative with poems that transport the reader to the lyric present. The poetry in *Recollecting and Such* thus prevents the narrative from reaching closure, filling in fissures of memory with sensory experiences in suspended animation.

The narrative begins in medias res, creating a rupture in memory. The opening lines show the narrator's awareness of the passage of time and detail the particular sensations that he remembers from a hospital stay several months earlier:

> At long last, I have returned to the hospital again. As I recall, the last time I spent mornings and nights here in the heat is already three months in the past. Back then, they had rolled out a reed screen that hung down about six feet from the second-floor eaves as an awning to shade the sunbaked veranda.[65]

The adverbial phrase "at long last" (*yōyaku no koto de*) indicates that the narrator's return has been delayed due to some strained circumstance or difficulty. The reader might assume that now misfortune has befallen the narrator as he makes his way back to the hospital "again" (*mata*). This "again" refers to the repetition of this physical return, which foreshadows the cyclicality of remembrance across the work's thirty-two installments. The narrator recalls the heat he had endured three months earlier, further distanced by the adverb "in the past" (*mukashi*). The language the narrator uses to talk about time in the passage reveals an anxiety about the discontinuity between present and past self. In order to recover the latter, he focuses on sensory details, remembering the "sunbaked" (*hoteri no tsuyoi*) heat on the veranda. Someone from the hospital had hung a screen from the second floor, shading the veranda from the sweltering heat. The narrator's focus on these details reveals an interest in describing the intensity of things—and in how those intensities fade over time.

The narrator realizes that physical return to a place is possible, but the reliving of a past experience is not. He continues to recall the details of his earlier hospital stay, mentioning various objects and people, but ends with the notion that memory is fallible and that he can never fully return to the same time or place in the past:

> Now everything has become the past: a fugitive past, uncertain as dream, never again to appear before my eyes.[66]

Everything that he has recalled to this point is as "fugitive" (*hakanai*) and "uncertain" (*futashika*) as a dream. These adjectives conjure the aesthetics of transience in Japanese literature and poetry informed by the Buddhist view that the world—including the subject's perception of his own experience—is an illusion. The tone here suggests that no matter how many details one can recall, they all become things of the past with no possibility of return.

The rupture in memory and the narrator's distrust of his own faculties to discern the reality of the present motivate him to supplement his recollections with a poem. The resulting haiku contains his feelings about a moment of paralysis in growing darkness, giving form to his memory of a past experience, which in the prose remains scattered as fragmented feelings and broken objects. The narrator remembers the day that he leaves Shuzenji (the hot-spring town on the Izu Peninsula where he vacations before falling ill again) and returns to Tokyo. He has been placed on a stretcher, where he experiences a deprivation of the senses:

> They covered the stretcher with tung-oil paper to keep off the rainfall at dusk. I felt like I had been put to sleep in a pit, and from time to time opened my eyes to darkness. My nose could smell the tung-oil paper. My ears could hear sounds in fragments, raindrops falling on the tung-oil paper, and the faint voices of people who seemed to be escorting me on the stretcher. But my eyes saw nothing. It seems that the chrysanthemum stem that Dr. Morinari inserted in the cloth purse by my pillow broke off in the confusion when we alighted the train.

> On the stretcher,
> No chrysanthemum in sight,
> Just tung-oil paper.

> *tsuridai ni / nogiku mo mienu / kiriyu kana*
> 釣台に野菊も見えぬ桐油哉

I later condensed the scene from that moment into these seventeen syllables.[67]

While lying on a stretcher, the narrator finds the darkness impairing his vision and forcing him to rely on his other senses, specifically smell and hearing. He likens the experience to having "been put to sleep in a pit" (*ana no soko ni nekasareta yō*), evoking an image of his own burial. The loss of sight hones other senses: he hears raindrops falling on the tung-oil paper, which he can smell. The sound of the raindrops blends with the faint voices of people around the stretcher, both of which he hears as a discontinuous flow of sound. His supine position limits his vision; he no longer sees the chrysanthemum that was once attached to the purse by his pillow.

Sōseki condensed the scene into seventeen syllables, which distills the preceding prose description, thereby furnishing space for a lyric response to sensory deprivation. Like the prose, the haiku focuses on the stretcher and the tung-oil paper, the narrator's knowledge of which registers through sound and smell. But he cannot see the chrysanthemum, a loss emphasized by the particle *mo*. It is his inability to see the chrysanthemum that makes him more aware of the paper that covers his stretcher, and he addresses this with the sad exclamation *kana*. In haiku, the chrysanthemum is a seasonal referent for autumn. Tung trees are as well, though not the water-repellent oil that comes from their seeds. The narrator's inability to see the chrysanthemum places him at odds with autumnal conventions in *haikai* poetry. In this way, the haiku becomes a lyric exclamation of sensory gain mixed with sensory loss.

The other installments in *Recollecting and Such* feature poetry in the center of prose passages like in *Pillow of Grass*, but in most cases feature poems as postscripts or codas. The poetic interruptions produce a pulse in the narrative. If a human being is alive, their pulse is still beating. The alternations between prose and poetry make that beat visible and audible in the form and content of the narrative. Prose passages give form to sensation through figuration and metaphor, while haiku and *kanshi* give form to sensation through similar figuration, through meter, and through the containment of poetic form. Although haiku are limited to seventeen syllables, *kanshi* appear in a variety of forms (quatrains, regulated verse, and ancient-style poetry), furnishing more space in which to mediate sensation and occasion irony. In this way, the prose and poetry in *Recollecting and Such* produce a pulse that varies in strength and speed, creating a living and breathing text that nevertheless doubts its own vitality.[68]

Sensory Renewal

Illness is the pretext for composing poetry in *Recollecting and Such*. The narrator's near-death experience results in memory gaps and sensory deprivation, precipitating feelings of longing for an older and more traditional aesthetic sensibility.[69] This loss of memory, of the senses, and of the value of the literati tradition inspires the narrator to compose haiku and *kanshi*, through which he seeks healing of body, mind, and soul.

As the narrator reacquaints himself with his senses, haiku begin to appear one by one in the prose, detailing a renewed sensitivity to sight, sound, and touch, as well as how these senses blend into one another. In installment 5, the narrator expresses his desire to communicate his "mood" (*jōchō*) to his readers—his wife, his children, friends, and others reading the newspaper—through poetry. His desire to impart an affect or affective atmosphere to visible and invisible listeners couches his poems in the intimacy of lyric address.[70] The narrator seeks sympathy from his readers, and restores his own sensory awareness, by composing two haiku that evoke the dissonance between images of placidity and noise:

> On the autumn river
> Pounding posts into the water
> Makes a boom.
>
> *aki no e ni / uchikomu kui no / hibiki kana*
> 秋の江に打ち込む杭の響かな [71]

The speaker hears wooden posts being pounded into the water, the sound of which makes a reverberating boom. The first image, "autumn river" (*aki no e*), is homophonous with "autumn painting" (*aki no e*), evoking a cold and placid landscape. This image is then disrupted by the sad exclamation "makes a boom" (*hibiki kana*), which transforms the image of calm water into one of undulating ripples. The visual image of ripples on the water's surface and the sound of the boom come together as a single disruption mediated through sight and sound.

Sōseki also composed another haiku that represents an autumn scene, blended with the subtle suggestion of sound:

> The autumn sky
> Clear as light blue-green;
> A cedar and an ax.
>
> *aki no sora / asagi ni sumeri / sugi ni ono*
> 秋の空浅黄に澄めり杉に斧 [72]

The verb *sumeri*—translated above as "clear"—describes the clarity of an image in air or in water, making it unclear whether the speaker is viewing the sky above or its reflection in a river below. He perceives light blue-green (*asagi*), an in-between color that serves as a metaphor for the way the poem represents a clear visual image while hinting at a sonic one. *Sumeri* can also describe the clarity of sound, and although the second measure ends with a pause, the image of light blue-green spills into the final measure, possibly serving as a descriptor for the imaginary sound made when two objects come into contact: the strike of an ax chopping cedar. With this possibility in mind, we might say that the poem refigures the clarity of the static light blue-green sky with the clarity of resonant disruption. These two haiku display the narrator's awareness of sight and sound as well as how those senses can blend or contrast like colors in a painting. As in the poems of Buson, thoughts blend in poetic form like paint on a canvas.

Sōseki also composed haiku that represent the sense of touch. Installment 12 opens with a scene of ceaseless rainfall: there is a lull in the narrator's pain, so he takes a bath and notices a group of young male performers staying downstairs. He observes them dancing in the nude, and admires their young, healthy, and mobile bodies. He concludes the installment with an autumn haiku that figures his illness as the weight of dew:

> My body ails
> Like the weight of dew
> On a bush clover.
>
> *hagi ni oku / tsuyu no omoki ni / yamu mi kana*
> 萩に置く露の重きに病む身かな [73]

The poem describes an early morning scene in late autumn when dew weighs on the delicate leaves of a bush clover.[74] Dew is a conventional trope for the pathos of impermanence; when it appears in a poem about an ill body, it makes the impermanence of life all the more keen and poignant. The poem also comments on the tenuous layering of objects: dew resting on bush clover leaves; illness figured as the weight of dew. Since dew eventually dissipates, the haiku evokes a liminal moment—which, in the context of the speaker's illness, can be interpreted two ways: like the dew, the narrator's illness may dissipate or the ill body may disappear entirely. In this way, the haiku represents a fleeting sense of touch holding both life and death in suspension.

The three haiku examined above figure sight, sound, and touch, show-ing how the author uses poetry to seek sympathy from his reader and to restore his own sensory awareness. Other poems in *Recollecting and Such* figure sensory recovery with philosophical reflection on tranquility—a common topic in literati culture—and, in the process, occasion irony. These poems are *kanshi* that explore the possibilities of movement in the narrator's enfeebled mind, while his ill body lies immobile. As Angelia Yiu has observed, "the very form and language that hold together the appar-ent tranquility in these poems also undermine it by betraying an underly-ing anxiety."[75]

In installment 13, the narrator describes liquids entering and exiting his body. He is bed-ridden at the inn, and Dr. Sugimoto pays him a visit. The narrator describes the act of drinking—the texture and taste of fluids going down his throat—and the process of digesting ice cream—how ice cream begins as semi-solid substance that then melts once it travels down the throat and then ends up as a congealed lump in the stomach, which pro-duces a strange sensation. The narrator also learns that he has fallen unconscious for half an hour. Reading his wife's diary, he learns that he has coughed up a large amount of blood and he calls her to his bedside to learn more about what had happened when he fell unconscious.

The prose narrates a dramatic scene of events that the narrator does not remember having experienced, including spewing blood on his wife's yukata. He concludes the installment with a heptasyllabic quatrain (*shichi-gon zekku*) that aestheticizes the blood and reveals his feelings about the declining state of his body:

Dripping blood crimson, lettering from my bosom;
Coughed glinting in the twilight, a pool of twilled silk.
Night falls and I idly wonder, is this body bone?
Abed like stone, I dream of wintry clouds.

rinri taru kōketsu fukuchū no bun	淋漓絳血腹中文
haite kōkon o terashite kimon o tadayowasu	嘔照黃昏漾綺紋
yoru ni irite munashiku utagau mi wa kore hone ka to	入夜空疑身是骨
gashō ishi no gotoku kan'un o yumemu	臥牀如石夢寒雲 [76]

The opening couplet echoes the images of liquids that appear earlier in the installment but concentrates on the blood on the narrator's wife's yukata.

As the blood flows out from the heart of the speaker, it serves no longer as a marker of sickness or effluvium but as the aestheticized thoughts and feelings of a poet waiting to be read: the blood becomes a "pattern" (*bun*), a figure for calligraphy or a design on a garment. The "dripping" (*rinri*) describes the slow movement of blood as it exits the body; once expelled, it transforms into a liquid, beautifully patterned and as legible as words rendered by a brush. The "crimson" (*kō*) anticipates the description of the pool of blood as "twilled silk" (*kimon*) in line 2, as the Chinese graphs *kō*, *ki*, and *mon* are all etymologically related to fine silk. The opening lines comment on *Recollecting and Such* as a whole, depicting it as a text that transforms sickness and blood into the patterns of language that are beautiful and fleeting: the scene occurs at a liminal moment when day changes into night (*kōkon*), suggesting that the beautiful pool of blood, like silk gauze glinting in the twilight, will eventually be shaded in darkness.

The latter half of the poem is indeed set in darkness, and while it transports the speaker into celestial space, the poem does not allow his flight to go very far. In line 3, he idly wonders whether his body is all bone. In line 4, he says that lying abed is like being a stone, which echoes the static image that ends the previous line. In the haiku about the bush clover, the narrator laments the weight of his sickness through the figure of dew. Here, his awareness of illness does not forebode annihilation by evaporation but permanent stillness as a corpse. His identification with a stone suggests coldness, lack of emotive power, and immobility. The line ends with dreaming of "wintry clouds" (*kan'un*). Gaston Bachelard writes that "clouds are numbered among the most oneiric of 'poetic things'": they enable dream-like movement.[77] Here they provide the speaker with the possibility of oneiric transcendence to an eternal and celestial space beyond the waking life, beyond the senses. But the fact that these clouds are "wintry" (*kan*) suggests that he carries with him the numbing cold he feels as a body of bone or a slab of stone to an oneiric and celestial space where he is still immobile. Even the clouds cannot escape the fate that befalls the speaker's sensorium: frozen stillness.

Installment 22 offers another example of how Sōseki uses figurative language in prose and poetry to restore sensory awareness, again concluding with the narrator's feelings of grief. The installment opens with the narrator in between sleep and waking. The nostalgic sound of carp jumping in a pond wakes him, but his vision is impaired. He describes the faint illumination in the room and the ghostly figures seated before him:

> In my room there was light that glowed darker than twilight. The light bulb hanging from the ceiling was covered all in black cloth. The weak light seeping through the weave faintly shone on the eight tatami mats in the room. And in the gloomy glow sat two human beings dressed in white kimonos. Neither spoke. Neither moved. Both sat side by side with their hands in their laps, perfectly still.[78]

The narrator paints a monochrome scene of stillness. He compares the illumination of the room to twilight, imbuing the scene with the feeling of encroaching darkness. Seated before him are two people dressed in white, whom he later indicates are nurses. Speechless and motionless, their white uniforms contrast with the darkness of the room, evoking an eerie, funerary atmosphere.

While still in this liminal state, the narrator describes their swift and mechanical movements, and their ability to read him better than he can read himself. His immobility has left him completely vulnerable, forcing him to depend on his caretakers to respond to his every need:

> The women dressed in white had my mind all figured out: they reacted like a shadow to a body; they responded like sound reverberating on an object. It was eerie how these women dressed in bright white, under the dim light seeping through the black cloth, could see beyond my physical body, and unnoticeably, and methodically, move as one with my mind.[79]

The thought of their uncanny responsiveness frightens the helpless narrator. In his mind, the nurses are extensions of himself; they move as if his mind and theirs are one and the same. This leaves the narrator with what he describes later as a "weird feeling" (*kimi no warui kimochi*).

As soon as he opens his eyes and gazes at the dim light seeping from the covered bulb hanging from the ceiling, he sees the nurses dressed in white again. The prose portion concludes with an unnerving description of the nurses encroaching upon him when he is not paying attention. The scene ends with a disturbing feeling: the sense of being overcome by the nurses and losing control of mind and body. This is followed by a pentasyllabic quatrain (*gogon zekku*):

> The autumn wind moans in the forest,
> Mountain rain rattles the tall building.
> These frail bones are jagged like a blade;
> In the gloom of a green light, verging on grief.

shūfū banboku o narashi	秋風鳴萬木
san'u kōrō o yurugasu	山雨撼高樓
byōkotsu ryō toshite ken no gotoku	病骨稜如劍
ittō aoku shite ureen to hossu	一燈青欲愁 [80]

The poem refigures the narrator's paralysis and disembodiment as sensory embodiment by detailing a keen awareness of sight, sound, and touch. As a response to the prose that precedes it, the poem is a lyric cry that the narrator can still feel and, contrary to how the installment ends, he has not relinquished complete control of his mind and body to his caretakers. The first couplet evokes turbulent images of wind and rain wreaking havoc on the natural autumn landscape. In his poetic imagination, the sound of the wind can be heard in the sea of trees, while rain rattles the tall building where the speaker lodges, looking out at the dismal autumn landscape.

The latter half of the poem shifts the speaker's focus from the turbulence of nature to the frailty of his ill body, which he describes as "jagged like a blade" (ryō toshite ken no gotoku). If lines 1 and 2 figure the speaker's mind in the form of natural imagery, then line 3 figures his body as a mountain range: he has become so emaciated that he can feel his bones, rugged like crags, pressing against a thin layer of skin. The comparison between bones and a blade also evokes coldness; the jagged edge of the blade reinforces the sharpness of that cold.

The final line echoes the image of the bulb hanging from the ceiling of his room, the dimness of which the author uses to create the eerie atmosphere of darkness that permeates this episode in the narrative. The lamp is also a figure for the lyric mind in Romanticism and in classical Chinese poetry; the line evokes the image of a mind on the brink of emotional abandonment, "green...verging on grief" (aoku shite ureen to hossu). "Green lamps" (Ch. qing deng) appear in classical Chinese poems set in the early morning twilight, which accords with the time depicted in the preceding prose, but this line refigures the liminal moment between night and day as the mind at a threshold, about to fall into the throes of grief. Like the other poems in Recollecting and Such, the quatrain suspends sensory awareness—a crescendo moment during which the speaker restores his awareness of sight, sound, and touch—but couched in a penultimate moment that defers the grief about to overtake him to a later time in the future.[81]

The two *kanshi* examined above are representative of other poems in *Recollecting and Such* that betray doubts about their ability to promise sensory renewal. The fate of traditional poetry and of the narrator's health are thereby intertwined. The contingency of his recovery becomes an allegory for the contingency of literati tropes in modern times. Under these ill conditions, the narrator's lyric address is likely to fall on deaf ears because fewer and fewer readers can appreciate the *kanshi* form. By describing his poetry as cliché and outmoded in his explanation for including it in *Recollecting and Such*, Sōseki does not pretend to be in tune with the trends of the present age, yet simultaneously reveals his pretense in holding on to a tradition that has already reached its irrecoverable decline.

THE POETICS OF SUSPENSION

The immanent decline of literati culture is most evident when the narrator gives form to elegiac feelings, evoking nostalgia, melancholy, and death. The autumn setting and the number of autumn poems suggest that *Recollecting and Such*, in its very composition, is an elegiac ode to autumn or to melancholy. This sadness is figured in a combination of modern prose and traditional poetry, ironizing the tradition of pathos through a modern and Keatsian "negative capability," making suspension, uncertainty, and contradiction productive as poetry.

Contradiction arises when the narrator finds his own experience at odds with continuity. In installment 15, the narrator describes his thirty minutes of unconsciousness, the critical event that occasions the composition of *Recollecting and Such*. The opening of the installment echoes the feelings of self-alienation from the opening of the entire narrative, as the narrator highlights a discontinuity between two selves—the self before falling unconscious and the self afterward:

> I had believed that a solid continuity existed between the self that tried to turn over to the right, and the self that saw the raw blood at the bottom of the spittoon near my pillow. I was certain that I had been fully functional for every split second of that interval. When I learned from my wife shortly after that such had not been the case, and that I had lost consciousness for a whole thirty minutes, I was shocked.[82]

The narrator reflects on the loss of continuity and tries to piece together what happens before and after he falls unconscious. The phrases *ichibu no suki* (lit. "one-tenth of a gap") and *ippon no kamige* (lit. "one strand of hair") describe the minuscule measurements of space that challenge his conviction that the continuity of experience is invulnerable to even the slightest amount of disruption. Through these spatial descriptions the narrator draws our attention to how language measures continuity vis-à-vis discontinuity in time and space.

The narrator finds himself at a loss for words as to how to describe an experience that he does not remember having. Such a loss makes him doubt the continuity of experience: if he has no memory of losing consciousness, how does he know that he has lost it? He turns to figurative language and metaphor to fill in the lost time; the fugitive nature of the images he deploys points to the irony of metaphor's attempt to grasp the ungraspable:

> I was hard pressed to find the words that could best describe it. I did not even have the awareness of having awoken, nor did I have the feeling of having emerged from darkness into light. The faint whir of wings, the echo of things fading into the distance, the mood in a fugitive dream, the glimmer of an old memory, the trace of a waning impression—needless to say, I did not feel that I had passed through the numinous and awesome frontier that almost became visible after naming all the ways that could describe the unknown.[83]

The narrator lists sounds, images, and feelings that all suggest the fleeting: "the faint whir of wings" (*kasuka na ha oto*), "the echo of things fading into the distance" (*tōki ni saru mono no hibiki*), "the mood in a fugitive dream" (*nigete yuku yume no nioi*), "the glimmer of an old memory" (*furui kioku no kage*), "the trace of a waning impression" (*kieru inshō no nagori*). As his mind moves from one fugitive thought to the next, he stops after the fifth image. While the flow of poetic thought suggests that the list could continue, the author suspends these fugitive fragments of experience. Like the insertions of poetry throughout *Recollecting and Such*, the prose shifts into metaphor, bridging the gap between consciousness and unconsciousness, but the metaphor's lack of containment in the passage makes its disappearance immanent.

Such figurative language evokes the aesthetics of impermanence in the Japanese poetic tradition as well as the aesthetics of liminal thresholds that constitute poetic thought in Romanticism. In his discussion of Samuel Taylor Coleridge's poetics, Angus Fletcher writes that Coleridge "intensified the rendering of poetic thought, especially by inventing situations of liminal, or threshold, passage. In a sense, the liminal is key to the Romantic projection of the most intensely powerful effects of creative thought, including verbal virtuosity in Coleridge's work."[84] *Recollecting and Such* represents recollection through the contradiction of linear time, figuring memory in a liminal state of becoming outside teleological thinking in a manner that is reminiscent of the figuration of time in the Romantic tradition.[85] Fletcher asks: "Can a poet imagine a sequence that is devoid of any passing of time, when the poem shifts from space to space, point to point?" Doubting the continuity of experience, the narrator strings together images that resonate with one another, speaking to what Fletcher calls "one-after-the-otherness" in poetry—a sequence in which images are coeval and coterminous. In the liminal space between the narrator's consciousness and unconsciousness, the images all verge on vanishing.

Although the images, by their fugitive nature, eventually disappear, for the brief moment that they negate the passage of linear time, they eternally exist in a liminal state of motion, waning in intensity as though approaching a threshold. The words that give form to these slow and fleeting movements become the substance of the unknown space that the narrator describes as the "numinous and awesome frontier" (*reimyō na kyōkai*), making this space "almost visible" (*yōyaku hōfutsu subeki*). *Hōfutsu* describes liminal vision—an indistinct view of something formed when two opposing elements meet and merge, resulting in a view that is never one nor the other but something in between. As the narrator goes through a list of expressions in describing the gap in his experience, the poetic language hypostasizes the unreal, making the invisible almost visible, yet still indistinct.

The in-between-ness of vision—or *hōfutsu*-ness—evoked in the prose resonates with the feeling of suspension that looms within the poetry of *Recollecting and Such*. This suspension also emerges in the narrator's critique of philosophical understandings of time and space, including Zeno's paradox about Achilles's race with a tortoise in Greek philosophy. Zeno's paradox assumes that time and space are continuous and infinitely divisible. The tortoise is given a head start in the race because it is slower than Achilles, but because each moves at constant speed on a linear path, Zeno claims that both will remain the same distance apart.

The narrator describes an analogous paradox with eating a persimmon: if he eats half a persimmon one day, and then half of its remainder the next day, he could theoretically continue eating the same persimmon forever.

The narrator then ironizes the logic behind the two paradoxes by suppos-
ing that death works the same way: no matter how close he comes to
dying, he cannot die. He ultimately finds such logic "counterfactual" or
"false" (*hijijitsu*), as it does not accord with empirical knowledge—knowledge that the subject attains through personal observation and experience:

> We may be fooled by the counterfactual logic that no matter how close we
> come to dying we cannot die; but perhaps the road from life to death could
> be felt comprehensibly and most naturally by avoiding the incoherence that
> arises when theorizing about what it is to leap from one end and fall into
> another.[86]

Rather than leaving the problem of discontinuity and losing consciousness
for the mind to work out through "theory and philosophy" (*shisakujō*),
the narrator suggests a kind of understanding through sensory experience—one that "could be felt" (*kanjiuru*).

The way to "feel" the experience that the narrator does not remember
having is through sensory embodiment in lyric poetry. Sōseki composed a
heptasyllabic ancient-style poem (*gogon koshi*) of fourteen lines that can be
divided into three quatrains and a couplet.[87] Like other *kanshi* in
Recollecting and Such, the poem restores sensory awareness and suggests
its own failure. As the longest poem in *Recollecting and Such* it is the
work's keynote, revisiting themes and topoi from the narrative. It is the
only ancient-style poem (*koshi*) in the work and can be read as a metaphor
for the literati tradition. The poem narrates a dark journey through the
space of the unconscious, concluding the installment with feelings of wandering, failure, instability, solitude, decay, and lateness:

> Lost in a vastness beyond heaven and earth,
> I move in and out of life and death.
> Bereft in darkness of all reliance,
> Where does my heart and spirit go?
>
> 5   On my return, I search for the root of life,
> Only to end with an enigma too deep to fathom.
> I grieve alone and vainly circle dreams,
> Just like the sorrow stirred by a mournful wind.
>
> In the rivers and mountains autumn is already old,
> 10   My side locks are graying to the color of rice gruel.
> Vast and desolate heaven is still there,
> High trees have only bare branches left.

An old man's sensations are faint like this;
The world of wind and dew comes too late into his poetry.

hyōbyō taru genkō no soto	縹緲玄黄外
shisei komogomo shasuru toki	死生交謝時
kitaku meizen toshite sari	寄託冥然去
waga kokoro nan no yuku tokoro zo	我心何所之
kirai myōkon o motomuru mo	帰来覓命根
yōyō toshite tsui ni shirigatashi	杳窅竟難知
koshū munashiku yume o meguri	孤愁空遠夢
en toshite shōshitsu no kanashimi o ugokasu	宛動粛瑟悲
kōzan aki sude ni oi	江山秋已老
shukuyaku bin masa ni otoroen to su	粥薬鬢將衰
kakuryō toshite ten nao ari	廓寥天尚在
kōju hitori eda o amasu	高樹独余枝
bankai kaku no gotoku tan ni	晚懐如此澹
fūro shi ni iru koto ososhi	風露入詩遅 [88]

The first stanza describes the first half of the narrator's journey between antipodes, and evokes the feeling of being lost in space—as if he has fallen into a black hole. The words formed by the antipodes "heaven and earth" and "life and death" mark the spaces from which the speaker has absented himself: he is not within heaven and earth, or life and death, but without—in a space in between. The *hyōbyō* that opens the poem evokes the vastness and obscurity of this in-between space.[89] The word is an adverb for being beyond, but it is also an adjective that describes heaven and earth, and the colors that separate them: "black" (*gen*) for heaven and "yellow" (*kō*) for earth. They are the antipodes of dark and light, which in Daoist philosophy constitute the whole universe and human existence.

The narrator is beyond either antipode, a world outside and also between binary categorization. Line 1 describes the vastness beyond heaven and earth, evoking the indistinct line that joins but also separates them. Line 2 describes back-and-forth movements as the narrator moves "in and out of life and death," an action indicated by the adverb *komogomo*, which describes alternation and repetition. Lines 3 and 4 describe the uncomfortable separation of mind and body, as *kitaku* and *sari* mark the release and loss of the body. Disembodied, the speaker's mind wanders into *meizen*, a state of darkness.

The second quatrain describes his return. The gravity of the speaker's vertiginous and disorientating descent into oblivion in the first stanza is emphasized by his struggle to find life in the second. The first two stanzas take the form of the antipodes that constitute them, forming a wavering dialectic between life and death. In his discussion of the poetry of Edgar Allan Poe, Bachelard writes that when poeticizing vertigo there must be a rise and a fall.[90] The speaker's search for the root of life (*myōkon o moto-muru*) enables him to be conscious of his fall into alien space and to address the back-and-forth alternation between opposite states of being: life and death. While the couplet formed by lines 5 and 6 begins by indicating his return, his search for the "root of life" ultimately fails. Darkness (*yōyō*) obscures what can be known, retaining the enigmatic and boundless imagery of the alien space evoked in the first stanza. The narrator responds to this failure of knowing in the couplet formed by lines 7 and 8, which evokes feelings of loneliness and suspension: "I grieve alone and vainly circle dreams."[91] The adverb *munashiku* (vainly) imbues the line with irony, negating potentiality by revealing the futility of circling his dreams, grieving alone. Line 8 heightens this negativity with the metaphor of a mournful wind stirring sorrow.[92]

The third quatrain initiates a sharp shift in imagery from the world of darkness to the natural world. But the speaker's return to the world of the living is met only with decay and lateness. In line 9 he figures himself as the season of autumn, exposing his age in the rivers and mountains. The adverb *sude ni*, meaning "already," is emphatic and indicates the narrator's deeply felt disjuncture with time. He describes the passage of time through the metaphor of his graying hair. The image of gruel evokes a pale color as well as a substance that lacks form and stability. The adverb *masa ni* paired with the verb *otorou* indicates a transition—the speaker's state nearing decay. Lines 11 and 12 negate the fleetingness in lines 9 and 10 with a suggestion of permanence, but this is a permanence that does not last. Line 11 begins with *kakuryō*, meaning "vast and desolate," which modifies "heaven": *kaku* suggests a vastness contained within a limit;[93] *ryō* suggests an expanse of emptiness and sorrow. The latter half of line 11 establishes a sense of situatedness with permanence (*nao ari*).[94] Line 12 echoes the feeling of permanence with the solid image of towering trees, but then negates this soaring magnitude with sparseness and fragility, as these trees have only spare, bare branches.

Lines 13 and 14 form the final couplet and bring closure to the poem with a statement of truth tinged with irony and belatedness. The speaker declares that, in his late years, his "feelings and sensations" (*bankai*) are *tan*, or "faint," like the impressions he describes in the previous three stanzas.[95] *Tan* can mean "the slow undulation of waves," "movement," "silence," and "blandness." In this sense, *tan* encapsulates the rhythm and imagery of the entire poem: a modulation of presence and absence as the speaker describes his enfeebled journey in back-and-forth movements. Line 14 begins with *fūro*, "the world of wind and dew," which refers to the world of poetic convention. The speaker writes that this world entered his poetry too late (*ososhi*).[96] Here he questions how poetic diction creates meaning, arguing that poetry as convention—with its classical clichés and formal and topical constraints—ultimately fails to capture the immediacy of experience. In other words, in this poem, the world of wind and dew can only evoke its own belatedness—its own lateness in giving form and meaning to the poem. The line ironizes the form of *Recollecting and Such* as a whole, a prose poem that alternates between modern prose and traditional poetry. This alternation, as we have seen, produces contrapuntal motion in the narrative, a pulse betraying signs of renewal, but the final couplet ironizes that pulse, qualifying it as slow and faint, almost numb, revealing that the tropes have come "too late."

The final installment in *Recollecting and Such* echoes the irony occasioned by earlier poems. In installment 32, the narrator describes his return to Tokyo, and the narrative comes full circle: as in the opening installment, the narrator is carried on a stretcher in the rain, only the stretcher is covered in white cloth, reminding him of a funeral:

> It felt like a funeral. It is not apropos to use the word funeral for a living being, but the image of someone laid out on what was neither a stretcher nor a coffin and wrapped in white cloth could only be taken as a person to be buried alive. I kept repeating to myself the words 'second funeral.' I felt that I had been given no choice but to undergo twice what everyone else undergoes once.[97]

The thoughts and feelings in the passage evoke the opening stanza of a poem by Emily Dickinson: "I felt a Funeral, in my Brain, / And Mourners to and fro / Kept treading—treading—till it seemed / That sense was breaking through." In *Recollecting and Such*, the narrator, ironically and morbidly, figures himself as a living corpse. Like those of Dickinson, his senses seem to break through as his thoughts and feelings pace in the heart and mind like mourners at a funeral, but whether he achieves full sensory recovery remains to be seen. The sentiment of the passage speaks to *Recollecting and Such* as a recursive funerary prose poem, in which the lyric subject is between life and death—also suggested by the contradictory image of "a person to be buried alive" (*ikinagara tomurawareru*). The narrator finds himself repeating the words "second funeral" (*daini no sōshiki*), referring to his first encounter with death after falling unconscious for thirty minutes, and the second death that awaits him.

The installment ends with feelings of joy and expectation as the narrator looks forward to returning home, but the nostalgic reverie does not last, and the images disappear forever:

> When I saw the color of the bamboo grove, the red leaves on a persimmon, the potato leaves, the wild roses growing on the hedge, and the scent of ripe millet, I felt delighted to remember, as if I had been reborn, that now is the season, indeed, to expect such things. Furthermore, I alone took pleasure in imagining what new world I could expect to unfold at home, one that would revive faded and bygone memories. At the same time, the things that had occupied my mind until yesterday—the straw futon, the wagtails, the autumn grass, the carp, and the little stream—all completely vanished.[98]

The way that the images of autumn stir passionate feelings only to disappear speaks to the conceit of *Recollecting and Such* as a prose poem that conjures images of fullness only to deflate them later. The relationship between the images and the season that they indicate is clear and unequivocal, but the narrator's declaration of delight (*ureshigatta*) is contradicted by the fragility of his mental faculties. He describes the ability to recollect through metaphor, "as if I had been reborn" (*umarekaetta yō ni*), which speaks to the way narrative in *Recollecting and Such* is a reciprocal process of remembering and returning to consciousness, and vice versa. The fate of this process, however, is ironic: the narrator aims to "revive" (*sosei seshimuru*) old memories that pace back and forth in his mind, and then vanish (*kiete*) without the possibility of return (*shimatta*).

This irony is echoed in the poem that concludes the thirty-two installments of *Recollecting and Such*.[99] Sōseki composed a heptasyllabic regulated verse (*shichigon risshi*) that echoes the sentiments in the preceding prose, and as an ironic coda, caps the work with uncertainty:

> Now that it is done, I can catch my breath;
> How can I live the rest of my life, left over like cinders?

Wind passes over the ancient gorge, autumn sounds stir the air,
The sun sinks into secluded bamboo, stygian colors fall.
Thoughtlessly I said I would stay three months in the mountains,
Little did I know another sky stretched beyond the gate.
Let my return not be late for the season of yellow blossoms,
Chances are a roving spirit dreams of the old moss at home.

banji kyū seshi toki issoku kaeru	萬事休時一息回
yosei ani shinobin ya zankai ni hisuru ni	餘生豈忍比殘灰
kaze wa kokan o sugite shūsei okori	風過古澗秋聲起
hi wa yūkō ni ochite meishoku kitaru	日落幽篁暝色來
midari ni iu sanchū ni sangetsu todomaru to	漫道山中三月滯
nanzo shiran mongai ni itten hiraku o	詎知門外一天開
kiki okururu nakare kōka no setsu	歸期勿後黄花節
osoraku wa kikon no kyūtai o yumemuru aran	恐有羈魂夢舊苔 [100]

The poem opens with the affirmation that the narrator has survived the worst of it, referring to his miraculous return from the dead. He figures his recovery through the image of "breath" (*issoku*). The "return" (*kaeru*) or cyclicality of breath indicates the vitality of the lyric subject and speaks to the role of lyric poetry in *Recollecting and Such*: poems and poetic language recur with a pulse like an endless cycle of breath. Although his breath has returned, the narrator contradicts its vitality by figuring the remainder of his life as "left over like cinder" (*zankai ni hisuru ni*), evoking the image of ashes after a funerary cremation. The image is ironic—the remnant glow of cinder will eventually go out—and conjures the opening line to another Dickinson poem: "The Poets light but Lamps—/ Themselves—go out—."[101] Like this speaker, Sōseki's narrator displays an awareness of life's limitations as well as the limitations of poetry, which may not have an afterlife.

The couplet formed by lines 3 and 4 evokes the sounds and sights of autumn: the mourning wind, and the darkness of twilight. The narrator claims that what began as a three-month convalescence in the mountains led to a discovery that a new horizon awaits him on the other side of consciousness. This alludes to his reverie in the preceding prose, where he talks about the new world that awaits him at home. But as the prose and poem suggest, this home is illusory and is still contained by the poetic imagination. The narrator's inability to join the real world precipitates doubt about his own future. He writes: "Let my return not be late for the season of yellow blossoms." The season to which he is referring is, of course, autumn, when the chrysanthemums are in bloom. In the event that his body is too late for the autumn blossoms, the final line reveals that his mind, figured as a "roving spirit" (*kikon*), will continue to dream of home. The speaker's decision to end the poem with nostalgia contained in a dream deflates the hopeful expectancy suggested by *osoraku wa* (chances are) but also speaks to the precariousness of whether such a possibility will ever come to fruition.

By leaving its conclusion open ended in this way, *Recollecting and Such* can be said to lack literary closure, suggesting that the literati tradition, as a disembodied spirit, can only sustain itself through dream. And, as the opening of the narrative declares loud and clear, recollection is uncertain and fugitive—just like dream.

NOTES

1. Kermode, *The Sense of an Ending*, 101.
2. In this way, I follow the path of other scholars who have examined narrative form in Sōseki: Austead, *Rereading Sōseki*, Sakaki, *Recontextualizing Texts*, Vincent, *Two-Timing Modernity*, Austead, "Reading Sōseki Now," and Bourdaghs, *A Fictional Commons*.
3. Grief psychotherapist Julia Samuel observes that "grief is the emotional reaction to a loss," and the process of grief is "in the movement—the back and forth—between the loss and restoration." She also describes grief as a paradox: "The paradox of grief is that finding a way to live with the pain is what enables us to heal. Coping with grief doesn't involve immersion theory; rather, it is enduring the pain as it hits us (this often feels like a storm crashing over us), and then having a break from it through distraction, busyness, and doing the things that comfort and soothe us. Every time we alternate between two poles, we adjust to the reality that we don't want to face: that the person we love has died." Samuel, *Grief Works*, xvii–xviii.
4. Colebrook, *Irony*, 49. Colebrook on the idea of the "ironic fall" and Romantic irony in the writings of Karl Wilhelm Friedrich Schlegel (1772–1829): "An ironic 'fall' realizes…that there was no paradise before the sense of loss. The idea of an original plenitude is an image created *from* life. 'All life is in its ultimate origins not natural, but divine and human.' The idea of a fall is, however, essential to irony and life as irony. It is in creating images of a lost paradise that we create ourselves *as fallen*, and thereby create ourselves at all. For to be selves or personalities we must be limited or delimited from some grander whole." Colebrook, 49–50. *Pillow of Grass* and *Recollecting in Such* both emerge from loss:

the former aims to reconstruct an idyllic space; the latter attempts to restore lost experience.

5. Sōseki wrote in an essay from November, 1906: "Once this 'haiku-style novel'—odd as the name may be—is complete, it will break new ground in the literary world. In Japan, let alone the West, there has never been a novel like this. When it makes its appearance in Japan, the first thing one could say is that a new movement in the world of fiction started in Japan." Natsume Sōseki, *Sōseki zenshū*, 25: 209–212. From here on *SZ*. Translations are mine unless otherwise noted.

6. For more on how *haikai* informed Late Edo *kanshi*, see Sugimoto, *Edo kanshi*, 155–171.

7. Backus, "What Goes Into a Haiku," 736.

8. Miyoshi, *Accomplices of Silence*, 65.

9. Freedman, *The Lyrical Novel*, 3.

10. Muecke, *The Compass of Irony*, 159.

11. *SZ*, 3: 3. I have consulted the two English translations by Alan Turney and Meredith McKinney.

12. "Kusamakura" is a poetic epithet (*makurakotoba*, or "pillow word") for travel from *Collection of Ten Thousand Leaves* (ca. 759 CE; Man'yōshū):

> Grass for a pillow—
> The traveler on his journey
> Along the way
> May don the colors
> Of the bush clovers in bloom.
> 草枕旅行く人も行き触ればにほひぬべくも咲ける萩かも

Man'yōshū, 333.

13. The meaning behind these terms has been the subject of debate. Scholars have read *Pillow of Grass* alongside Sōseki's own literary theory, expressing contrasting views about the relationship between *hininjō* and the genres of writing that constitute the novel. Anette Thorsen Vilslev has suggested that both the prose and the poetry in *Pillow of Grass* mediate the narrator's detached stance, what the novel calls *hininjō*, enabling him to describe the natural landscape and human emotion with objectivity. Daniel Poch has examined *Pillow of Grass* in the context of Sōseki's experiments with *shaseibun*, a new genre of prose writing inspired by Masaoka Shiki's haiku reforms that called for realism and immediacy in poetry. Poch argues that the detached stance of the narrator enables him to deconstruct the emotion-packed lyric genres that appear in the narrative. These poetic genres link *Pillow of Grass* to the *ninjō* tradition in premodern literature, in which poetry was featured prominently to mediate

romantic feelings between characters. Vilslev, "Questioning western universality"; Poch, "Kanjō hyōgen"; Poch, *Licentious Fictions*, 179–208.

14. As Miyoshi wrote, "Paradox is the narrator's modus operandi in argument." Miyoshi, *Accomplices of Silence*, 65.
15. Karatani, *Sōseki ronshūsei*, 421–428.
16. The word *ninjō* also references the sentimental fiction (*ninjōbon*) in vogue during the early nineteenth century. If we take *hininjō* at its literal meaning, "that which is not *ninjō*," then we might understand the polarity between *ninjō* and *hininjō* as analogous to the polarity between "genre" and "anti-genre." In Chapter 9, the narrator has a conversation with Nami about a cherry tree's "variation" (*henka*) of motion in a stream. Nami wishes that humans could move with such variation, to which the narrator replies, "You have to be *hininjō* to move like that." *SZ*, 3: 114. What constitutes *hininjō* is the ability to change, to diverge from an established form, or a literary institution.
17. Although the narrator tries to maintain a clear distinction between Eastern and Western aesthetics, and wants to favor the former, he fails because they often overlap in his examples. This failure fuels the irony of the novel, while also revealing the fusion of multiple literary traditions in Sōseki's writing. The influence of Shakespeare, Milton, Romanticism, and nineteenth-century English novels can be found in his oeuvre—from his critical writings to his novels to his traditional poetry.
18. *SZ*, 3: 6.
19. *SZ*, 3: 7.
20. Sōseki's literary translation of Shelley's stanza also stands on its own as a "new-style poem" (*shintaishi*)—a genre that emerged after the importation of Romanticism in the late nineteenth century: "*mae o mite wa, shirie o mite wa / monohoshi to, akogaruru kana, ware. / hara kara no warai to iedo / kurushimi no, soko ni aru beshi. / utsukushiki kiwami no uta ni, kanashimi no kiwami no omoi, komoru to zo shire.*"
21. Sandy, *Romanticism, Memory, and Mourning*, 97.
22. *SZ*, 3: 10–11.
23. Nakajima, *Kindai bungaku ni miru kanjusei*, 640.
24. *SZ*, 3: 14.
25. Ibid.
26. *SZ*, 3: 14–15.
27. Muecke, *The Compass of Irony*, 189.
28. O'Neill, *Romanticism and the Self-Conscious Poem*.
29. *SZ*, 3: 36. Translation is a modified version of McKinney.
30. *SZ*, 3: 37. Translation is a modified version of McKinney.
31. *SZ*, 3: 74. Translation is a modified version of McKinney.
32. *SZ*, 3: 74.

33. Ibid.
34. Ibid.
35. The narrator writes that the power of his elation is not commensurate with the image of a boundless blue sea: "My state lacks the power that this image suggests, but I find joy in that. In the manifestation of great power, lurks the concern that that power will eventually be exhausted. In its everyday form, no such worries attend it. But in my present state of mind, more 'bland' than usual, I am not only far away from woes about whether my vigorous strength will whittle away, I have also transcended the quotidian realm where the mind discerns what is permissible and what is not." *SZ*, 3: 74. Such observations about the relationship between power (*katsuryoku*) and the subject tempt us to consider the conceit of *Pillow of Grass* as allegory for the power of imperialism (and later fascism) during the early twentieth century. The narrator succumbs to a trance that frees him of the ability or necessity to judge right from wrong. Such language may just be Sōseki's effusive paean to aesthetics, poetry, and painting; but the language also forebodes a potentially frightening scenario in which such language is used to mobilize subjects of the empire. For a study on aesthetics and fascism, see Tansman, *The Aesthetics of Japanese Fascism*.
36. Karatani Kōjin has speculated that Sōseki likely read *Lyrics of Chu* before writing *Pillow of Grass*. Karatani, *Sōseki ronshūsei*, 427. In 1972, Furukawa Hisashi discussed the similarities between the two texts, arguing that *Pillow of Grass* may be an inversion of *Lyrics of Chu*. When Japanese readers think of *Lyrics of Chu*, they are generally thinking of Qu Yuan's long poem "Encountering Sorrow," which has been read in traditional commentary as political allegory for a court official—Qu Yuan—who has fallen out of favor with his ruler. In late Qing criticism, Qu Yuan was celebrated as the "lyrical poet" par excellence, a sentiment that continued in early twentieth-century Japanese literary criticism. In Qu's poem, the lyric subject, feeling distraught and misunderstood, has a fantasy wherein he encounters a goddess with whom he fails at consummating a relationship. Although temporality in the poem is out of whack, the imagery and sorrow overall evoke late autumn. *Pillow of Grass*, however, is an ode to spring. In this way, Furukawa has argued that Sōseki turns lament into paean. While this interpretation is simplistic, as *Pillow of Grass* also brims with grief, Furukawa's point that *Lyrics of Chu* and *Pillow of Grass* share common diction is well taken. Furukawa, *Natsume Sōseki*, 114–125.
37. *SZ*, 3: 74.
38. Saitō Mareshi has argued that such diction exemplifies how Sōseki drew from classical Chinese poetry, while also affording him the means to construct a new "separate world" (*betsu kenkon*) in the modern Japanese novel. Saitō, "Sōseki no kanshibun—shūji to hihyō."

39. Burke: "It is the nature of grief to keep its object perpetually in its eye, to present it in its most pleasurable views, to repeat all the circumstances that attend it, even to the last minuteness; to go back to every particular enjoyment, to dwell upon each, and to find a thousand new perfections in all, that were not sufficiently understood before; in grief, the *pleasure* is still uppermost; and the affliction we suffer has no resemblance to absolute pain, which is always odious, and which we endeavor to shake off as soon as possible." Burke, *A Philosophical Enquiry*, 34–35 (original emphasis). Sōseki did not own this work, but he did own a collection of Burke essays and *Reflections on the Revolution in France* (1790).

40. Rebecca Comay on Freud's idea that melancholia is an attachment to an unknown loss: "Melancholia would thus be a way of staging a dispossession of that which was never one's own to lose in the first places—and thus, precisely by occluding structural lack as determinate loss, would exemplify the strictly perverse effort to assert a relation with the non-relational…. Trauma would itself in this way be mobilized as a defence against an impossible enjoyment: the melancholic derealization of the real here functions, as Giorgio Agamben has compelling argued, not only to aggrandize the subject of fantasy, but in so doing ultimately to hypostatize what is unreal (or phantasmatic) as a new reality." Comay, "The Sickness of Tradition," 89; Agamben, *Stanzas*.

41. Another word that comes to mind is *saudade* from Portuguese: "longing, melancholy, nostalgia, as a supposed characteristic of the Portuguese or Brazilian temperament." (*OED*)

42. Boym, *The Future of Nostalgia*, 16.

43. Matsuoka, *Sōseki no kanshi*, 80.

44. SZ, 3:152. For *kundoku* and annotations, see *SZ*, 18: 194–198.

45. SZ, 18: 198.

46. Ikkai Tomoyoshi—editor of vol. 18 of *SZ*—observes that the opening line evokes the Yuefu tradition, known for its many songs on longing. He also cites early Tang poet Song Zhiwen's (656?–712 CE) "Song of Descending the Mountain" (Xia shan ge), a poem that deploys diction from *Lyrics of Chu*:

Descending Song Mountain—much on the mind;	下嵩山兮多所思
Accompanied by the fair one—we plod along slowly.	携佳人兮步遲遲
The bright moon between the pines, it will be like this forever;	松間明月長如此
But to roam again with you—when will the next time come?	君再游兮復何時

47. Stephen Dodd has examined nostalgia in the context of Japanese literature about the *furusato*, or "native place." Such works feature a protago-
nist from the city who returns to his native place, where he reflects on the
evils of urbanization and reminisces about the idyllic past of his childhood. In this kind of literature, *furusato* can be literal or figurative: either
referring to the writer's actual native place or what Dodd describes as a
metaphorical "other" that allows the writer to "articulate both a criticism
for society and an idealized alternative." Dodd, *Writing Home*, 1. Dodd
argues that the *furusato* "emerged in Meiji as a newly invigorated symbol
of desire and discontent," a place to which writers wished to return but
also one that was falling to ruin and, hence, required restoration. *Pillow
of Grass* can be read alongside *furusato* literature because it longs for a
home that is disappearing or already gone.

48. Goodman, "Uncertain Disease," 199–201.

49. Ibid.; Dodman, *What Nostalgia Was*.

50. Goodman, "Uncertain Disease," 204.

51. Sōseki's representation of sense perception speaks to the kinds of nostalgia that Boym identifies in her study: restorative and reflective, the former
being a "transhistorical reconstruction of the lost home," and the latter,
"the longing itself," which "has the capacity to awaken multiple planes of
consciousness." Boym writes: "Restorative nostalgia does not think of
itself as nostalgia, but rather as truth and tradition. Reflective nostalgia
dwells on the ambivalences of human longing and belonging and does
not shy away from the contradictions of modernity. Restorative nostalgia
protects the absolute truth, while reflective nostalgia calls it into doubt."
Boym, *The Future of Nostalgia*, 49–50, xviii.

52. Sigmund Freud in *Mourning and Melancholia* (1917) distinguishes
"mourning" from "melancholy," writing that the former refers to a feeling of loss when a person has died, whereas the latter refers to a feeling of
loss whose object is lost in the mourner's consciousness.

53. Földényi, *Melancholy*, 255.

54. Ibid., 252.

55. Ibid., 215.

56. In the "Mastering Life" (Da sheng) and "The World" (Tian xia) chapters,
Zhuangzi critiques the epistemological basis on which such ethical judgments are formed, arguing that forgetting of right and wrong renders the
mind at ease, freeing the subject from the entanglements of knowledge.
Judgment about what is "right" vis-à-vis what is "wrong" is based on
received and institutionalized knowledge. Watson, *The Complete Works*,
206–207, 370. Sōseki's poem seems to be arguing that freedom from
such categories and distinctions is both to be free of ideological contain-

ment and to consider non-teleological and more open-ended conclusions.

57. François, *Open Secrets*, xvi.
58. *SZ*, 3: 171.
59. *Recollecting and Such* was serialized in the Tokyo *Asahi* newspaper from October 29, 1910 to February 20, 1911, and in the Osaka *Asahi* newspaper from October 29, 1910 to March 5, 1911. In March through June of 1910, Sōseki's novel *The Gate* (Mon) was serialized in the same newspaper. Not long thereafter, Sōseki came down with severe abdominal pain, admitted himself to the hospital and was diagnosed with a stomach ulcer. After receiving treatment, in August of that year Sōseki vacationed at Shuzenji on the Izu Peninsula. He suffered a relapse of the ulcer, which hemorrhaged, resulting in blood loss and a coma. He survived and convalesced at Shuzenji until he was able to return to the hospital in October. It was at the hospital where he began writing *Recollecting and Such*.
60. In her introduction to the translation, Flutsch describes the multitude of forms contained within the work: "In its form, unique among Sōseki's works, *Recollections* could be said to present a microcosm of his whole oeuvre. This is because it contains miniature versions of every literary form Sōseki ever used, moulded together into a new genre." Natsume, *Recollections*, 6.
61. Marcus, *Reflections in a Glass Door*, 12.
62. *SZ*, 12: 416.
63. *SZ*, 12: 400.
64. Here one thinks of the relationship between cold and numbness in John Keats's *The Fall of Hyperion*:

> ...the leaves were yet
> Burning, when suddenly a palsied chill
> Struck from the paved level up my limbs,
> And was ascending quick to put cold grasp
> Upon those streams that pulse beside the throat.
> I shriek'd, and the sharp anguish of my shriek
> Stung my own ears; I strove hard to escape
> The numbness, strove to gain the lowest step.
> Slow, heavy, deadly was my pace: the cold
> Grew stifling, suffocating, at the heart;
> And when I clasp'd my hands I felt them not.

Keats, *Complete Poems*, 376.
65. *SZ*, 12: 357–451.
66. Ibid., 357.

67. Ibid., 358.

68. I mean "vital" in the poetic sense that describes the life force contingent on breath, like in Wordsworth's *Vernal Ode*, "And though to every draught of vital breath, / Renewed throughout the bounds of earth or ocean," and in Shelley's *Adonais*, "Dream not that the amorous Deep / Will yet restore him to the vital air."

69. The narrator describes the reason for writing *Recollecting and Such*: "*Omoidasu koto nado* is nothing more than quotidian and dull reminiscences and descriptions of my own illness, but among them you should find many rare pleasures, albeit old-fashioned. I recollect things quickly, and write them down in haste, so that I can savor these old fragrances in the company of those who embrace the present and those who are suffering in it." *SZ*, 12: 368.

70. William Waters has examined the value of poetry as lyric address in the way that lyric poems mediate contact between poet and reader: "When poems address their readers, the topic of the pronoun *you* and the topic of reading (what it is like to be a person reading a poem) become two sides of a single coin. This, then, is the end to which my investigation of lyric address leads: the claim that we as readers may feel in second-person poems, in a poem's touch, an intimation of why poetry is valuable, why it matters to us, and how we might come to feel answerable to it." Waters, *Poetry's Touch*, 2. Helen Vendler has described lyric address as intimacy between the poet and his future, unseen, reader. Vendler, *Invisible Listeners*.

71. *SZ*, 12: 371.

72. *SZ*, 12: 371.

73. *SZ*, 12: 395.

74. The bush clover is one of the seven flowers of autumn (*aki no nanakusa*) that poets have written about since ancient times. Sōseki featured the "white bush clover" (*shirohagi*) in another haiku from 1910:

> Since becoming ill
> Dew on the white bush clover
> Has been falling heavily!
> 病んでより白萩に露の繁く降る事よ

   SZ, 17: 408.

75. Yiu, *Chaos and Order*, 188.

76. *SZ*, 12: 397. For annotations, see *SZ*, 18: 248–249.

77. Bachelard, *Air and Dreams*, 185.

78. *SZ*, 12: 421.

79. *SZ*, 12: 422.

80. *SZ*, 12: 423. For annotations, see *SZ*, 18: 237–239.
81. The conclusion of the poem speaks to Comay's discussion of how fetish-ism defers loss to the future, exemplified in a passage by Lessing on Laocoön: "the sculptor has captured the pregnant moment just before the full horror strikes—the father's mouth open but not yet screaming, the serpent's venom not quite completely penetrated, the agony not quite yet at its climax: the gaze fixes on the penultimate moment so as to block the revelation of the monstrous void. Penultimacy—incompletion as such—becomes a defence against a mortifying conclusion." Comay, "The Sickness of Tradition," 95–96.
82. *SZ*, 12: 401.
83. Ibid.
84. Fletcher, *Colors of the Mind*, 167.
85. Here I refer to what Sharon Cameron has called "lyric time" or "apoca-lyptic time" in Emily Dickinson's poetry. For Cameron, lyric is unmedi-ated by narrative and operates in a time of its own: "Unlike the story, novel, or drama, the lyric enjoys an independence from authorial inter-ruption (those breaks in the action that remind us all action inevitably ends), and it is free as well from the speech and thought of other charac-ters. As pure unmediated speech it lies furthest of all the mimetic arts from the way we really talk. Lyric speech might be described as the way we would talk in dreams if we could convert the phantasmagoria there into words. But as the present is neither the past nor the future, as desire is not equivalent to the object of its longing, as there is a space predicated between the landscape and the human subject who regards it, between language and what it hopes to word into being, so the same radical inequality is manifested between lyric speech and the voice or voices it represents." Cameron, *Lyric Time*, 207.
86. *SZ*, 12: 403.
87. This is my interpretation, as the structure of Sōseki's poem resembles that of a Shakespearean sonnet. Sōseki was a careful reader of Shakespeare and English poetry, so it is likely that English poetics informed his *kanshi*.
88. *SZ*, 12: 403. For annotations, see *SZ*, 18: 263–272.
89. This is also the same word that the narrator uses later in installment 20 to describe the sublime state of "boundlessness" he feels after having merged with the sky. In this poem from installment 15 and in the prose from installment 20 are the sole two places where the word *hyōbyō* appears in the narrative. The vast darkness of *hyōbyō* conjures the dark and strange space in between in Coleridge's "Limbo":

> 'Tis a strange place, this Limbo!—not a Place,
> Yet name it so;—where Time and weary Space

Fettered from flight, with night-mare sense of fleeing,
Strive for their last crepuscular half-being;—
Lank Space, and scytheless Time with branny hands
Barren and soundless as the measuring sands,
Not mark'd by flit of Shades,—unmeaning, they
As moonlight on the dial of the day!

Coleridge, *The Complete Poems*, 357. Coleridge's poem is more haunting, but both he and Sōseki were interested in representing the experience of being in liminal space. For Sōseki on Coleridge, see *SZ*, 27: 67–70.

90. Bachelard: "The storyteller feels...that he cannot give the impression of this essential fall, at the very limits of death and the abyss, unless he tries to make associations with the effort to *rise up again*.... It is these *efforts* to rise up again, these efforts to become conscious of the vertigo, that give a kind of undulating effect to the fall, that make the imaginary fall an example of that undulating psychology in which the contradictions between the real and the imaginary constantly change places, reinforce each other, and interact with each other as opposites. Then vertigo becomes stronger in this dialectics wavering between life and death; it reaches the point of that *infinite fall*, an unforgettable dynamic experience that so deeply affected Poe's soul." Bachelard, *Air and Dreams*, 96–97 (original emphasis). For Sōseki on Poe, see *SZ*, 25: 340. In his essay "Poe's Imagination" (Pō no sōzō), Sōseki argues that Poe has a scientific imagination.

91. The line alludes to Bashō's death poem:

Sick on a journey,
But over withered fields dreams
Are running all around.
旅に病で夢は枯野をかけ廻る

Trans. Robert Backus. Backus, "What Goes Into a Haiku," 754. *Bashō kushū*, 216. Iida Rigyō has noted the Bashō reference. Iida, *Sōseki shishū yaku*, 201. The frail minds and bodies of Bashō and the poet in *Recollecting and Such* are wandering in a space of darkness and absence. Bashō's haiku pairs sickness and death with oneiric vitality: dreams that will continue to run around the fields. In the haiku, such a pairing suggests potentiality for life in death. But in the narrator's *kanshi* that potentiality is ironized.

92. Many annotators comment that this line alludes to the first lines in "Nine Changes" (Jiu bian) in *Lyrics of Chu*.

Alas for the breath of autumn!
Wan and drear: flower and leaf fluttering fall and turn to decay.
悲哉!秋之為氣也. 蕭瑟兮, 草木搖落而變衰.

Hawkes, *The Songs of the South*, 209. *Soji*, 282. *Lyrics of Chu*, a poetry collection that transports its reader on a journey into the spiritual realm, seems to have informed Sōseki's poetic diction when describing movement in ethereal space.

93. The Chinese graph *kaku* 廓 originally refers to the domain of a castle town. The meaning of this word resembles the meaning of "circumference" in an Emily Dickinson poem:

> The Poets light but Lamps—
> Themselves—go out—
> The Wicks they stimulate
> If vital Light
> Inhere as do the Suns—
> Each Age a Lens—
> Disseminating their
> Circumference.

Dickinson, *The Poems of Emily Dickinson*, 397–398. Lines 7 and 8 end the poem with the suggestion that the lens of future readers enables the circulation of light (poetry), but with the firm assertion that such circulation has a limit, as "circumference" refers to the enclosing boundary of a circle.

94. This line alludes to a couplet in "Far-off Journey" (Yuan you) in *Lyrics of Chu*:

> In the sheer depths below, the earth was invisible;
> In the vastness above, the sky could not be seen.
> 下崢嶸而無地兮, 上寥廓而無天.

Hawkes, *The Songs of the South*, 199. *Soji*, 270.

95. Iida Rigyō, Wada Toshio, and Nakamura Hiroshi read the Chinese graph 澹 as *awaku*. Iida, *Sōseki shishū yaku*, 198. Wada, *Sōseki no shi to haiku*, 299. Nakamura, *Sōseki kanshi no sekai*, 159. Yoshikawa Kōjirō and Ikkai Tomoyoshi retain the Chinese reading: *tan*. Yoshikawa, *Sōseki shichū*, 126.

96. Yoshikawa and Ikkai have interpreted *ososhi* to mean "slow," reading the line as more of a comment about the emergence of a poetic feeling than the actual result of coming to grips with dulled senses. Furui Yoshikichi has also read the line in this way, praising Sōseki's usage of the adjective *ososhi*, writing that the line comments on the length of time required to feel the charm of autumn. Furui, *Sōseki no kanshi o yomu*, 77.

97. *SZ*, 12: 450.
98. *SZ*, 12: 451.
99. Sōseki published an essay entitled "Spring in the Hospital" (Byōin no haru) in the Tokyo *Asahi* newspaper on April 13, 1911 (April 9 in Osaka). *Recollecting and Such* was anthologized in book form in *Kirinukichō yori* (From the scrapbook) on August 18, 1911. In the volume, the essay appears as installment 33 of *Recollecting and Such*. The extra installment can be read as but another coda to a prose poem of codas.
100. *SZ*, 12: 451. For annotations see *SZ*, 18: 249–252.
101. See note 93.

CHAPTER 6

Coda: Echoes in the Ether

Poetry should really only be philosophized.
—Giorgio Agamben, "The End of the Poem" (1999)

I end this study with an examination of Sōseki's final *kanshi*, the one lyric form from literati culture that he shared with Buson, Saikō, and Shiki. On the night of November 20, 1916, Sōseki composed an untitled heptasyllabic regulated verse (*shichigon risshi*) that laments the decline of literati poetry and the death of *kanshi* in the modern period. His poem presents an allegory for the rise and fall of Japanese literati culture from the eighteenth through early twentieth centuries, a period during which four eccentric writers transformed the lineaments of lyric expression, forging new poetic forms through which each participated ironically in the literati tradition. Sōseki's final poem also presents an allegory for the future of literati culture in the absence of *kanshi*: its paradoxical ending suggests that the lyricism afforded by *kanshi* might survive only as a disembodied echo beyond Sōseki's moment, into our own.

As Giorgio Agamben has observed, "poetry lives only in tension and difference between sound and sense, between the semiotic sphere and the semantic sphere."[1] A poem, in other words, is a poem as long as there is

dissonance between sound and sense, a dissonance produced by enjambment.[2] Agamben argues that this tension finds resolution when the poem
ends, but what if a poem ends by not ending? Sōseki's final *kanshi* presents
a case of poetic closure that goes beyond closure—what Barbara Herrnstein
Smith describes as "anti-teleology" or "anti-closure."[3] His poem shows
how paradox allows this dissonance to continue forever as a sound that is
"both spatial and temporal, stable and unstable, finite and infinite, closed
and open."[4] This final image is evoked by the word *gin*, a "song" or "ode"
that the speaker sings without his body to white clouds in the void. The
ambiguous meaning of *gin* here suggests that poetry may continue even
after the poem has ended:

> The true path is desolate, dark and hard to find,
> Wanting to keep an open mind, pacing the past and present.
> Emerald hills and emerald streams, how can they have an ego,
> When all of heaven and all of earth have no feeling?
> Misty evening shades, the moon trapped in the grass,
> Motley autumn sounds, the wind caught in the trees.
> I ignore both eyes and ears, and let go the body,
> Chanting in the sky alone an ode to the white clouds.

shinshō wa sekibaku yō toshite tazunegataku	眞蹤寂寞杳難尋
kyokai o idakan to hosshite kokon o ayumu	欲抱虛懷步古今
hekisui hekizan nanzo ware aran	碧水碧山何有我
gaiten gaichi kore mushin	蓋天蓋地是無心
iki taru boshoku tsuki kusa ni kakari	依稀暮色月離草
sakuraku taru shūsei kaze hayashi ni ari	錯落秋聲風在林
ganji futatsu nagara wasurete mi mo mata ushinai	眼耳雙忘身亦失
kūchū ni hitori tonau hakuun no gin	空中獨唱白雲吟 [5]

The poem paints an autumnal landscape: dark, desolate, and dreary.
Considering Sōseki's declining health at the time of its composition, many
critics have read the poem as autobiography.[6] To be sure, his impending
death on December 9, 1916, may have inspired the conflict that runs
through the poem's imagery—the rhythm between past and present, the
discord between self and nature, the precariousness of life figured by the
atmospheric opacity and mournful sounds of autumn, and the estrangement of mind from body.[7]

The lyric subject in the poem tries to resolve these conflicts across eight lines comprising four couplets. The opening word "true path" (*shinshō*) refers to the path that the speaker followed to represent a self that was "true" or "real" (*shin*) in his literary works. It also refers to the path that he leaves behind—his literal "tracks" or "footprint" (*shō*) in literary history as a modern *bunjin*, a metaphor for the trail-blazing performed by all four artists treated in this book. What makes the path or footprint of any artist "true" and "real" over the course of the long nineteenth century increasingly meant a representation of the self and the world that was true to life and that privileged the visual apprehension of the world.

By describing this path (both followed and left behind) as "desolate, dark and hard to find," the speaker ironizes this quest, calling into question whether "true" or "real" (*shin*) representation is ever possible by purely visual means. By rendering the "true path" obscure, line 1 opens a space for the poem to resolve this problem of representation—which, the reader realizes by the end of the poem, is a non-representational means of communicating sense and feeling: sound.

Line 2 extends this openness (or desire for openness) by qualifying that "path" (or, more literally, "foot traces") as a journey through past and present.[8] This journey through time in the act of reading and composing poetry is mediated by an "open mind" (*kyokai*), and evokes traditional Chinese theories on literary craft and composition.[9] By linking the "path" to poetic creation, beginning with the idea of its elusiveness, the opening couplet already anticipates the way the poem ends: with a song whose human imprint is no longer visible.

As the speaker reflects on the meaning of poetry through the rhythm of past and present, repetition, like a stutter, breaks the integrity of the poem's concepts, slowing the affirmation of meaning, and allowing sound to disrupt sense.[10] Lines 3 and 4 form a couplet that speaks to a central question in traditional Chinese and Japanese poetry as well as in Anglo-European Romantic poetry: What is the relationship between humanity and nature? In traditional Chinese thought, humanity and nature are one: natural objects have feelings as do human beings because both exist on the same metonymical plane.[11] Romanticism, however, is a response to the loss of connection between man and nature, which is why the Romantic tradition features prosopopoeia, anthropomorphism, and other figurations that grant natural objects human attributes.[12]

The second couplet questions this figuration through repetition and parallel construction: the words *heki* (emerald) and *gai* (lit. "vault," translated as "all") qualify the binaries *sansui* and *tenchi*, "the natural landscape" and "the human world," respectively. The repetition of *heki* and *gai* adds to the rhetorical force of each line but also compromises the integrity of the binaries by severing them. Thus the couplet throws the world of poetic representation on its head, asking how landscape can have a "self" or "ego" (*ware*), when its world has "no feeling" (*mushin*). The couplet blends the Buddhist idea of *mushin* ("no mind" or "no-mindedness") with the modern concern for the self, the Romantic idea of the isolated lyric subject, and the modern human being's alienation from the natural world. In the parallelism and the repetition of the couplet, the poet utters a plaintive cry over this loss; it is in these formal features that the music and rhythm of poetry is heard.

The speaker renews his connection with nature in foreboding images of visual and sonic indistinctness in the couplet formed by lines 5 and 6.[13] The humanization of nature through figures of moonlight on the grass and wind blowing in the trees evokes the twilight moments and opaque atmospheres of Romantic poetry as well as the eerie and jarring sounds and sights of autumn that poets across multiple traditions have used to forebode death. The fact that the moon's image is "caught" in the grass and the wind is "trapped" in the trees imbues the couplet with a feeling of perpetual penultimate-ness, of being on the threshold of an imminent crescendo: the end of the poem.[14]

In the wake of visual and sonic indistinctness comes the deflation of the speaker's sensory embodiment and the humanization of nature as an estrangement of mind from body. In the penultimate line, the speaker abandons his eyes, ears, and body, thereby effacing his material existence in the world and becoming a disembodied spirit or mind floating in the ether.[15] This abandons the promise of empirical investigation from Late Edo through Meiji—that the world could be felt and perceived through one's own eyes and ears—and instead aspires to embrace the conceit of the Daoist immortal who has transcended the vulgar realm and the Zen practitioner whose mind has abandoned the material world for a place of higher existence.

And yet the speaker's transcendence is ironized by the image of a disembodied voice and its ghostly echo in the void, turning the poem into a comment on lyric and metaphysics.[16] Transcendence is here attained through pure sound in emptiness. The word *kūchū* means "in the sky" but also carries the Buddhist notion of "inside emptiness." This nuance evokes the "open mind" in line 2 as well as the rift created by the repetition of qualifiers in lines 3 and 4: *kū* (also *sora*) refers to the space between "heaven" (*ten*) and "earth" (*chi*), and is also the state of mind that stirs poetic creativity. By figuring his voice in liminal states denoted by "in the sky" and "inside emptiness," the poet allows his ode to come to fruition. The adverb *hitori* (alone) indicates his solitude but the term also means "just" or "only," meanings that make his "chanting" (*tonau*) ironic and suggest cynically that chanting in endless repetition will fall on deaf ears.

The final image—"ode to the white clouds" (*hakuun no gin*)—echoes this irony by figuring an audience that is formless and indifferent.[17] Whether the ode is being sung "to" the white clouds or "on (the topic of)" the white clouds is unclear. As a verb, *gin* means "to groan," "to sigh," "to cry," and "to sing"; as a noun, it refers to a Chinese poem to be sung aloud—likely, given the former meanings, a poem both mournful and elegiac.[18] As such, Sōseki's poem concludes on a somber note, with an image of sound separated from sense (song without a singer; poem without a poet), and hovering as an eternal echo in the ether.

The question raised by this ending is whether sound can be heard if the disembodied lyric mind is floating in liminal space among indifferent white clouds—form without content. Can sound be heard without a body to sense it? The paradox offers a solution to a *crise de vers*, which Agamben argues all poems face upon ending: "At the point in which sound is about to be ruined in the abyss of sense, the poem looks for shelter in suspending its own end in a declaration, so to speak, of the state of poetic emergency."[19] The poetic emergency—the feeling of "ending"—is evoked in the form and content of Sōseki's poem as well as in the extra-textual contingency of his own mortality.

The word *gin* evokes the rhyme that gives order to the poem; as a word that denotes a song to be sung, it speaks to the ontology of poetry itself.[20] In its Chinese form, Sōseki's poem rhymes (*jin, kin, shin, rin, gin*) and adheres to the meter (*hyōsoku*) of heptasyllabic regulated verse. Such metrical limits operate in opposition to the semantic movement facilitated by enjambment. When Sōseki's poem ends, therefore, its poem-ness theoretically ends too. However, the paradox suggested by the metaphysical ending—whether the ode can be heard in formlessness—allows the disjunction between sound and sense to continue in deafening silence.

If the end of a poem is a poetic impossibility, as Agamben argues, then the paradox of a potentially endless chanting audible only as perpetual silence offers a way for poetry to continue in thought—in the poetic imagination. This *gin* evokes a rhythm that continues as a form without content, like the white clouds figured with it; by the end of the poem, it has returned to its start, with the uncertainty and obscurity of meaning. It is through dissonance in meaning—the continued disjunction between sound and sense through paradox and contradiction—that the poem stirs thought.

In his essay on US poet Hart Crane (1899–1932), Allen Grossman argues that a good poem is a "cognitive triumph": "Poems are 'good' from my point of view, insofar as they respond to *real problems of mind to which there is no other solution than poetry.*"[21] If Sōseki's poem is a distillation of his entire enterprise as poet and painter, an allegory for the history of *bunjin* culture and its future, then its seamless blending of multiple literary traditions through an allusive tapestry of images displays its self-consciousness as a modern poem in ancient form—a mind in contradiction. This is precisely the problem of modern literary form, for which one (or perhaps the only) solution is poetry: a form that questions the limits of thought, sound, and sense, leaving answers open. In Sōseki's poem, that openness rests on the final word *gin*, the paradoxical sound of presence and absence. To echo Grossman on the open-endedness of the last lines in Crane's poem "The Broken Tower": "The poem has done what poetry can do. It has given rise to thinking."[22]

I would hope that my examination of Buson, Saikō, Shiki, and Sōseki has shown what poetry can do. That is, how poetic form can mediate the perceptions and feelings of a lyric subject with openness and indeterminacy—or, put simply, poetic language in the state or process of thinking. The four writers treated here thought about how they could make a claim to the literati tradition—two during its rise and two during its fall. They all forged new poetic forms of irony through which they anxiously longed to be the poets they wanted to be.

In the late eighteenth century Buson represented the sound of anxious longing as the placid and plangent waves of a spring sea heaving eternally, all the day long. By Sōseki's time in the early twentieth century, when the literati tradition's end was immanent, that soothing hymn and plangent song could only be heard in a void, as an echo in the ether. Via the paradox of the word *gin* and through the form of rhythm, Sōseki's last poem continues to think and to long with neither poet nor containment of the poem—a contradictory image that keeps the reader at home thinking too and longing for more.

NOTES

1. Agamben, *The End of the Poem*, 109.
2. In Anglo-European poetry "enjambment" refers to "the continuation of a syntactic unit from one line to the next without a major juncture or pause; the opposite of an end-stopped line. While enjambment can refer to any verse that is not end-stopped, it is generally reserved for instances in which the 'not stopping' of the verse is felt as overflow, especially in relation to some poetic effect." *The Princeton Encyclopedia of Poetry and Poetics*, 435. Considering this definition, "enjambment," in the syntactical sense, rarely occurs in traditional Chinese poetry. I use "enjambment" to refer to the "incompleteness" in the flow of thought in one line that seeks "completion" by forming a mutual dependency with another line. This is the continuation or carrying-over of sense, in opposition to sound, from one line to the next in a Chinese poem. This idea is akin to what Milton describes in his preface to *Paradise Lost* (1764) as "the sense variously drawn out from one verse into another." For a discussion of this line by Milton, see Fitzgerald, *Variety*, 15.
3. Smith, *Poetic Closure*, 234–271.
4. Ibid., 271.
5. Natsume Sōseki, *Soseki zenshū*, 18: 476–477. From here on *SZ*. Translation mine. The *kundoku* is a blend of versions by Yoshikawa Kōjirō, Iida Rigyō, and Ikkai Tomoyoshi. Iida, *Sōseki shishū yaku*, 584; Yoshikawa, *Sōseki shichū*, 301–302. Ikkai is editor of vol. 18 of *SZ*.
6. Most Japanese annotations read the poem as a "poetic presage" (*shishin*) of Sōseki's imminent death. For a heartfelt discussion on the poem and Sōseki's final days, see Matsuoka, *Sōseki no kanshi*, 267–269. One exception is Makizumi Etsuko, who has examined the poem in the context of Sōseki's oeuvre and argues that the poem, like other Sōseki *kanshi*, is about reaching as close as possible to the realm of the "no-self" (*muga*). Makizumi, "Natsume Sōseki no Fūryū," 64.
7. The fatalism in Sōseki's poem speaks to William Wordsworth's "The World Is Too Much With Us." Wordsworth, *Selected Poems*, 144–145.
8. There is also a subtle irony in the resonance between "path" (*shō*) and "pacing" (*aruku*), as if the poet's journey into literature of the past and present is already futile because the "path" or "foot-prints" left by his literary forebears may not exist. He seems to be lamenting that only their traces remain.
9. As Liu Xie (465–522 CE) argues in the "Spirit Thought" (Shen si) chapter in *The Literary Mind Carves Dragons* (Wenxin diaolong), "In the shaping of literary thought, the most important thing is emptiness and stillness within." Owen, *An Anthology of Chinese Literature*, 346. Once the writer

finds his peace of mind (through a process of meditation), he enters the ideal state for literary creation. As Lu Ji (261–303 CE) observes in "Poetic Exposition on Literature" (Wen fu), in this tranquil state of mind the writer can scan the thousands of volumes of classical literature, and simultaneously traverse the past and present: "He [the writer] sees past and present in a single instant, / Touches all this world in the blink of an eye." Owen, 337. The speaker in Sōseki's poem, however, tells us that keeping this "open mind" is but an unfulfilled wish, not a certainty.

10. Here I invoke Craig Dworkin's essay "The Stutter of Form," in which he compares the dissonance between sound and sense in poetry to the dissonance between sound and sense in a stutter or a stammer. In his discussion of the stuttering in *Blert* (2008) by contemporary Canadian poet Jordan Scott, Dworkin invokes Paul Valéry's definition of a poem as "a prolonged hesitation between sound and meaning." Perloff and Dworkin, *The Sound of Poetry*, 166–183.

11. Yu, *The Reading of Imagery*.

12. The way nature is figured in Sōseki's poem speaks to Karl Kroeber's reading of nature in Wordsworth's "The World Is Too Much With Us." He argues that the way Wordsworth humanizes natural elements without full personification "demonstrates how modern man, without returning to an outworn attitude, may not merely observe nature and enjoy the gratifying sensations it provides but can, in a sophisticated, creative fashion, humanize his natural environment, make it belong to him, make it 'ours.'" Kroeber, "A New Reading," 186.

13. In the same way Wordsworth writes "Little we see in Nature that is ours," Sōseki humanizes nature in this couplet by acknowledging man's distance from it. Kroeber writes: "By not pretending that nature is human—the 'pretense' of full personification, a favorite neoclassic device—and by admitting that 'little we see in Nature …is ours,' we can become in 'tune' with nature, can associate natural objects and human feelings." Kroeber, "A New Reading," 188.

14. Annotations by Ikkai and many others read the Chinese graph 離 in line 5 as *hanare* ("separated," from *hanaru*, "to separate"), not *kakari* ("trapped," from *kakaru*, "to cling"; "to hang"). Following Iida and Makizumi, I read the graph as *kakari* because it also means "to encounter (something undesirable)," as in Qu Yuan's "Encountering Sorrow" (Li sao). This association speaks to the mournful tone of the poem. Iida, *Sōseki shishū yaku*, 584–586. Makizumi, "Natsume Sōseki no Fūryū," 63.

15. This image resonates with the ending of the last poem in Recollecting *and Such* (1910), wherein the poet figures his mind as "a roving spirit dreaming of the old moss at home." *SZ*, 12: 451.

16. Here is an example of how Sōseki blended Buddhist and Daoist philosophy with the ideas of Andrew Marvell (1621–1678) and other seventeenth-

century metaphysical poets, creating new images of dissolution and self-annihilation. The way that Sōseki ends the poem with a disembodied psyche may be interpreted as a statement of truth about the "self" in metaphysical thought. As David Boym writes: "This 'self' is viewed, in the first instance, as a physical body, sharply bounded by the surface of the skin, and then as a 'mental entity' (also called the psyche or 'the soul') which is 'within' this physical body and which is taken to be the very essence of the individual human being. The notion of a separately existent 'self' thus follows as an aspect of the generally accepted metaphysics, which implies that *every*thing is of this nature." Boym, *On Creativity*, 120. Original emphasis.

17. Sōseki's other poems often represent "white clouds," a poetic figure for imaginative transport as well as cold and indifferent listeners. See Preface.

18. We may interpret the images that constitute the poem as metaphors that speak to concerns of lyric expression at the present moment of composition and also in the future. The word *gin* evokes the afterlife of *kanshi*, if not of literati culture overall, in the oral performance art known as *shigin*, or "Chinese poetry recitation." In *shigin*, poetry meets prayer, conjuring the space of ritual in which poetic meaning derives less from words and more from sound, rhythm, and repetition.

19. Agamben, *The End of the Poem*, 113. Agamben views the end of the poem as an object of ontological inquiry, arguing that the ends of poems cease to be "poetry" because they foreclose the possibility of enjambment—the continuation of meaning from one line to the next that facilitates movement in verse. As David Ben-Merre observes: "Agamben takes up the negative ontological state of the final line of a poem, but also the eschatological end of lyric poetry in the twentieth century." Ben-Merre, "Falling into Silence," 90.

20. Agamben: "the poem is an organism grounded in the perception of the limits and endings that define—without ever fully coinciding with, and almost in intermittent dispute with—sonorous (or graphic) units and semantic units." Agamben, *The End of the Poem*, 110.

21. Grossman, *True-Love*, 156. Original emphasis.

22. Ibid., 162.

REFERENCES

Agamben, Giorgio. *The End of the Poem: Studies in Poetics*. Translated by Daniel Heller-Roazen. Stanford, CA: Stanford University Press, 1999.

Ben-Merre, David. "Falling into Silence: Giorgio Agamben at the End of the Poem." *Mosaic* 45, no. 1 (March 2012): 89–104.

Boym, David. *On Creativity*. New York: Routledge, 1996.

Fitzgerald, William. *Variety: The Life of a Roman Concept.* Chicago: The University of Chicago Press, 2016.

Grossman, Allen. *True-Love: Essays on Poetry and Valuing.* Chicago: The University of Chicago Press, 2009.

Iida Rigyō. *Sōseki shishū yaku.* Tokyo: Kokusho Kankōkai, 1967.

Kroeber, Karl. "A New Reading of 'The World Is Too Much With Us.'" *Studies in Romanticism* 2, no. 3 (Spring, 1963): 183–188.

Matsuoka Yuzuru. *Sōseki no kanshi.* Tokyo: Asahi Shinbunsha, 1966.

Makizumi Etsuko. "Natsume Sōseki no Fūryū—Sōseki ni totte no kanshi." In *Kanbunmyaku no Sōseki,* edited by Yamaguchi Tadayoshi, 63–85. Tokyo: Kanrin Shobō, 2018.

Natsume Sōseki. *Soseki zenshū.* 29 vols. Tokyo: Iwanami Shoten, 2003.

Owen, Stephen, ed. and trans. *An Anthology of Chinese Literature: Beginnings to 1911.* New York: W.W. Norton, 1996.

Perloff, Marjorie, and Craig Dworkin, eds. *The Sound of Poetry/The Poetry of Sound.* Chicago: The University of Chicago Press, 2009.

Smith, Barbara Herrnstein. *Poetic Closure: A Study of How Poems End.* Chicago: The University of Chicago Press, 1968.

The Princeton Encyclopedia of Poetry and Poetics. Edited by Roland Greene, et al., Princeton, NJ: Princeton University Press, 2012.

Wordsworth, William. *Selected Poems.* Edited by Stephen Gill. New York: Penguin, 2004.

Yoshikawa Kōjirō, ed. *Sōseki shichū.* Tokyo: Iwanami Shoten, 1967. Reprint, Tokyo: Iwanami Shoten, 2002.

Yu, Pauline, ed. *Voices of the Song Lyric in China.* Berkeley: University of California Press, 1994.

Correction to: Anxiety and Grief in the Prose Poems of Natsume Sōseki

CORRECTION TO:

Chapter 5 in: M. Mewhinney, *Form and Feeling in Japanese Literati Culture*, https://doi.org/10.1007/978-3-031-11922-4_5

The book was inadvertently published with missing references in Chapter 5.

Agamben, Giorgio. *Stanzas: Word and Phantasm in Western Culture*. Translated by Ronald L. Martinez. Minneapolis: University of Minnesota Press, 1992.

Austead, Reiko Abe. *Rereading Sōseki: Three Early Twentieth-Century Novels*. Wiesbaden: Harrassowitz, 1998.

———, et al., eds., "Reading Sōseki Now," Special Issue, *Review of Japanese Culture and Society* 29 (2017).

Bachelard, Gaston. *Air and Dreams: An Essay On the Imagination of Movement*. Translated by Edith Farell and Frederick Farell. Dallas: The Dallas Institute Publications, 1988.

Backus, Robert L. "What Goes Into a Haiku." *Literature East and West* 15, (1972): 735–764.

The updated original version of the chapter can be found at
https://doi.org/10.1007/978-3-031-11922-4_5

Bashō kushū. Edited by Ōtani Tokuzō, et al. Vol. 45, *Nihon koten bungaku taikei*. 102 vols. Tokyo: Iwanami Shoten, 1962.

Bourdaghs, Michael. *A Fictional Commons: Natsume Sōseki and the Properties of Modern Literature*. Durham, NC: Duke University Press, 2021.

Boym, Svetlana. *The Future of Nostalgia*. New York: Basic Books, 2001.

Burke, Edmund. *A Philosophical Enquiry Into the Origin of our Ideas of the Sublime and Beautiful*. Edited by Adam Phillips. New York: Oxford University Press, 2008.

Cameron, Sharon. *Lyric Time: Dickinson and the Limits of Genre*. Baltimore: John Hopkins University Press, 1981.

Colebrook, Claire. *Irony*. New York: Routledge, 2004.

Coleridge, Samuel Taylor. *The Complete Poems*. Edited by William Keach. New York: Penguin, 1997.

Comay, Rebecca. "The Sickness of Tradition: Between Melancholia and Fetishism." In *Walter Benjamin and History*, edited by Andrew Benjamin, 88–101. New York: Continuum, 2005.

Dickinson, Emily. *The Poems of Emily Dickinson*. Edited by R.W. Franklin. Cambridge, MA: The Belknap Press of Harvard University Press, 2005.

Dodd, Stephen. *Writing Home: Representations of the Native Place in Modern Japanese Literature*. Cambridge, MA: Harvard University Asia Center, 2004.

Dodman, Thomas. *What Nostalgia Was: War Empire, and the Time of a Deadly Emotion*. Chicago: The University of Chicago Press, 2018.

Fletcher, Angus. *Colors of the Mind: Conjectures on Thinking in Literature*. Cambridge, MA: Harvard University Press, 1991.

Freedman, Ralph. *The Lyrical Novel: Studies in Hermann Hesse, André Gide, and Virginia Woolf*. Princeton, NJ: Princeton University Press, 1963.

Földényi, László F. *Melancholy*. Translated by Tim Wilkinson. New Haven: Yale University Press, 2016.

François, Anne-Lise. *Open Secrets: The Literature of Uncounted Experience*. Stanford: Stanford University Press, 2008.

Furui Yoshikichi. *Sōseki no kanshi wo yomu*. Tokyo: Iwanami Shoten, 2009.

Furukawa Hisashi. *Natsume Sōseki: bukkyō, kanbungaku to no kanren*. Tokyo: Hotoke no Sekaisha, 1972.

Goodman, Kevis. "'Uncertain Disease': Nostalgia, Pathologies of Motion, Practices of Reading." *Studies in Romanticism* 49, no.2 (Summer 2010): 197–227.

Hawkes, David, trans. *The Songs of the South*. New York: Penguin, 1985.

Iida Rigyō. *Sōseki shishū yaku*. Tokyo: Kokusho Kankōkai, 1967.

Karatani Kōjin. *Sōseki ron shūsei*. Tokyo: Heibonsha, 2001.

Keats, John. *Complete Poems and Selected Letters of John Keats*. New York: The Modern Library, 2001.

Kermode, Frank. *The Sense of an Ending: Studies in the Theory of Fiction*. New York: Oxford University Press, 2000.

Man'yōshū. Edited by Kojima Noriyuki, et al. Vol. 7, *Shinpen Nihon koten bungaku zenshū*. 88 vols. Tokyo: Shōgakukan, 1995.

Marcus, Marvin. *Reflections in a Glass Door: Memory and Melancholy in the Personal Writings of Natsume Sōseki*. Honolulu: University of Hawaii Press, 2009.

Matsuoka Yuzuru. *Sōseki no kanshi*. Tokyo: Asahi Shinbunsha, 1966.

Miyoshi, Masao. *Accomplices of Silence: The Modern Japanese Novel*. Berkeley, CA: University of California Press, 1974.

Muecke, D.C. *The Compass of Irony*. London: Metheun & Co., Ltd., 1969.

Nakajima Kunihiko. *Kindai bungaku ni miru kanjusei*. Tokyo: Chikuma Shobō, 1994.

Nakamura Hiroshi. *Sōseki kanshi no sekai*. Tokyo: Daiichi Shobō, 1983.

Natsume Soseki. *Kusamakura*. Translated by Meredith McKinney. New York: Penguin, 2008.

———. *The Three Cornered World*. Translated by Alan Turney. Washington D.C.: Gateway, 1988.

———. *Recollections*. Translated by Maria Flutsch. London: Sōseki Museum in London, 1997.

———. *Soseki zenshū*. 29 vols. Tokyo: Iwanami Shoten, 2003.

O'Neill, Michael. *Romanticism and the Self-Conscious Poem*. Oxford: Clarendon Press, 1997.

Poch, Daniel. "Kanjō hyōgen toshite no 'bun' no kindai—Natsume Sōseki ni okeru shiika to shizen to 'Rōmanshugi.'" In *Nihon ni okeru "bun" to "bungaku*," edited by Kōno Kimiko and Wiebke Denecke, 221–233.Tokyo: Bensei Shuppan, 2013.

———. *Licentious Fictions: Ninjō and the Nineteenth-Century Japanese Novel*. New York: Columbia University Press, 2020.

Rilke, Rainer Maria. *Letters on Cezanne*. Translated by Joel Agee. New York: North Point Press, 2002.

Saitō Mareshi. "Sōseki no kanshibun—shūji to hihyō." In *Kanbunmyaku no Sōseki*, edited by Yamaguchi Tadayoshi, 5–29. Tokyo: Kanrin Shobō, 2018.

Sakaki, Atsuko. *Recontextualizing Texts: Narrative Performance in Modern Japanese Fiction*. Cambridge, MA: Harvard University Asia Center, 1999).

Samuel, Julia. *Grief Works: Stories of Life, Death, and Surviving*. New York: Scribner, 2017.

Sandy, Mark. *Romanticism, Memory, and Mourning*. Farnham, Surrey, England: Ashgate Publishing Limited, 2013.

Soji. Edited by Hoshikawa Kiyotaka. Vol. 34, *Shinshaku kanbun taikei*. 121 vols. Tokyo: Meiji Shoin, 1970.

Sugimoto Motoaki. *Edo kanshi: eikyō to henyō no keifu*. Tokyo: Perikansha, 2004.

Tansman, Alan. *The Aesthetics of Japanese Fascism*. Berkeley: University of California Press, 2009.

Vendler, Helen. *Invisible Listeners: Lyric Intimacy in Herbert, Whitman, and Ashbery*. Princeton, NJ: Princeton University Press, 2005.

Vilslev, Annette Thorsen. "Questioning western universality: Sōseki's *Theory of Literature* and his novel *Kusamakura*." *Japan Forum* 29, no. 2 (2017): 257–278.

Vincent, J. Keith. *Two-Timing Modernity: Homosocial Narrative in Modern Japanese Fiction*. Cambridge, MA: Harvard University Asia Center, 2012.

Wada Toshio. *Sōseki no shi to haiku*. Tokyo: Merukumārusha, 1974.

Waters, William. *Poetry's Touch: On Lyric Address*. Ithaca, NY: Cornell University Press, 2003.

Watson, Burton, trans. *The Complete Works of Chuang Tzu*. New York: Columbia University Press, 1968.

Yiu, Angelia. *Chaos and Order in the Works of Natsume Sōseki*. Honolulu: University of Hawaii Press, 1998.

Yoshikawa Kōjirō, ed. *Sōseki shichū*. Tokyo: Iwanami Shoten, 1967. Reprint, Tokyo: Iwanami Shoten, 2002.

Index